10-26-2016

FOR LUCY —
A KINDRED SOUL
TO BE SURE

WITNESS TO A CHANGING WORLD

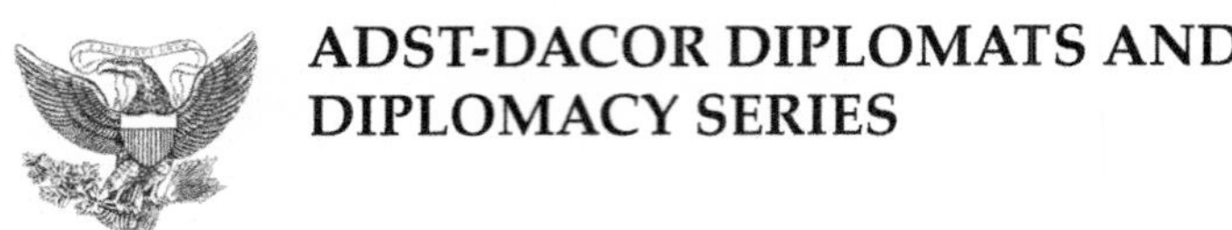

ADST-DACOR DIPLOMATS AND DIPLOMACY SERIES

Since 1776, extraordinary men and women have represented the United States abroad under all sorts of circumstances. What they did and how and why they did it remain little known to their compatriots. In 1995 the Association for Diplomatic Studies and Training (ADST) and Diplomatic and Consular Officers, Retired, Inc. (DACOR) created the Diplomats and Diplomacy book series to increase public knowledge and appreciation of the role of American diplomats in world history. The series seeks to demystify diplomacy through the stories of those who have conducted U.S. foreign relations, as they lived, influenced, and reported them. David Newsom's *Witness to a Changing World* fulfills these aims in depth, with grace and wit.

OTHER TITLES IN THE SERIES

Gordon Brown, ***Toussaint's Clause: The Founding Fathers and the Haitian Revolution***
Herman J. Cohen, ***Intervening in Africa: Superpower Peacemaking in a Troubled Continent***
Charles T. Cross, ***Born a Foreigner: A Memoir of the American Presence in Asia***
Brandon Grove, ***Behind Embassy Walls: The Life and Times of an American Diplomat***
Parker T. Hart, ***Saudi Arabia and the United States: Birth of a Security Partnership***
Michael P. E. Hoyt, ***Captive in the Congo: A Consul's Return to the Heart of Darkness***
Hume, Cameron R., ***Mission to Algiers: Diplomacy by Engagement***
Dennis Kux, ***The United States and Pakistan, 1947–2000: Disenchanted Allies***
Bo Lidegaard, ***Defiant Diplomacy: Henrik Kauffmann, Denmark, and the United States in World War II and the Cold War 1939–1958***
Jane C. Loeffler, ***The Architecture of Diplomacy: Building America's Embassies***
Robert H. Miller, ***Vietnam and Beyond: A Diplomat's Cold War Education***
Richard B. Parker, ***Uncle Sam in Barbary: A Diplomatic History***
Ralph Pezzullo, ***Plunging into Haiti: Clinton, Aristide, and the Defeat of Diplomacy***
Howard B. Schaffer, ***Ellsworth Bunker: Global Troubleshooter, Vietnam Hawk***
Ulrich Straus, ***The Anguish of Surrender: Japanese POWs of World War II***
James Stephenson, ***Losing the Golden Hour: An Insider's View of Iraq's Reconstruction***

WITNESS TO A CHANGING WORLD

David D. Newsom

An ADST-DACOR Diplomats and Diplomacy Book

Washington, DC

New Academia Publishing, 2008

The opinions and characterizations in this book are those of the author and do not necessarily represent official positions of the United States Government, the Association for Diplomatic Studies and Training, or Diplomatic and Consular Officers, Retired.

Printed in the United States of America

Library of Congress Control Number: 2008940922
ISBN 978-0-9818654-6-1 paperback (alk. paper)
ISBN 978-0-9818654-7-8 hardcover (alk. paper)

New Academia Publishing, LLC
P.O. Box 27420
Washington, DC 20038-7420
www.newacademia.com - info@newacademia.com

CONTENTS

PREFACE

The last eight decades of the twentieth century were a time of profound global change. Certainly, every generation has struggled to adjust to change; but it is not hard to argue that the effects on human life of the political, technological, scientific, social, and economic upheavals in the twentieth century were as profound as any in history.

I was born January 6, 1918, in the small city of Richmond, California, on San Francisco Bay. At that time—

World maps in school textbooks were largely colored red—for the British Empire. The world counted fifty-seven independent nations.

Racial segregation marked much of the world, including parts of the United States, and racial epithets were common. "Political correctness" was an unknown concept.

Jews and Catholics and Negroes and women were unwelcome in many organizations; in California, "Orientals" faced housing discrimination.

Homosexuality was a matter for whispered gossip.

Mental illness was subjected to shame, not treatment.

Divorce was frowned upon "in the best circles." So was living together before marriage.

Profane expressions and candid views of ordinary life were censored in the new world of motion pictures.

Electricity had not yet come to the rural areas of California, including the Dunlop pear ranch in Diamond Springs, California, my mother's family home.

Social customs among the wealthier followed a strict code. Men wore hats. When my mother went shopping in San Francisco ("the city"), she always wore a hat and gloves.

The prohibition of alcoholic beverages had just come into force.

All of these elements of society were to change in the next eighty years.

As a student, a newspaper reporter, a naval officer, a newspaper publisher, an American diplomat, and a university professor, I was a witness—and sometimes a participant—in these changes.

This is the story of that witness, written at the request of my family, largely from memory and from personal and family letters—all fallible sources—augmented by official documents and other writings. I accept full responsibility for any errors.

David D. Newsom
Charlottesville, Virginia
January 2008

ACKNOWLEDGMENTS

On the evening David and I were celebrating the completion of this manuscript he fell ill. It was an illness from which he did not recover. It has thus fallen to me to write these Acknowledgments on his behalf. I will try, to the best of my ability, to recognize those who have contributed to this book, by name when possible but in spirit and gratitude to all those who played a part in the stories that constitute his memoir.

When David was organizing his papers for the preparation of his memoir, he developed a medical condition similar to carpal tunnel syndrome that seriously affected his ability to use the computer keyboard. Our son John introduced his father to a software program called "Dragon Naturally Speaking," which allowed him to dictate his words. In a short space of time, with patience and a few unprintable phrases, David was able to persuade the computer to accept his pronunciation, tone, and manner of speaking, and the results were remarkably successful. All this took place in John's kitchen in his house in Redmond, Washington, during the beautiful spring season of 2007.

We returned to Charlottesville a few weeks later and, surrounded by boxes containing files of photographs, newspaper clippings, carbon copies of his correspondence, and an abundance of saved e-mail messages, David began dictating his memoir. It became clear that he would need some assistance with assembling and organizing this overwhelming supply of resources, and he was fortunate to find a young library assistant, Kathy Judge, ready and eager to be part of the project. Kathy continued to assist after the manuscript was completed by indexing the book. Her skills and her patient attention to detail were essential as the project drew to a close. David and his family owe her a warm debt of gratitude.

David's book would not have moved forward without Margery Thompson's willingness to edit the manuscript and supervise its production as a publication in the Diplomats and Diplomacy series cosponsored by the Association for Diplomatic Studies and Training (ADST) and Diplomatic and Consular Officers, Retired, Inc. (DACOR). During his years at the Institute for the Study of Diplomacy at Georgetown University in Washington, D.C., David and Margery shared many responsibilities in the Institute's publishing efforts. He was particularly pleased when Margery agreed to resume that relationship with "Witness to a Changing World."

As a retired diplomat, David sought the assistance of the Freedom of Information office in the Department of State in order to access documents not yet publicly available. He was enormously grateful for the cooperation of Margaret Grafeld, Jane Diedrich, and Charles Daris of the Office of Information Programs and Services. Their assistance helped ensure the accuracy of David's view of the events he was including in the book.

Many of David's former colleagues and friends gave helpful responses to his request for their review of his description of international issues occurring in the seven countries where he served. Ambassadors Roscoe Suddarth, Philip C. Wilcox, and James Blake were among this group of reviewers, but many others were also warmly responsive.

We also encouraged David's family of three sons and two daughters to read and comment on the account of their father's life and work. Nancy, Katie, John, Daniel, and David all made helpful —often lighthearted—suggestions that David incorporated into the story. I had the pleasure of hearing David's voice as I read through the manuscript prior to its submission. I felt his presence strongly as I lived again, through his words, the sixty-five years of our marriage.

Jean Newsom
Charlottesville, Virginia
October 2008

WITNESS TO A CHANGING WORLD

1

WHO WAS CONNIE MACK?

On May 17, 1947, our first son, John, was born. That was also the day I took the oral examination for the United States Foreign Service, the diplomatic arm of the Department of State.

Among the three of us awaiting the examining panel in the San Francisco Federal Building that day was a young man who spoke of his experiences in Europe, his fluent French, and his knowledge of international affairs. With that kind of competition, I did not feel that I, who had not formally studied international relations, stood a chance.

I later discovered that the young man with his demonstrated knowledge failed the exam, while the third man, Hugh Appling, and I passed. When I had an opportunity some years later to speak with the chair of the committee, I asked him whether he remembered that day in San Francisco.

He replied, "I remember that young man well. You will recall that one member of the examining panel asked you a baseball question."

I did remember. The panel member, when he saw on my record that I had once been a sports reporter, asked me a technical question about scoring a fielders' choice.

"Well," said the chairman, "the member asked this young man who Connie Mack was. [Cornelius McGillicuddy Mack, was, for many years, manager of the Philadelphia Athletics.] The young man did not know, so we began asking him more questions about life in the United States. It was clear to us that he knew little about his own country. And, after all, American diplomats are sent abroad to explain this country."

In my hometown of Richmond, California, at that time, there would have been few people who did not know who Connie Mack was. Richmond was a great baseball town. The city had a semipro twilight league, and everyone followed the Oakland Oaks and the San Francisco Seals of the Pacific Coast League. Lefty Gomez, a pitcher for the New York Yankees, had gone to Richmond High School. In the days before the majors moved to the West Coast, we were mostly Yankee fans.

But, in Richmond, California, in the 1920s and 1930s, I learned about more than baseball. I learned about politics, prejudice, power, patronage, diversity, and faith.

My windows into the world of experience were my family, my school, my neighborhood, my church, and, ultimately, my university.

My father, Fred Stoddard Newsom, was the most important early influence in my life. He was popular whether in a family, community, or business setting. He would spin out absorbing stories to my cousins. In Richmond he became a civic leader and president of the Chamber of Commerce, an active member of the Lions Club and the Republican County Central Committee, an elder in the Presbyterian Church, and a Sunday school teacher.

With other members of my mother's family, my father built cabins on the Dunlop Ranch property. He loved fishing in the Sierras and duck hunting with Richmond friends, including the son of his business partner, John Galvin.

I was an only child, and my father and I were very close. In my earlier years he read to me from many works of literature and poetry. We built things together and, frequently, when he returned from work, played catch. We followed the fortunes of the University of California Bears sports teams. In my teen years he employed me in various capacities on the *Richmond Independent* and encouraged my interest in journalism. I was twelve when I published my first newspaper, a typewritten Dunlop family newsletter.

My father must have had a difficult childhood, although he did not speak much about it. He was born in 1885 in San Jose, California. His father, Ira Newsom, was a carpenter and probably an alcoholic. We have a 1906 letter from the wife of a saloon owner in Oakland, California, to my grandmother, describing how Ira Newsom had come in, feeling ill, and how they had put him on a cot in the rear of the saloon, where he died. His wife, my grandmother, Nettie Swazey Newsom, and, presumably, my father and his brother, Albert, had been living in Healdsburg at the time. I do not know why Ira and Nettie were separated. Albert was somewhat mentally retarded and depended on my father to find him employment. The last job I remember his having was as a janitor at the Richmond Post Office.

Nettie was a "character." My father provided her and Albert with a small house, where she lived in the company of seven cats and mementos of various kinds, including costumes for pageants that she used to stage at the First Christian Church. My fastidious mother was always appalled at the condition of Nettie's house and, upon Nettie's death in 1947, had everything inside the house destroyed. That "everything" included important Civil War mementos from Nettie's father as well as valuable letters and documents that might have given me a clearer idea of my father's early life. I was overseas at the time and was unable to prevent this cleaning out.

My father worked to support his mother and brother from an early age. He described how he picked hops in fields near Healdsburg when he was twelve. An early achiever, he was able to put himself through the University of California at Berkeley and the Pacific School of Religion. He graduated from the latter in 1911 and was ordained a minister in the Church of Christ. His first pastorate was in the Geyserville Christian Church near Healdsburg. He was not there long before he was called to the First Christian Church of Richmond

He left the ministry in 1913. My mother's explanation was that "his nerves could not stand the ministry." Shortly thereafter he was employed by the Richmond Real Estate Company.

Richmond in 1911 was a boom town. The Acheson, Topeka and Santa Fe Railroad had established a major terminal there in 1899, and Standard Oil of California had built a major refinery in 1902. The real estate firm was busy selling Richmond lots, including some that were under water, to people around the world. My father's Christian scruples must have been tested by the somewhat less than candid salesmanship of the firm.

That was not the end of the story of the underwater lots. Years later at the beginning of World War II, Richmond became the site of the Kaiser shipyard, building Victory ships. Landfill for the shipyard required locating the owners of property under water. It so happened that my father was then involved as a member of the Chamber of Commerce in helping prepare for the shipyard. In that capacity he had to institute a worldwide search for the buyers of those lots, some as far away as Thailand.

Next door to the real estate office was a new newspaper, the *Richmond Independent*, published by an enterprising young Irish Catholic, John Galvin. The *Independent* was at that time one of four newspapers in the new community. Over time, two of the four went out of business, leaving only the *Independent* and the *Record-Herald*. Galvin subsidized the *Record -Herald* to shut out other competition—my introduction to the market system.

My father left the real estate company in 1915 and joined the *Independent* as sales manager for commercial printing, but not before attracting the attention of one of the secretaries at the real estate office, my mother, Ivy Dunlop. Fred and Ivy were married on September 9, 1915. As he said in a biographic note he wrote for the Lions Club, "The only things I got out of the real estate firm were a note at the bank and the stenographer."

My father disclaimed any knowledge of his ancestry, but a few years ago my oldest son and I did some genealogical research and discovered an interesting past. We learned that, like most Americans, we were descended from immigrants—people who made what must have been agonizing decisions to leave a familiar continent for unknown shores. On August 21, 1635, two brothers, William and Richard Newsom (also known as Newsham), sailed from Dublin, Ireland, for Jamestown, Virginia, on the ship *George*. Born in Lancashire in England, they were probably Catholic and may have fled to Ireland. Being younger sons, they had little hope of inheritance and were seeking their fortunes in the new colonies. Shortly after arrival, William obtained a 550-acre grant of land in Surry County, Virginia, across from Jamestown.

William's descendants followed the country's westward path, moving successively to North Carolina, Indiana, and Iowa, becoming Quakers at some point. My grandmother, Annette Swazey, was born in Farmington, Iowa, in 1856; her father had been a captain in the Iowa Volunteers on the Northern side during the Civil War. After the war, the family moved west to San Jose, California, where my father was born.

Meanwhile, another family story was developing in Scotland, one that carried genes that have given me a curiosity about the world, a taste for adventure, and a love of the sea.

We pick up this other trail in Scotland in 1857, one year after Annette Swazey was born. In that year, a 19-year-old native of Glasgow, John Patterson Dunlop, who would become my maternal grandfather, was enlisting in the British East India Company militia. Shortly after enlistment, he departed for India to assist in quelling a mutiny of Indian soldiers against the British, famous as the Indian Mutiny. The mutiny was over by the time his contingent arrived, but he stayed on in India for two years. Upon his return from India, after studying mechanical engineering, he joined the Royal Navy as an engineering officer in the early days of the conversion to steam. His logs show that, in a career of twenty-seven years, he visited every continent. The logs also reflect the technological transition. They note that, in a voyage from Calcutta to Madras, 5407.7 hours under steam, 35 hours under steam and sail, 202 hours under sail. In a note in one of his diaries, my grandfather wrote that he did not object when the engines broke down. "It was much quieter under sail."

In 1888, having reached the rank of Commander, he decided to retire and weighed whether to retire in Egypt or in California. He chose California.

In 1889, he and his wife and three children proceeded by freighter to New Orleans and by train to San Francisco. My mother, the youngest of the three had been born six months earlier at a naval base at Chatham, outside London.

In San Francisco, Commander Dunlop arranged to purchase a pear ranch of 160 acres near Placerville, in the foothills of the Sierra Nevada Mountains, for which he paid $3500.

Commander Dunlop died in 1924 when I was six. I remember him vaguely, an old man in a skull cap sitting in a rocking chair on the front porch of the ranch house. I recall his marveling at the automobile that can "go the speed of an express train." How he, who had seen the transition from sail to steam, would have been fascinated by the changes to come.

The Dunlop and Newsom trails came together in Richmond.

My mother was an amiable person with a pleasant sense of humor but a Victorian sense of propriety, inherited from her Scottish father. She was active in Presbyterian women's organizations and taught a Sunday school class. She was also a regular member of a bridge group and a teetotaling member of the Women's Christian Temperance Union. She liked good clothes and spent much of her time shopping in San Francisco. She was always conscious of her appearance and hated to be conspicuous. She avoided banks and libraries. Like her sisters, she was an excellent cook. In later life, after my father died, she showed considerable adaptability and courage as she visited me and my family in two of our most difficult Foreign Service posts, Karachi and Baghdad. She died of pancreatic cancer in 1956.

My mother had two brothers and three sisters. Although I was an only child, I was part of a large family of twenty-one cousins who gathered frequently at the ranch house in Diamond Springs. We were closest to my mother's youngest sister, Agnes, always known as Dolly; she had been born prematurely and as a tiny baby had been put in with the chicks in the incubator behind the ranch stove. She had a difficult and often tragic life. She served as a nurse in the front lines in France in World War I. In the Depression she and her ailing husband lived at and managed the Dunlop Ranch, while she also worked as the principal nurse in the hospital in Placerville. Her husband and two sons all predeceased her, but her spirits never flagged. She lived to be ninety-three, and in the final years of her life still drove her Mustang, ate only desserts, and played the slot machines at Harrah's Club at Lake Tahoe. She rationalized the slots by saying that she always put her winnings in the church collection. Her stories of life in the Placerville Sanatorium entertained us for many years. Typical was this bit from one of her letters: "The latest addition to the sanatorium is an oldster who says he 'kain't keep nothing' on his stomach but squirrel soup. I asked him if gopher stew would do and he was mad!"

My path to that morning in 1947 at the San Francisco Federal Building was circuitous, yet each step added more to my knowledge of the world and of the United States. An understanding of the nature of politicians and politics is essential to an understanding of that world, and my early life in a small California town introduced me to both.

Edmund Muskie, when he moved from the U.S. Senate to become secretary of state in 1979, was asked whether he found diplomacy different from politics. He replied, "Diplomacy is just politics on a wider scale."

If one defines politics as the process by which people govern themselves, a small town is an excellent place to observe that process. It is also an excellent place to see our country in microcosm. In Contra Costa County I gained an understanding of the egos, ambitions, fears, and temptations that are part of governing everywhere.

My father ultimately became part owner of the *Richmond Independent*. Although Richmond was not the county seat, it was the largest city in Contra Costa County and much of the political maneuvering of the county swirled around the institutions of Richmond: the Lions and Rotary clubs, the Elks Club, the Masonic lodges. I have learned over the years in many lands how important it is to provide avenues for individual recognition and prestige. In small-town America, these clubs and lodges provide such opportunities. They were also important politically. In Richmond, a city of 30,000 in the 1930s, there were 205 clubs and lodges of various sorts; many politicians belonged to a sizeable number.

The years of my youth were years of dramatic changes in the world about us. We thrilled over Lindbergh's flight. We listened with fascination to the early crystal-set radios and read with wonder the predictions of the future in *Popular Mechanics*.

On the Dunlop ranch where my cousins and I spent summers, we observed in the 1930s the coming of electricity to rural America. The smoky oil lamps and noisy gasoline lanterns became things of the past. We saw blocks of ice replaced by the refrigerator and the primitive communications of the early telephone, "the farmer's line." The Dunlop ranch was three short rings and one long one. That didn't mean much. Most customers picked up the phone whenever it rang to listen in on a neighbor's doings.

We also saw the years of depression. On the pear ranch, if the frost did not get the buds and the trees survived the blight, the prices fell in the New York market. But it cost the farmers money to raise their crops. The struggle of farmers in El Dorado County during the depression was as near to agriculture as I have wanted to get, but that experience helped me later in understanding problems of economic development in other areas of the world.

It would have been difficult even to give the ranch away in 1935. But the long view in El Dorado County was better. My cousins, who subsequently bought out the rest, sold the ranch in 2000 to Wal-Mart for a price in excess of a million dollars. My Scottish grandfather, who bought it for $3500, would have been impressed. But, sadly for those of us who had great memories of the old 1888 ranch house, the Placerville Fire Department was invited in to burn down the house as an exercise.

Boyhood in Richmond also introduced me to the melting pot and baseball.

For a time, we lived next door to an Italian family. It was during Prohibition and the father next door used to make wine, stamping the grapes with his feet in a large barrel in the backyard. Players on our high school football team represented eleven different national origins. At an early age, I was conditioned to diversity.

But, as I look back through a career that dealt with Africa and Asia and with human rights in my country and others, I realize how unconscious I was in those days of race issues. We had a number of Hispanics in our town, but few African-Americans. Also, as I look back, I recall the undercurrents of prejudice in the derogatory epithets used as a matter of course — including by my own parents — to refer to those who were different. The presence of Jews and Catholics in certain settings was met with raised eyebrows, and both were excluded from some local organizations. Chinese had difficulty buying homes.

Only when I went east to Columbia University in New York did I begin to realize the deep emotions relating to race. In a trip south from New York, I observed for the first time the phenomenon of separate facilities. Later, in the 1960s, when I was dealing with African affairs in the State Department, I had to carefully arrange trips for new black African diplomats between Washington and New York so that they did not encounter the embarrassment of separate facilities.

The Civil War was a distant historical event in California, but not for Douglas S. Freeman, a biographer of Robert E. Lee and one of our professors at the Columbia School of Journalism, or for my roommate from Gloucester, Virginia, John Mawhinney. For them, "The War of Northern Aggression," or "The War between the States," or "The Late Unpleasantness" had not yet been concluded. My education on race discrimination was further amplified when some of my Japanese-American friends were sent to relocation centers after Pearl Harbor.

Richmond and Contra Costa County had their own power structure. In part, it revolved around the principal industry, the Standard Oil refinery. The manager of the refinery occupied one of the better houses in Mira Vista, on the hill to the east of the city, and he and his wife had status. He ranked with local bankers, lawyers, and doctors in the social hierarchy. They symbolized wealth and jobs in the town.

Politics revolved around the *Independent*. My father was a member of the Republican County Central Committee. His partner, John Galvin, was a Democrat. One of the principal political operatives, attorney Tom Carlson, was a tenant in the *Independent*'s building. My father owned a building across the street in which the local assemblyman was a tenant. At home our dinner table conversation often involved discussions of which candidates the paper should support for supervisor, assemblyman, or governor or how to get jobs for friends and relatives. From time to time, my father also mentioned the growing tensions between the newspaper and the increasingly powerful unions of printers, stereotypers, and pressmen. Later, I was to experience this directly when for a short time my wife and I owned a newspaper.

During elections—beginning with the Hoover-Smith contest in 1928—I was one of those sent out by the *Independent* to gather results from local polling stations, observing as the judges counted the ballots and entered the results in great sheets. Then, before television, the results were entered on glass slides and projected on a giant screen in front of the *Independent* office.

At an early age, I became aware that politics combines power, influence, and services—a mixture of calculation and compassion. And politics in Contra Costa County were often colorful. The sheriff's brother ran the local slot machine syndicate. Slot machines were, on the books, illegal. The district attorney, when he was unhappy with the sheriff, would have his deputy raid clubs that had slot machines. Once, as a stunt during an election campaign, the sheriff released a group of prisoners from the county jail, then formed a posse to round them up.

Just outside the city limits of Richmond were some "houses of ill repute," as they were delicately called. Periodically the ladies employed would be rounded up and brought before the justice of the peace, the same justice who was frequently one of their customers.

I first encountered Earl Warren, later California governor and U.S. Supreme Court chief justice, when he was district attorney of neighboring Alameda County. I was working as a reporter on the *Independent*. A group of clubs, with bingo games and slot machines, had developed along the border between the two counties. Warren found a state statute that authorized county authorities to take action against nuisances within 200 yards of the county line. On that basis, he raided the clubs with his deputies, much to the consternation of Contra Costa authorities.

Once, later, when returning to Richmond on a visit, I spoke to the local Rotary Club and mentioned that growing up in Contra Costa County had made it easier for me to understand the politics of the Middle East. Not all the members were pleased with my remarks.

My father not only introduced me to politics; he shared with me the fascination of the newspaper—the linotype, presses, the great rolls of paper, contact with the community, the excitement of deadlines. In the days before television, the Internet, and the twenty-four-hour news cycles, the *Independent* would print "extras" when significant events occurred. I remember selling "extras" in 1935 when Will Rogers and Wiley Post were killed in an airplane crash in Alaska. The newspaper connection also showed me the perilous life of the small-town merchant, whose advertising was so important to the life of the newspaper—and to our own.

On one occasion during a summer break from college, I was given a job selling one-inch ads that were to form the border of a city map. I approached one merchant in San Pablo, a small suburb of Richmond, and tried to sell him an ad. I shall always remember his reply. "Son, I don't have enough hay to feed my nightmares, let along buy an ad from you."

My father also generated in me an appreciation for words. He had majored in English at the University of California at Berkeley. During my childhood, he would read to me not only the poetry of Wordsworth, Shelley, and Keats, but also the novels of Dickens, James Fenimore Cooper, Sir Walter Scott, and others. Perhaps indicating a wanderlust gene that later turned up in his son, my father was also fond of the travel books of Richard Halliburton and the novels of international intrigue of E. Phillips Oppenheim. He retained his love for the Bible, particularly the letters of Paul, which he also read to me.

Much of our family life centered around the First Presbyterian Church. My father was an elder, my mother was active in the Ladies Aid. Both taught in the Sunday school. I still love and occasionally play the hymns learned during that period of my life. It was there, also, that I first met Jean Frances Craig, who eventually, after some years of friendship and pursuit, became my wife—and my partner in diplomacy.

The Craig family, recent immigrants from Canada, introduced me to another political perspective: the Democratic left. Jean's father, Clarence, worked for the Santa Fe Railroad and was an official in the Brotherhood of Railroad Trainmen. The family was staunchly Democratic. Clarence had at one time, I believed, voted for Norman Thomas, the Socialist candidate for president. Our budding friendship was sorely tested by arguments over the gubernatorial election in California in 1942, when Republican Earl Warren was running against a leftist Democrat, Culbert L. Olson.

In my early years, my destiny was clearly to be a newspaperman. My father never liked the word "journalist." He would say "a journalist is a newspaperman out of work." But there were hints that my ultimate destiny might be different, hints of links to a world beyond Richmond and California.

One hint of that world came in 1933, when a group from Richmond sailed on a Standard Oil tanker for an island in the Persian Gulf called Bahrain to explore for oil. Friends from that year's high school graduating class were on board. Over the coming years, Richmond would have close links with the growing U.S. oil presence in both Bahrain and Saudi Arabia. Many years later, I became officer-in-charge of Arabian Peninsula Affairs in the Department of State and worked with some of the oil pioneers of that early period.

I must have inherited from Commander Dunlop a love of the sea. I never tired of walking down the Embarcadero in San Francisco and looking at the liners that used to grace that port: the *Lurline* and *Mariposa* of the Matson Line, the *California* of the United States Lines, the round-the-world President liners, and the Dollar liners. I was deeply disappointed when the State Department decided in the 1960s that all diplomats must go to their posts by air.

My first taste of the sea was on a coastal steamer that used to run between San Francisco and Los Angeles. My mother and I made such a trip in the late 1920s. With my father, we made two trips through the Panama Canal on banana boats. Then, in 1938, when I had just graduated from Berkeley, my mother and I sailed for England on the Cunard liner *Saturnia*. My father followed later on the *Aquitania*.

The 1930s was the period of Franklin D. Roosevelt, whom my Republican mother always referred to, somewhat derisively, as "that man." It was a time, also, of turmoil and depression.

The University of California at Berkeley was in the 1930s, as in the 1960s, a center for agitation. Harry Bridges, leftist (some said communist) leader of the International Longshoremen's Association in San Francisco, was seeking to enhance the power of the unions. Some students supported the strikers, some were strikebreakers. A major confrontation with the Board of Regents occurred when one group of students invited Earl Browder, head of the Communist Party, to speak at the university gate.

I, or rather my parents, paid the $26 per semester fee that enabled me to attend Berkeley. As an English major with journalistic ambitions, when I was not engrossed in Shakespeare, Spender, or Milton, I was active on the *Daily Californian*. As one also active in the youth group of the First Presbyterian Church, I was involved in the antiwar movements of the day.

In an essay I wrote some years later, I described the Berkeley scene: "Through four years of college, I followed the trend of university thought. I wrote pacifist plays, gave pacifist talks, and served on a university committee for peace propaganda. America in 1917, I learned, had been dragged into a war which was not hers by British propaganda, American money interests, and a national hysteria. From a professor who had been a framer of the treaty, we learned that Versailles was one of the greatest crimes of the age. We were shown motion pictures of the horrors of war. We applauded *Johnny Johnson, Bury the Dead,* and *Idiot's Delight* (antiwar plays of the era)."

Except for courses continuing my high school French, I paid little attention otherwise to the international scene. That was to change in 1938, when my mother and father and I headed for Europe.

Thinking back on that trip, I am amazed at how oblivious we seemed to be to what was happening around us. We were there in the year before the lights went out all over Europe, but all seemed normal. We were in Paris during a visit to France by King George V and Queen Mary. Paris was alive with the Tricolor and the Union Jack.

My perspective changed, however, when I ended the visit staying with a cousin, John Dunlop, who was doing graduate work in Cambridge. (John and his wife were sharing a house with John Kenneth Galbraith and his wife. Both later became Harvard professors and John served as Secretary of Labor under President Gerald Ford.)

There I encountered the bitter debates among British students over whether to accept or oppose what was happening in Germany and over the divide between the admirers and denouncers of Stalin and the Soviet Union. There, also, for the first time, I was subjected to bitter criticisms of my own country, the United States, whether for its pacifism, its capitalism, or its intellectual shortcomings.

I fear I was more fascinated by the antics of the Cambridge students. Many were Alpine climbers who practiced their art on the Gothic buildings of the university. The story was still fresh about the students who, during the Italian war against the Ethiopians, climbed the steeple of King's College Chapel and implanted the Ethiopian flag. Soldiers were brought in the next day to shoot the flag down. The morning after, the campus awoke to see a chamber pot where the flag had been at the top of the spire.

I returned from Europe in June of 1938 and went to work as a reporter on the *Richmond Independent*. But, as I sat and looked out through the Golden Gate, a wider world beckoned. In August I sailed on a freighter, the *Fred Luckenbach,* for New York and the Columbia University School of Journalism, where doors opened to that wider world and to a diplomatic career for which I had never planned—or dreamed.

2

JUST LIKE CENTRAL PARK

One night in November 1939, three students at the Columbia University Graduate School of Journalism were walking down Lenox Avenue in Harlem in New York City. Herbert Price was from Utah, Vivian Richter was from South Africa, and I came from California.

We stopped on a corner and chatted with a police officer who asked where we were from. When Vivian mentioned that he was from South Africa the policeman asked him a number of questions about Africa. Then, with a kind of a dreamy expression on his face, he said, "Gee! I've always wondered what Africa must be like. I imagined that it was full of wide open spaces and forests—just like Central Park." Further discussion with this officer revealed that he had never been outside Manhattan.

With fifty-nine others (including fifteen women and two foreign students), I had entered the School of Journalism in September. Our walk up Lenox Avenue was part of our discovery of New York. The city was our laboratory. We were sent on assignments throughout the city and came to know its dynamism, its diversity, and the mix of its people.

As a young man from the West, I was enthralled. At one point, I wrote home:

> The greatest thing about the education is this city. It is not a place to stay forever—all those here admit that. It is, however, a well to return to and draw upon and a well to provide the spark that will make other places and other jobs alive in the same way. Wherever we go from here, we will be able to see a vision of a greater world of which this city is now the center. New York in many ways is the most provincial of all

cities; in other ways it exemplifies the infinite possibilities of ideas and visions.

We learned many things about the city. It was a city of villages, neighborhoods often centered around the local deli. Many of its residents, like the policeman in Harlem, seldom ventured beyond Manhattan. It was, and is, a city of the arts. At the Metropolitan Opera I heard Zinka Milanov (whom I was later to meet in person in Norway) in *Aida*, and stood to hear Laurence Melchior and Kirsten Flagstad in *Tristan and Isolde*. In the theater, I was privileged to see Maurice Evans in *Hamlet* and Lillian Hellman's hit, *The Little Foxes*, and witnessed the heartlessness of Manhattan audiences as people, talking all the way, strolled out of one of Jerome Kern's few failures, *Very Warm for May*. The New York World's Fair of that year introduced us to a technological future that was just coming into focus.

I was witness to the city's contrasts. When the actress Mary Pickford was invited to speak at a student dinner, I was elected to pick her up from her lavish apartment at the Sherry-Netherlands Hotel in a chauffeured limousine. I described her in a letter home:

> Mary Pickford is a small woman, beautifully dressed in a silver fox cape and a ring with a half-inch-long diamond on one finger. Her face shows the wear of her years as a public celebrity, but she still has a beauty and a charm. Her voice is rather harsh but still very 'little girlish.' She is still the child actress in her manner and her appearance as much as is possible. She is very gracious and completely without pose. She spoke briefly to us, but very well. She told us that she always had a soft spot in her heart for newspapermen. She had always been treated very fairly by them. Some of the other film people try to avoid them, but she realized that her life was not a private one and that the press had to be accepted as an integral part of it.

Immediately after the Pickford dinner, in sharp contrast, I went to the McCauley-Cremone rescue mission on West 42nd St. I was part of a group from the Broadway Presbyterian Church conducting a night service for the mission. One hundred twenty-five men were packed into the room. I led the singing. I commented, "They all had the ashes of a wasted life written on their faces and clothes," but they sang better than any group I had ever led.

Taking advantage of the presence of some of the great preachers in New York, I had a variety of religious experiences. These included hearing Harry Emerson Fosdick at Riverside Church, Norman Vincent Peale at Marble Collegiate Church, George Buttrick at Madison Avenue Presbyterian Church, the evangelist Gypsy Smith, and Father Divine at his No. One Heaven in Harlem.

I participated in active journalism of sorts, writing copy for the *Washington Heights Observer*, a free-distribution weekly paper for that area of upper Manhattan. One of my tasks was to proofread the final copy before the press run. This led me to various parts of New York as the publisher constantly sought a cheaper printer. He finally settled on a print shop in Coney Island. I still have recollections of walking down the snowy boardwalk, late at night, and climbing a flight of rickety stairs to reach the print shop.

The focus of national sports interest in those years was on the East Coast, and for those of us from Richmond, California, the New York Yankees were our team. One memorable afternoon, to do a story for the *Richmond Independent*, I was able to visit Yankee Stadium and to meet the greats of that team, Lou Gehrig, Joe DiMaggio, manager Joe McCarthy, and Lefty Gomez, "with whom I talked for fifteen minutes." In my article in the *Independent*, I reported:

> The New York Yankees, three-time winners of the World Series and four-time winners of the American League pennant in four years, are little different from the countless other minor league and semipro teams in the country. They play the game with the same spirit, swear as vigorously, and seem to enjoy playing as much as any other team.
>
> There are just three differences, however, that set these young men off from other baseball players and made one realize that they were national heroes, admired and talked about by little kids, big kids, and grown-up kids from the Pacific to the Atlantic. The first was the presence of numerous photographers, calling one after another of the stars in from the field to pose in a variety of positions. And the young

> men took just as much interest in seeing and laughing at pictures of their teammates and themselves as bush leaguers do on the rare occasions when they are photographed. The second was a constant hounding by autograph hunters, with baseballs, books, programs, and all sorts of papers. The third difference was in the way they played. It was not hard to see how they became world champions. The fielding of Joe Gordon, who picked up a fast grounder and, with scarcely a motion of his arm, cut the man off at first, or of Frank Crosetti, who executed two double plays with Gordon, and the hitting of Keller and DiMaggio, so relaxed and easy that one marvels that the ball traveled so far, were beautiful things to watch.

I discovered that New York never slept. In my second semester at Columbia I rented an apartment on West 114th St. One morning at about ten o'clock, I heard a voice calling down to a visitor in the stairwell below, "Damnit what are you doing waking me up in the middle of the night?"

A variety of dining opportunities made New York a world in miniature. At least once a week we closed our eyes and placed a finger on the restaurant list. This led us to establishments from the Russian Kretchma on East 14th St to the German restaurants in Yorkville on East 86th. The war had not yet changed the character of these restaurants or stilled the voices of the singing waiters. The prices, by 2007 standards, were incredible. A dinner in one of the better restaurants could cost five dollars. At the other end of the scale, at the New Asia, a nice clean Chinese restaurant, lunch cost thirty-five cents, and dinner (tomato juice, soup, entrée, vegetable, drink, and dessert) fifty cents. Breakfast at the university dormitory cost twenty-five cents.

One of our classmates was Hermes Secondari, son of the president of the Italian Line. One evening he took us to a restaurant where slabs of dough with vegetables and cheese were cooked in great open ovens. It was my introduction to pizza.

But, beyond the fascination of the city, there was the school—and the world.

World War II had just started, accelerating both political and technological changes that would have profound effects on the practice of journalism. We were at the end of an era that had been dominated by the printing press. The structure of the one-year course was built primarily on the production of print media for a domestic audience. The principal feature of the curriculum was the production of a daily newspaper centered around a mock copy desk directed by a copy editor from the *New York Times*.

The faculty included key editors from the *Times*, Bob Garst and Ted Bernstein; Henry Pringle, Pulitzer Prize biographer of Theodore Roosevelt; Douglas Southall Freeman, editor of the *Richmond News Leader* and biographer of Robert E. Lee; Harold Cross, a specialist on media law; Roscoe Ellard, former dean of the Missouri University School of Journalism; Walter Pitkin, a writer; and Herbert Brucker, an authority on newspaper history.

Of these, the two I remember most vividly are Pitkin and Freeman. Pitkin taught classes in magazine and feature writing. Somewhat disheveled in appearance, deaf, and loud of voice, Pitkin's approach to writing was strictly commercial. In our first class he shouted at us, "Anyone who thinks about writing is an idiot. Only 10 percent of manuscripts that are written are ever reviewed and only 2 percent of those make any money." He seldom praised any student papers and on one occasion said that most of the reports the class had been doing for him "smelled."

He described how he decided to write his best-known book, *Life Begins at Forty*. He had placed the *World Almanac* table of the population breakdown by age in the United States against the best-seller list and realized that no book on the list appealed directly to the 40–60 age category. So he wrote one.

To pass the course we each had to sell an article to a magazine. We had help from the school's numerous contacts. I sold a piece on a new approach to elementary school examinations in the New York schools to *Parents' Magazine*.

In the process, Pitkin gave me a valuable lesson in writing. I showed him what I felt was my finished draft. He applied a blue pencil to the first page of about 300 words and, slashing it down to 75, tossed it back to me and said, "Tell me if I have left anything out." I had to agree that nothing meaningful had been left out. I have never forgotten the exercise and have passed on the lesson to students in diplomacy who would let verbosity get in the way of clarity.

Over and over again he emphasized what we called Pitkin rules: "Don't use so many words. Be telegraphic in style. People want to read what's in the article; they don't want to read words. The fewer words they go through to get at the meat, the better they like it. Get away from compound sentences. Get punch into your writing. Use questions—they are good for effect."

Professor Freeman was another memorable influence. A man who structured his life by the clock, he came one day a week by night train from Richmond, Virginia, to teach courses in editorial writing and feature writing. He would give us a lecture and an assignment in the morning, return in the afternoon to critique our papers, and then close the day with a homily about the South. I had the privilege of spending a weekend at his home in Richmond and visiting the attic in which he worked, an attic covered with maps of military campaigns, a war room of the Confederacy.

On one occasion I was the designated note-taker for the class. I recorded this homily:

> [Freeman] spoke of the threat and possibility of war and of the world that would come after the war. He attempted to show that this world would not be as hopeless a place as sometime pictured. He pointed to the South in the period following the War Between the States (he never called it anything else) as an example of a nation that came back after a terrible war. The South collapsed completely. Railroads stopped, mails stopped, telegraph lines were down. The sons coming home from the war were phantoms of those who had gone. Black as the picture was, the South had resources. They had men to lead and women to follow. Those men and women went to work. Big men took menial jobs. They put the evil days behind and looked to the future. They trained their sons and daughters for the future. They had faith in America.

He also frequently commented on current affairs. One of my letters observed,

> Freeman sounds most of the time like a Rotary Club speaker, "Gentlemen this and gentlemen that." He completely ignores the ladies in the class. The highlight of the day, however, was his description of the Senate in the present neutrality debate. He says all senators feel this is the time to make a speech rivaling those of Daniel Webster and they all wait for the day when they can speak. All the others get bored and leave and all those that remain are the deaf ones, who can work at their desks while the debate is going on, and the clerk, who is asleep. The others gather in the coffee room downstairs and wonder, "When is that damn fool going to shut up and sit down?"

The school's curriculum reflected only peripherally the profound changes in the offing. The school did have an international outreach. Dean Carl Ackerman was much interested in Latin America, and the school sponsored the Cabot prizes for journalism relating to that region. The Pulitzer traveling fellowships were another manifestation of international interest. Within the school, however, there were no specific courses relating to international news coverage or international political developments.

Radio was already making its mark as a source of news and competitor in advertising. The broadcasts of Edward R. Murrow from London during the war were dramatizing the power of this new medium. Showing the growing interest in radio by small newspapers, my father, because of his part ownership of the *Richmond Independent*, wrote me to find out as much as I could about the pros and cons of small newspapers owning radio stations. He had always fulminated against the threat of radio. "No one wants to listen to an ad when they can see it in print."

Television was already on exhibit at the New York World's Fair. On April 30, 1939, Franklin D. Roosevelt spoke on television from New York's W2XBS. The summer of 1939 saw the first television broadcasts of a Princeton-Columbia baseball game, a heavyweight boxing match, a major league baseball game, and a college football game. Yet I do not recall any discussion of television and its possible future impact on the collection and dissemination of news. Some attention was paid to radio, but it was peripheral.

Dr. Freeman devoted part of a course to a discussion of how to write for and speak on radio. Freeman had already become a radio personality in Richmond. He referred to the teaching of radio news as "a pioneering work in which the standards have not yet been set." He divided the students on the basis of voice tests between those who have a voice for radio and those who do not. His comments on the psychological and political consequences of radio at this early stage in its development were prescient: "Firstly it puts voice in the hands of demagogues; secondly, radio represents passive reception as against active reception through reading. Thirdly, there is no way of recapturing what is said or correcting error." Tests with students, he said, showed that what the student did not remember from a broadcast he supplemented with his own knowledge of the subject. The margin of error for radio increases as the story is repeated, with supplements from the teller's own information. "Because of this," he said, "there was much misinterpretation at the start of the war. But radio is here to stay and it is a potent part of the information machinery of the world."

Paul White, an official of the Columbia Broadcasting System, also gave a short course on the business of radio. The computer and Internet were still distant dreams.

What is even more striking, looking back at the curriculum, is the absence of any serious attention to foreign news coverage and to the knowledge necessary to an understanding of the developing world crisis. The School of Journalism was no more ready for the catastrophe that lay ahead than was the rest of the country.

My time at Columbia (1939–1940) coincided with the period of the "phony war" in Europe. It was a time, also, when the nation was engaged in a debate over whether the United States should enter the conflict. In Washington, sitting on the steps of the Capitol on September 21, 1939, I listened to President Roosevelt's neutrality speech. President Nicholas Murray Butler of Columbia spoke at the fall convocation that year with praise for the German people and a vitriolic attack on the villain who was at their helm.

The war impinged only occasionally on our lives. Active public interest was low. In a letter I wrote home on November 1, 1939, I noted, "Everyone seems very tired and bored with the war and there is little feeling one way or the other concerning it." On November 19 I wrote:

> At the German restaurant where we ate tonight the orchestra played, among other pieces, "It's a Long Way to Tipperary," "Annie Laurie," and "When Irish Eyes Are Smiling." Last week when Jack Gleason and I went to the show down here, the newsreel showed a picture of Leslie Hore-Belisha (Britain's Secretary of State for War) making a speech in Washington asserting the British war aims, and the boos and the applause were about equally distributed. If anything boos were in the majority. Last night the *World Telegram* had only four stories in the entire paper about the war. Only the *Times* seems to be keeping the conflict in the foreground.

In March of 1940, the half-finished British liner *Queen Elizabeth* slipped secretly out of its Scottish berth and sped across the Atlantic. Through our press contacts we were alerted to its impending arrival. I was able to join reporters at the Quarantine Station to watch this great grey hull emerge from the early morning mist. The ship would join other famous liners, the first *Queen Mary* and the French liner *Normandie,* tied up in the East River for the duration of the war.

On another occasion, I was sent to the Metropolitan Museum of Art to write a story about a collection of Greek statues that had been sent for safety from Europe. The lead on my story was a bit poetic: "War means nothing to five Greek treasures now at the Metropolitan Museum of Art. They were created in war, buried in war, and now, two thousand years after their creation, are again at the mercy of war."

The courts and the burning issue of communism were not neglected. I was sent to cover the trial on passport charges of Robert William Wiener, financial secretary of the Communist Party and lieutenant to Earl Browder, the party head. I was able to attend the jury selection in which "every banker they called up was challenged by the defense and every union man was challenged by the government. The jury finally narrowed down to insignificant people like a subway attendant, a museum attendant, a housewife, etc."

The School of Journalism also provided opportunities to meet prominent personalities of the day who came for special monthly dinners. Mrs. Franklin Roosevelt charmed us with her personality and her heartfelt comments on the nation's needs. I wrote home, "She has a certain quiet charm about her and is really not bad-looking in real life. . . . She speaks in a quiet voice with a directness of approach and few diversions from her subject or attempts at humor. She speaks of social problems in a platitudinous sort of way and has a singular way of avoiding incrimination as she answers questions at the close of her speech. If she were not the First Lady, she would not command the audience she does. When she does command the audience as the First Lady, however, she holds it with a definite power of her own—an assuredness and a self possession that must have been necessary in her constant rounds of activities. In short, it was interesting to hear her, but I should not go out of my way to do so again."

After a talk by Alexander Wolcott, I wrote:

> New York has often been called a small town, and though it is large in size it still has many features of the small town. Everyone speaks of it as a town—not a city. As in a small town, too, there is a "set" about whom everyone gossips and around whom most of the life of the town centers. It is not composed of the politicians or predominantly of the millionaires but of authors, playwrights, actresses, lecturers, radio stars, commentators, producers, and other millionaires or figures who by their color and character rank with the artists of the town. Everyone talks about these people; the columnists write about them; and the lecturers discuss them.
>
> Tonight I heard one of the members of this set discussing the others. The man was Alexander Wolcott, newspaperman and lecturer. He discussed people only about half of whom are nationally known. You can read the *New Yorker*

> and get the same effect. He said so many funny things I can recall only the closing one. This was a dramatic criticism he considered the best he had ever read: "George Mason played King Lear last night at the Adelphi Theater. The chief trouble was that Mason played the King as if he were expecting someone else to play an ace."

Our class spent a half-hour with the dynamic mayor of New York, Fiorella La Guardia, in his office at City Hall. From time to time we listened to him read the comics on local radio.

Naturally, as the year drew to a close, we were all particularly interested in speakers who might hire some of us. One such speaker was Paul C. Smith, a dynamic young man who had become publisher of the *San Francisco Chronicle*. I wrote home that "I don't think the Dean knows quite what to make of this young man from San Francisco and his rambling remarks. The Dean is naturally a formal person and very conservative and was a bit puzzled by the informality and liberalism of this young man." Being from San Francisco I was chosen to introduce him. He subsequently hired three graduates: Bill German, who subsequently became managing editor, David Perlman, who became science editor, and me.

My job problem was resolved in a most unexpected way.

At the end of the year, I was one of three fortunate recipients of a Pulitzer Traveling Fellowship, a grant of $1,500 "to enable each of [the recipients] to spend a year abroad to study the social, political and moral conditions of the people and the character and principles of the foreign press." Two other winners—Ross P. Schlabach Jr. and Nona Baldwin—and I shared a full page in the *New York Times* with the Pulitzer prize winners of the year: Carl Sandburg (history), William Saroyan (drama), John Steinbeck (fiction), Mark Van Doren (poetry), S. Burton Heath (reporting), Otto Tolischus (foreign correspondence), Edmund Duffy (cartoons), Ray Stannard Baker (biography), and Bart Howard (editorial writing).

That travel fellowship would ultimately lead not to a career in journalism but to one in diplomacy, farthest from my mind in 1940. But I subsequently realized that journalism was not a bad preparation for diplomacy—although adjustments were required. Generally, the journalist is on the outside looking in, judging, but without responsibility for action. The journalist is working against deadlines set by the process. The diplomat, with the onus of responsibility, seeks—and hopes for—the time for deliberation. For the diplomat, events, not the daily production of a paper, drive deadlines.

Diplomacy also involves changes of environment and the need to adjust to new surroundings and new personalities—and Columbia provided both. Columbia also provided a rigorous training in the use of words, another essential in diplomacy

I decided to use the grant to go around the world. The cheapest round-the-world ticket was $600 on a Japanese line, the Osaka Syoshen Kaisha (OSK). With Europe at war and the tensions with the Japanese, the time for such a voyage did not seem auspicious, but I was not going to let this opportunity pass.

My original itinerary was to include Japan, Singapore, Colombo, Mombassa, Beira (in Mozambique), Cape Town, Buenos Aires, and Rio de Janeiro. By stopping off and waiting for the next ship, I was able to visit North China, the Dutch East Indies, India, South Africa, and Chile. I acquired a fascination with the world and its often intractable problems that never left me.

3

A NEW ORDER IN ASIA

In traveling through Asia in 1940, I was experiencing the final days of European domination in that continent. While I did not realize it at the time, I was observing the beginning of the process of decolonization, a process that was to dominate my life as a diplomat seven years later.

Japan was proclaiming its "New Order" in Asia, an order challenging European imperialism. Its invasion of French Indochina had already begun. The Sino-Japanese conflict that started in 1931 continued. The attack on Pearl Harbor was only fourteen months away.

In the major British colonies, the strong momentum of independence movements was clearly felt. The war in Europe that was to have such profound effect on the imperial system was already underway. Western Europe, except for Britain, Sweden, and Switzerland, was under German occupation. German influence was strong in the nominally neutral countries of Spain and Portugal and in the Axis ally Italy. Air battles raged over British and German cities. Conflict between the Axis and Britain had begun in North and East Africa. The British were retreating before Rommel in North Africa. Having attacked the Russians, the Germans were moving toward Stalingrad. On September 26, Japan began the invasion of Indochina and, on September 27, joined Germany and Italy in a tripartite pact.

I sailed from Los Angeles on the Japanese liner *Brazil Maru* on July 30, 1940. A new luxury vessel, it carried only eighteen passengers on a ship designed for a thousand. Twelve of the eighteen were Japanese returning from Brazil, who kept largely to themselves. Of the rest, four others were American—three missionaries returning to Africa and Karl Kup, traveling to China to collect specimens of early Chinese paintings and prints for the New York Public Library.

The voyage was ghostly. Karl Kup and I walked at night on empty decks; the ghostly impression was enhanced by periods of fog. We peered into spacious lounges, eerie in their emptiness. Stewards, with so few passengers to care for, monopolized the deck sports.

We arrived in Yokohama on August 18. I joined Karl Kup at the Imperial Hotel, the famous Tokyo landmark designed by Frank Lloyd Wright. I decided to stay when I discovered it was only 50 cents more a night than the YMCA.

Initially my first impression was of a relatively friendly country. I experienced no overt anti-American manifestations. But, as the days went on, I began to realize the implications of Japan's involvement in China, referred to as "the China incident." There were blackouts to conserve fuel and shortages of many items, including paper and gasoline. Taxis and buses coasted with their motors off at every opportunity, and taxi drivers pushed their cabs up in a hack line. Taxis were hard to get because their drivers were told to take Japanese first.

Air raid drills and blackout tests were common. One evening I went for a walk and got caught in an air raid drill just as I was passing through the geisha district.

The atmosphere was marked by the symbols of the Greater East Asia Co-Prosperity Sphere and by other indications of the war with China. Flags were everywhere, and the Greater East Asia Co-Prosperity Sphere march was blaring from loud speakers on Tokyo corners.

I still recall the tune of the Greater East Asia Co-Prosperity Sphere march. Thirty years after this first visit to Japan, I returned as a U.S. official to discuss assistance to Africa with the Japanese Foreign Ministry. After our formal discussions, we adjourned for dinner at a geisha house where the custom was to sing after dinner. I was asked if I knew any Japanese songs. After some hesitation, I said, "Well, I do remember one tune from a previous visit, that of the Greater East Asia Co-Prosperity Sphere March." My hosts were much amused. The older ones also remembered, and we joined in a rendition of that march.

On September 9, 1940, in a letter to Dean Ackerman, I wrote:

> Japan is going through a drastic revolutionary period under her new government. Japan's "New Structure" has been born during the four weeks I have been here. I have been able to see at first hand the adoption of a rigid system of economic, political, social, and moral control by a great nation.
>
> A Cabinet Planning Board to centralize authority has been organized. A Central Bureau of Information is being organized to control all press, radio, newsreels, and movies. Newspaper articles urge earlier marriages to increase the birth rate. The worship of deities is being encouraged and enforced through the establishment of a special board of heavenly and earthly deities. Clubs are merging and dissolving. Rotary clubs have severed their international connections to work for the new "Asiatic Order." Strict money control has been established.
>
> The most stringent part of the new order is the anti-luxury law. After October 7th sales will be prohibited of expensive silk cloth, jewelry, silverware and ivory ware, of ready-made suits over 80 yen [at that time $20], neckties over 40 yen, watches over 50 yen, tables over 100 yen, and bouquets and wreaths over 10 yen, to mention a few of the articles. Women may no longer wear fancy brocaded clothes. The use of cosmetics and fancy coiffures is being discouraged. Geisha houses cannot open until 5 p.m. Dance halls are being closed throughout Japan. In Kobe, a taxi cannot be used to take people to places of amusement. The Episcopal Church has cast off foreign connections and is becoming Japanese-centered. All girls between sixteen and twenty-five are being forced to join a new Girls League.
>
> The new structure has been brought about partly because of Japanese aspirations, but more certainly by tremendous shortages in the country. After October, private citizens will get four gallons of gasoline per month.

> September 16th has been set aside as Rabbit Day in memory of the rabbits who have given their skins to make shoes for the Army. All stray dogs in Tokyo were being rounded up and slaughtered to be used for meat for animals, shoe leather, and fertilizer. It is going to become a crime in Tokyo to kill a puppy. That puppy can be brought up for "the good of the state." Small boys have left other jobs to go to work for industries; small girls have taken their place in offices. Caddies are being abolished on golf courses. No more automobiles are being sold in Japan. Many things are rationed, including textiles, vegetables, fruit, wheat, rice, tin cans, hemp, coal, isinglass, sugar, electric power, and matches. A family of five gets seven hundred matches a month.
>
> The worst shortage has been rice. Last year's rice crop was one of the lowest in history, because of the shortage of manpower and because of a bad drought. Rice in Tokyo is 70 percent foreign rice mixed in with Japanese rice. Foreign rice makes the Japanese ill. Siam sent a special mission to Japan to show her how to make Siamese rice palatable. Acorn wine has been developed to take the place of sake.

One explanation given to me for the anti-luxury ordinances was the desire to conserve all luxury articles for export to get badly needed foreign exchange. With the entrance of British and French colonies into the war, much of Japan's textile trade stopped. Japan had large stocks of goods that it could not sell. While cotton was being rationed, one million yards of such cloth was stocked in warehouses in Osaka and Kobe, awaiting shipments to foreign markets that no longer existed.

More than I realized at the time, Japan was preparing for something beyond China.

Signs of the Axis relationship were everywhere. Germans, both officials and visitors, were wearing the Swastika. German ships, interned for the moment, were visible in Yokohama harbor. And Japanese compared their role in Asia to that of Germany in Europe. One Japanese citizen proudly told me, "We are keeping the peace in China as Germany is keeping it in Europe."

On September 14th I wrote to Paul C. Smith of the *San Francisco Chronicle*: "It is it agreed among all Americans here that the Germans and Italians are doing a most clever piece of fifth column work. The German news agency in Tokyo for instance, now has twelve correspondents; most other agencies have only one or two at most. According to other correspondents, most of the twelve have never seen a newspaper. Germans and Italians wear their party emblems openly and get the best service everywhere. Japanese frankly say that they do not like the Germans and Italians as well as they do the British and Americans. But they believe that the former are going to win the war and, in their victory, they see Japan's only salvation."

The following editorial appeared in the Japanese-dominated *Peking Chronicle* on the first anniversary of the start of the European war: "Britain, after a dishearteningly long chain of reverses, not only in Europe, but anywhere in the world where the manifest decline of British prestige and power has raised hitherto dormant hopes and aspirations, and, after deliberately rejecting several opportunities for a peaceful settlement, must face, probably, the very hard realities of a situation for which she bears full responsibility. The Axis powers, on the other hand, fortified by hard-fought victories and conscious of the greatly widened responsibilities which have become theirs can look confidently into the future."

I was treated courteously, with no outward signs of anti-American feeling, wherever I went in Japan and North China. The embossed letter of introduction from Columbia University seemed to have a magic quality. At one point, I had to tell a Japanese immigration official who Joseph Pulitzer was. He took copious notes in his little notebook.

Other Americans who had been longer in Japan told a somewhat different story. The General Motors manager, who had resided in Japan for 36 years, said that, for the first time in his life, he was spit upon one day as he walked down a street in Kobe. At a dinner, also in Kobe, the American hostess explained that the meat was burned because the cook's husband had beaten her that day because she was working for foreigners.

I was encouraged to give newspaper interviews on the grounds that such interviews brought the visitor's business out in the open and made a police visit unnecessary. To refuse an interview was apparently a sure way to be called upon by the police the next day.

One saw visible signs of the Japanese sacrifices in China. On August 21 I wrote: "Yesterday I saw another phase of the China incident as I went through the Tokyo Station. Forty-eight soldiers came marching through the station, each with a little square box tied against his stomach by sashes of white linen. Following them was a parade of other soldiers, women with vendors, and women carrying flowers. There was not a single show of emotion on any face. There could well have been, too, because in each little box were the ashes of a Japanese soldier who had fallen in China. They had just arrived from the 'continent' by ship and were being taken north for burial."

China

In September, I traveled to Japanese-occupied North China, It was my first view of a military occupation.

I sailed from Yokohama on August 26 on the *Haruda Maru,* an ancient vessel built in 1905 for the English Channel service. It was sold to the Japanese in 1925 and still had the British coat-of-arms on the glass doors to the salon.

Early in the morning, I stood on the deck of the ship and watched our approach to the mountainous shoreline of China. Our ship proceeded up the bay into the harbor of Tsingtao, passing the U.S.S. *Augusta,* part of the U.S. Navy East Asiatic fleet. Beyond was the dark outline of a Japanese destroyer. Around me were more than 200 Japanese fellow passengers, army officers, businessmen, and settlers coming to supervise, work, and pioneer in the land they considered their frontier.

When we docked, Japanese and Chinese officials surged on board, and we were lined up for the examination of our passports and papers. We were entering China, but the seal of the Japanese Imperial Consul General was stamped in our landing permits.

My first view of one phase of the occupation came as our ship moved slowly into the dock. Gangs of Chinese coolies, twice the size of their Japanese bosses, were handling the lines and the cargo. Suddenly, there was a commotion on the pier. A coolie, a small object in his hand, broke from the gang and ran toward the street.

Japanese guards were at once everywhere. Three of them stopped the coolie, striking him. The bulky Chinese dropped to his feet and begged for mercy. His cries went unheeded and he was dragged, screaming, into a warehouse. For some minutes the agonizing cries could be heard; then there was silence. The guards came out but the coolie did not.

On my first Sunday in Peking, I attended a worship service in a British Chapel in the Legation Quarter. The congregation was small. Only that week had the last British troops garrisoned in Peking left the city. I was there at a historic moment.

Throughout North China at the time, one flag dominated—a hollow, winged red circle on a white field, the flag of the Japanese-owned North China Railway. A majority of the troops wore similar insignias on their caps. The North China Railway was the moving force in Japanese-occupied China. Not only did it run the railways, but it built the factories and protected the new settlers. A Chinese, speaking guardedly to me on the train, told me that the Japanese soldiers and people could not leave the railroads and the large cities. "They would not come back," he said.

The trains were frequently derailed and bridges dynamited. Trains were blacked out and carried six to eight Japanese soldiers in each car. Armed guards with fixed bayonets patrolled the platforms of dimly lit stations. With barbed wire around each station, Chinese were only admitted with tickets and after being searched. At the time, the Japanese were trying to get Chinese to work in the factories in Manchukuo. Unable to round up workers themselves, the Japanese paid Chinese who would collect people by promising them better wages in another part of China. Those responding were then shipped to Manchukuo.

Soon after we left Tsingtao, a White Russian official of the railroad came through to inspect our passports. As one foreigner put it to me, "These people [the White Russians] are without a country and have become the pawns of the Japanese in North China."

I obtained a visa for Manchukuo in Peking. It took me two and a half hours of waiting in a crowd of Mongolians, Russians, American missionaries, Chinese, and Japanese. At one point the chair on which I sat collapsed. In my two weeks of travel through North China, my passport was inspected twelve times. My baggage was opened and searched six times, and I filled out thirteen elaborate forms, mostly in processes conducted by White Russians.

Returning to Japan from Peking, the train passed through Korea. I was in Korea for 18 hours but was only able to set foot on Korean soil twice for five minutes at stations. Yet to do that I had to show my passport twice, fill out a long form, answer ten minutes of questions, open my baggage, and change all my money. When we reached the Korean border at 5:15 a.m., I had to get up, put on my bathrobe, and stand in line in the station for fifteen minutes to change my money. I went back to bed, and at 6:30 the passport inspector came through and made me get up and dress.

English was widely spoken, and language was only occasionally a problem. On the *Haruda Maru* one morning, I asked for hot water. A steward other than mine brought a can. Then a few minutes later my own steward brought a can. I tried to tell him that I already had some. He looked blank and in a few minutes came back with a third can.

The railway was heavily guarded, curtains were drawn across all the windows on the train, and station platforms were dark. A publicity folder from the North China Railway acknowledged the difficulties: "Every village within 10 kilometers of the railway has been proclaimed a railway-loving village, and its inhabitants are being urged to cooperate in the protection of the railway against Communist bandits. Periodic railway-loving trains with food and entertainment are sent to the railway-loving villages to encourage cooperation with the railway."

In a column I wrote for the Cape Town (South Africa) *Argus* on December 28,1940, I described the situation in Peking:

> In Peking I had my first view of a city under foreign occupation. Chinese who had once held white-collar jobs were working as rickshaw boys. Prices had soared to four times their normal levels. . . . Signs saying "Down With The British" and "Support The New Order in China" had been erected everywhere by the Japanese.
>
> Peking is a rundown city. Its national monuments are being covered by grass and are falling into ruin. Many of its treasures have gone, taken by fleeing Chinese troops. The

hotel where I stayed in the city was falling to pieces. While I was writing my letters, the chair at the desk collapsed under me.

In a letter, written on the Dutch freighter that took me from Japan, I observed: "Japanese soldiers were everywhere in Peking, driving American cars dangerously through crowded streets, their horns a constant blare, riding through streets, fully armed, in American trucks, forcing Chinese to accept low prices in shops and rickshaws. Japanese businessmen stride arrogantly into the best hotels and restaurants, ill-dressed, ill-mannered, and demanding a maximum of service. And last night on this ship at dinner, the little Japanese who is a fellow passenger told us that Japan has not occupied China, 'We only keep the peace.'"

In my brief visit to Peking I traveled in blacked-out trains over tracks recently repaired after guerillas had attacked. The famous Summer Palace in Peking was crowded with Japanese soldiers in white kimonos, recuperating from the wounds of battle.

Train travel in Japanese-occupied North China was frequently interrupted by guerilla attacks. My letter records the trip from Peking through Manchukuo and Korea to Pusan and the boat back to Japan. "Our train was the second train out of Peking in 36 hours. There had been no train service to Tiensin the day before. Guerillas had torn up the tracks. You ask a Chinaman what time a train leaves and he will tell you the time and then say, 'Maybe it no run,' and a big smile will come over his face. Nothing makes the Chinese happier than a day when the trains don't run."

Rereading my letters home as I write this leaves me somewhat puzzled. Letters I wrote from Japan show little realization of the growing militarism of the country or of the possible threat to U.S. interests. Instead, they are full of praise for Japanese politeness and for the beauty and charm of the country. Perhaps I was conscious of possible censorship because later, in a letter written from Singapore, I said, "The more I see of the 'new order' here in Asia and the representatives in Asia of the 'new order' in Europe, I am convinced that it is something America must stop, even if it means war for us."

I returned from China via Manchukuo and Korea and prepared to leave Japan to move farther into Asia.

4

FADING EMPIRES

In the desire to see still another imperial domain, I booked passage on a Dutch freighter for the Dutch East Indies. The freighter *Tjimanoek* was part of the fleet of the Japan–China–Java line (JCJL). Because its ships never stayed long in any port, it was known as the "Just Came, Just Left" Line.

The *Tjimanoek* was an old, slow freighter, its average speed six knots an hour. The crew fished from the stern. Besides myself, there were ten other passengers, including a young Dutch soldier of fortune, Maximilian Von Stockum, one of the more unforgettable characters I met on the trip. He could have fitted in a Grahame Greene novel.

Von Stockum was twenty-two, the same age as I, and apparently had all he wanted in his life. He had an automobile at twelve and an airplane at fifteen with which, to hear him tell it, he terrorized the neighboring country folk. He had fought in Spain and in Finland and following that spent four months in Stockholm "with a different girl every four days." He offered to fight for Britain but was refused because he had fought for Franco in Spain. He said he would not fight for the Chinese Nationalists because they did not pay enough. The invasion of Holland evidently cut off most of his income, and he was forced to shift for himself. After buying the ticket to Java he had about $40 left and some pearls that he had purchased in Japan. When he entered the Dutch East Indies city of Surabaya, the customs took away his pistol and correspondence with his father in German. He smuggled in three strands of pearls by wearing them around his neck but was later unable to sell them in Java. The Dutch said he could stay in Java if he joined the Army for a year, but he refused. It was at that point that I left the story.

The voyage of the *Tjimanoek* was a constant reminder of the world at war. The ship was in blackout. Although passengers were told what time to be on board, the actual sailing time was never posted.

The war was never far from the minds of the officers of the *Tjimanoek*. I asked the Chief Officer (whose home was in occupied Holland) whether the Southern Cross was yet visible. "Oh," he replied, "We don't have that here any more. Hitler took it away to give to Goering. It was the only cross that Goering did not have."

We arrived in Surabaya in Java September 27,1940, after brief stops in Menado and Makassar, island ports that I was to visit again thirty years later. Dutch customs took two and a half hours. Every letter and paper was read and all letters intended for mailing had to be handed over for censorship. After my person and my luggage were thoroughly searched, I had to declare my money. I had a bit of explaining to do because I carried a letter of credit that I had not yet used. It took me a while to explain what an emergency was. I proceeded from Surabaya by train to Batavia (now Jakarta), the capital of the Dutch East Indies.

Just to the east of Java was the island of Bali. Even then it was known as a destination for American tourists. The Dutch viewed it with some contempt. I wrote home:

> Everyone in Java holds Bali in contempt as a bait for American tourists. American tourists seem to act as crudely down here as anywhere else and Bali has been set up as a sort of sucker's paradise for them. Few of the Dutch in Java have been there and those who have say there is not a great deal to see. One example of Bali's reception to Americans: the tourist photographs of Bali show the Balinese women bare to the waist. As the Dutch put it, a thrill for the grocers in Kansas. This is not the customary habit of the Balinese women but whenever they see an American tourist coming they remove their jackets preparatory to posing for photographs for which they ask the usual fee.

(Much later when I was ambassador in Jakarta, I visited Bali eleven times, mostly in connection with congressional visits.)

During the two days I spent in this major territory, Dutch officials were preoccupied with a Japanese economic mission. Dr. Walter A. Foote, the American consul, told me that the Japanese were seeking 3 million gallons of oil annually from the Dutch government and an oil concession in New Guinea. The Dutch replied that they had nothing to do with the oil fields and referred the Japanese to the companies. The Japanese invasion of the Dutch East Indies, on December 16, 1941, made moot whatever decisions were reached in these discussions.

The Tokyo delegation encountered language problems. They spoke no Dutch, and only a little English. They asked that the conference be conducted in German. The Dutch replied, "We are sorry. We forgot all the German we knew on May 10 [the day Germany invaded Holland]." According to Dr. Foote, to receive the diminutive Japanese delegation, the Dutch assembled a guard of honor of 100 soldiers, all over 6 feet, commanded by a lieutenant colonel, 6 feet seven.

The German capture of Holland made the East Indies even more vital to the Dutch. I was told, "This is now our only Holland. If we lose the Indies, we lose all." In an article for the *Star* in Cape Town, I wrote:

> Java is today a colony preparing for any emergency and supporting Britain financially and morally to the limit. In Britain lies their only hope for a free Holland. All tourists entering Java must undergo a thorough searching, both of their luggage and of their persons. The admittedly large fifth column element in Java before the invasion of Holland has made the government especially wary. All of the entrant's papers are taken from him and read by the censor before he can be admitted. Every male citizen in Java today must submit to a year's military service and to two weeks every year thereafter. All incoming Hollanders must complete military service before they can land employment in the Indies. There was little fear in Java, but there was a great

determination to maintain the freedom of the Indies at all costs.

During my visit to the Indies, I became suddenly aware that all the places I would be visiting next were parts of European colonial empires: Singapore, India, British East Africa, Portuguese East Africa, and South Africa. In visits to officials and newspapers, I was dealing largely with Europeans or with those of mixed blood, especially in the Dutch East Indies. A seed of curiosity about the future of empires was planted that was to be relevant to my later diplomatic career. In 1940, in Asia outside of Japan, it was only in India that I was to have extensive contacts with people of the country.

On October 5, I sailed from Batavia for Singapore on the *Plantius,* which was completely blacked out. Wallboard fronts had been erected around all of the entrances. Arrows cut in these fronts allowed just enough of the blue light shining inside to seep through to make the arrow visible. All of the windows were painted black, and white lines had been drawn on the deck to aid one in getting around. Black paint and heavy dark shades over all the windows made it extremely hot inside. Many fellow passengers had just come from the war zone or recounted news in letters they received of homes destroyed and friends lost.

My arrival in Singapore on October 7 was my entrance into the British Empire. I was viewing its last, bright days. My visit was slightly more than a year before the Japanese would conquer Singapore.

The war was never far away. Not long before my visit, the liner *Queen Mary* passed through with 15,000 Australian troops en route to Egypt. Local lore said the troops had stripped almost everything for souvenirs—including the crucifix from the chapel. Both Singapore and Colombo were full of Australian troops on their way to the African front. They enlivened both cities by their antics. One favorite was racing rickshaws with the Australians pulling and the rickshaw man in the seat.

On October 11 I sailed from Singapore for Colombo on the *Arabia Maru,* which I described as not as bad as the agent said it would be. This leg of the trip was my introduction to deck passengers.

About 180 Indians en route from Singapore to Colombo occupied the forward and after decks. They brought their own rice, coconuts, and vegetables and ate and slept on the decks, spreading out their mats and building little charcoal fires. Not all of the deck passengers slept on the deck. In a letter I described what happened:. "Last night we noticed a commotion down at the end of the hall and a purser, or a Japanese passenger who speaks Hindustani, and one of the stewards were pounding on the door of a cabin. They opened to find eight Indians sleeping on the floor. Two Indians had purchased a first-class cabin and had let out space in the cabin at one dollar a night to deck passengers."

The *Arabia Maru* also had thirty-two Jewish refugees, who had come from Germany via the Trans-Siberian railway. Bound for Argentina, they were traveling steerage. My letter describes them:

> A pitiful lot are these people, poor, broken in heart, starving, but still with pride, graciousness, and a faith in their Jehovah. Across Siberia they have come on trains with food they could not buy and could not eat to a Japan where food is scarcer yet and onto third-class accommodations on this tub, where the food is scarcely enough to keep them alive. They must sleep in the great, hot, smelly steerage room, enduring the persecution of the stewards, who are amazingly unkind to them. Many of them were poor in Germany, but many more were wealthy and prominent. There is a former perfume manufacturer, a former merchant, and so on. The former merchant had fought for Germany in the world war.
>
> Mr. Barger (one of the other passengers) went ashore to a refugee commission and got a large supply of food to hand-distribute to them last night. . . . Up from below they came, grateful, with tears in their eyes, to get what we could give them. All but one came. The merchant was too ashamed. Never before had he had to accept charity.
>
> Yesterday was the Sabbath, and Mr. Barger intervened with the purser to get the use of the first-class lounge for the refugees to hold their service in. A dramatic thing that

was, too—these old, persecuted people, gathering to pray and plead with their Jehovah for mercy.

Although I only reflected it obliquely in my letters, I remember being conscious of the Japanese mixture of cruelty and love of beauty. My room steward on one ship told me, without feeling, that he had been an executioner, cutting off heads in China. I observed sailors amusing themselves by torturing captured sea gulls. Yet, whatever the drabness of the surroundings, one always found a flower arrangement; sailors cultivated flowers in pots on the ships.

The only overt anti-American feeling I encountered was from a few British residents in Bombay. "Some," I wrote, "criticized America blatantly for sitting on the sidelines and said that nothing angered the British more than American expressions of 'how brave the British were,' uttered from the security of our non-belligerency. . . . British even go so far as to blame [President Woodrow] Wilson for this whole darn war."

I arrived in Colombo, Ceylon (now Sri Lanka), on the S.S. *Arabia Maru* on October 18 and proceeded by train (second class) to Bombay, via Madras. My records show that the trip took sixty hours. I was fortunate in Bombay in having a contact with Robert Stimson, deputy editor of the *Times* of India. He put me in touch with the family of Sir Benegal Rama Rau, who was Indian High Commissioner in South Africa.

Lady Rama Rau was an ardent nationalist. Her daughter Santha had studied at Wellesley and later wrote a book, *Home to India,* that received some attention. In that book, she recounts an incident that happened while I was in Bombay. In England, she had come to know a young Englishman, who later came to Bombay. He invited Santha to join him at the exclusive Bombay Yacht Club. She was refused entry because she was a "native."

Robert Stimson not only introduced me to important Indians, but he also gave me insights into India itself. One of the phenomena of pre-independence India was the existence of some five hundred princely states. Stimson was writing a book about one of the richest of the princes, the Nizam of Hyderabad. He shared with me some of the results of his research: "He doles out food to his 120 wives, tells servants when guests have had enough, and personally counts all monies and jewels. All guests are expected to bring a gold present. On one occasion, he received two truckloads of Indian rupees, but did not have the time to oversee the counting. The trucks were locked up in a garage, but by the time the Nizam got around to counting the money, white ants had eaten the entire truckloads."

Indian news and conversation in 1940 were dominated by two subjects: India's effort in the war and the growing power of the pro-independence Congress party, led by Mahatma Gandhi and Jawaharal Nehru. The attitude of the Congress party toward the war meant that the two subjects merged.

India's contributions to the British war effort were substantial; it is doubtful that Britain could have won the war without that contribution. Indian troops fought in nearly every theater of the war. India's air force and navy took over British responsibilities in the Indian Ocean. In addition, a rapid program of industrialization in India meant the supply of substantial industrial items, including weapons, to the war effort. During the first nine months of the war, India produced ships, radios, canned goods, dressings, surgical instruments, rubber goods, artificial silk, and chemical acids. In the same period the production of lethal stores increased seven times and shell manufactures increased twelve times. In 1940, plans were being made for the production of automobiles, tanks, and armored cars and newsprint.

The Congress party objected to the war on grounds that the viceroy declared India's participation without consulting the representative assembly. Many members of the Congress refused to have anything to do with the war. Others saw it as India's war and gave their support. Typical was one comment of a speaker in Bombay: "I support the war, not because of any great love for the British or because I am unconscious of the grave wrongs they have done to us who are slaves at home and humiliated abroad. We have been disarmed and emasculated. But neither do I have any delusion about what would happen to us if Germany won the war. India would be worse off than she is now."

I had raised with Robert Stimson the possibility of my seeing Gandhi. I was delighted one morning to return to Stimson's apartment to find the following note, "Let me know as soon as you're back. Gandhi wants to see you tomorrow."

I traveled to Gandhi's ashram in Central India. A letter home describes the setting: "Gandhi's village is a beautiful little valley, now green with corn and cotton fields. It might be El Dorado County (in California) with its red dirt, low brush foliage, scattered trees. It is a quiet spot undisturbed by automobiles, although an occasional one does come in now and he rides in one. Gandhi's compound of about fifteen dirt-floored bamboo wall and tile roof buildings lies about a quarter-mile from the village. In the compound are a school, a weaving house, and the living quarters of about forty followers."

An extensive quote from my report to Dean Ackerman tells of my meeting with Gandhi:

> Although I was not concentrating on the independence problem in India, I was nevertheless desirous of meeting and talking with Mr. Gandhi. . . . I asked Mr. Stimson about the possibilities. I was told they were slim. Mr. Gandhi had just suspended publication of his weekly, the *Harijan,* in protest against a government press order prohibiting newspapers from mentioning the non-violence and civil disobedience movements. . . . It was a time of crisis in Mr. Gandhi's movement. Nevertheless, Mr. Stimson wired the request for an interview. We were both pleased when Mahatev Desai, Mr. Gandhi's secretary, granted the request.
>
> Of Mr. Gandhi himself I shall remember one thing above all: the utter simplicity of the man. At the appointed time for the interview, I was taken to one of the larger houses on the compound. I entered, expecting that the small room before me was an entrance hall and that Mr. Gandhi would be in the larger room within. I was surprised, then, when a voice at my feet said, "Good afternoon." I looked down to find Mr. Gandhi lying on a sheet just inside the door. His sole garment was a dhoti, a single sheet of cloth wrapped around the hips and hanging generally down to the ankles. Beside him were his spinning wheel and a small bookcase. A small table holding medicines was on the other side of his rude bed. . . .

Mr. Gandhi speaks clearly and deliberately, without fire or excitement. He has a noticeable trace of an Indian accent in his English and a lisp. The latter is by reason of his having no teeth. He does not appear as thin as photographs would lead one to believe. He is in good health, walks five miles a day to a nearby cottage for his quota of goat's milk. He was lying down, as he told me, "not because I am ill, but because I do not wish to be ill." He has a delighful smile . . . and a delightful sense of humor. Mr. Nehru, who delights a little in poking fun at Gandhi, explained to me afterwards that Gandhi was lying down because he had a mustard plaster on his stomach. "He has two vices," Nehru said, "mustard plasters on the stomach and on the head." Mr. Gandhi and Mr. Nehru had just completed a seven-hour discussion of their campaign of civil disobedience before my interview. Nehru was arrested the next day.

I asked Mr. Gandhi three questions. It is customary to write out questions and hand them to him before an interview. . . . I asked him first: "It is your hope that someday India may be in a position to defend itself nonviolently against an aggressor. What are the characteristics necessary for a people that would defend itself by nonviolence? Do you believe it possible for a highly industrialized nation like the United States to be nonviolent?"

His answer in essence was this: "The nation that would defend itself nonviolently must have the opposite of all those characteristics of a violent nation; it must have patience, kindness, good will, faith, and a much greater degree of courage than a violent nation. I consider it possible for a nation to defend itself nonviolently. After an enemy has chopped off a million heads, he will become tired of chopping off heads. Our nation will have won a victory without committing the sin of taking a human life. . . . Industrialism itself has something in it of violence. We could not defend Bombay nonviolently. Bombay is a creation of the British mind. Our defense would be in the villages."

> My next question asked: "You have expressed a desire to keep industrialization from the villages of India. Do you consider industrialism a retrogression?"
>
> His answer was: "For India, I consider it wrong."
>
> My last question was, "What type of government do you envision for an independent India?" He answered that he envisioned a government embodying all the principles of nonviolence upon which he would build India and a government with its basis in the villages."
>
> Mr. Nehru, who sees a socialist free India describes Gandhi's idea of government as a "benevolent Christian anarchy."

I was given a personal view of the workings of Indian censorship on the night Nehru was arrested. My report to the Dean told the story:

> Bob Stimson's wife was in Allahabad, the city where Nehru was arrested. Early in the evening, she phoned the office, telling of the arrests and of seeing Nehru after the arrest. Nehru told her at that time, without committing her to confidence, that Gandhi had written a letter to the Viceroy threatening a fast. That news, were it to be published, would have profoundly affected the Indian political picture. It would have been a sign that Gandhi had, at last, determined to take steps in support of his antiwar program.
>
> I relayed this news to Mr. Stimson when he returned home. His first instinct was to print the story without asking the censor's permission. Unfortunately—or perhaps fortunately—when he phoned the office, he learned that the night desk man had phoned the censor already to ask his advice. The assistant censor in Bombay telephoned Delhi for advice. An hour and a half later, the answer came back. There was no order against printing the story, but there was a veiled hint that the *Times*'s relations with the government would continue on an easier level if the *Times* would wait until the Viceroy made a statement. After considering all things, the fast story was dropped.

I had another view of Indian attitudes from a prominent high-caste woman in Bombay:

> We do not need your Western ways, your Western ideas to make of India a great nation. India, centuries before the nations of Europe existed, was great. She will be again. The British here have only emasculated us, made us weak and impotent. They have despised our centuries-old ways and given us nothing good in return. British officials have refused to receive us dressed in our own costumes; they have refused to eat with us in our own way. They have excluded us from the best clubs of our own land, many of us more cultured, more refined than they. The sari is as graceful, as beautiful a dress as any Western design. Our poetry is as beautiful as yours. India will be a great nation again some day, some day when we are guiding our own destiny. India, with a reawakened China, will lead the world.

From India, I proceeded to Africa, a continent with which I was to be much concerned in later years. Sailing at that time on Japanese ships certainly had its risks, but economy and a taste for adventure prevailed over prudence. The OSK ships were the subject of special scrutiny and delays in British Empire ports. Because of delays, we did not enter two East African destinations, Dar Es Salaam and Zanzibar. Ships were blacked out when in British ports. After stops in Mombassa in Kenya and Beira in Mozambique, I disembarked at Lourenço Marques (now Maputo). My report to the dean gave my impression of colonial differences, an aspect of Africa that has always been of interest to me.

> With my visit to Portuguese East Africa I have visited now the colonies of three different European nations, Holland, England, and Portugal. There seems to be a striking difference between the British colonies and the colonies of the other two nations. [I had not, then, had an opportunity to see the colonies of two other European empires, France and Belgium.] The Dutchmen in Java and the Portuguese in Africa have made, architecturally, little bits of their own nations

on these foreign shores; the British, in Singapore, India, and Colombo, have left the cities to a much larger extent characteristic of the land in which they are situated. Batavia and Sourabaya are transplanted cities of Holland; Singapore, except for the British-like municipal buildings, is a Chinese city. In the same way, Mombassa seems much more African than the bits of Portugal in Beira and Lourenço Marques.

Paradoxically, this outward appearance seems to be reversed in the spirit of the people. [By which I then meant the Europeans.] The Dutchmen and the Portuguese break their strong ties with the mother country and call Java or Africa home; to the Englishman, wherever he may be, England is always home. This difference has deep ramifications. It means more imposition of the European order on the native in Dutch and Portuguese colonies; he has less chance for his own national development. . . . There is less chance for political strife in Dutch and Portuguese colonies because the native is given less chance to think and live for himself.

That relatively rosy assessment was to change radically within just a few years; I was to witness that change.

From Lourenço Marques, I took the train for Johannesburg in South Africa. I was to meet up with the *Africa Maru* in Cape Town two weeks hence.

The Union of South Africa, which within a few years was to be consumed by the question of race and apartheid, in 1940 was still racked by the divisions of the Boer War. At the turn of the twentieth century, Britain fought to crush the separatist goals of the earlier Dutch settlers, the Afrikaners, or Boers. The scars of that war were further inflamed by the growing global war. Afrikaners were conspicuously pro-German and sought to frustrate South African support for the war. On one occasion on the train to Cape Town an Army sergeant of Scottish origin shared my compartment. At one stop an Afrikaner boarded the train and entered our compartment. As I wrote in my letter, "To show the distrust of the Britisher for the Afrikaner, this sergeant asked me to stay in the compartment with the Afrikaner while he (the sergeant) went to dinner. He had some valuable papers in his suitcase which he didn't want the Afrikaner getting into."

The country was held together during this period by the prime minister, Jan Christian Smuts, himself an Afrikaner who had fought the British in the Boer war. I heard him speak. My letter offered this description: "Smuts is a tall, dignified man of 70 with a white Vandyke beard. He speaks in a clear, quiet voice, first in English, then in Afrikaans. The people gave him a tremendous ovation when he rose to speak. And my national pride welled up when the band saluted him with a medley of Stephen Foster airs."

But I saw another side of South Africa as well. I visited a gold mine. (Johannesburg, surrounded by tailings from mines, reminded me of Folsom in California.) I commented in my letter:

> All labor for African mines is recruited from native country by recruiting stations of the Mine Association. Because many of them come from backward areas where they have never before seen automobiles, there are large signs reading "Beware of the Natives" and "Look Out for the Natives" on the roads through all the mines. The natives live on compounds, where they are fed and cared for by the mine owners. They receive 75 cents a day and board and lodging. Eleven thousand lived on the compound which I visited. I was there at feeding time when huge dishpans of mealie meal, meat, and vegetable meal were being dished out—a dishpanful to a man. This and bread and milk in the morning constitute their two meals.

In a later report to the dean I commented, "Not yet serious, but with all the elements that can make it a serious problem is the racial question in South Africa today. Eight million natives, colored people (half-castes), and Indians live in a land ruled by two million whites. German agents have already made inroads into native minds, but much of the Axis work was destroyed by Italy's invasion of Ethiopia. Black men looked upon that as their last stand. They do not forget that Italy took it from them."

The recording of my impressions of South Africa was somewhat hampered by the seizure of all my notes by officials when I left the country. They went through all my effects and took all written materials. The confidentiality of my notes was, perhaps, protected somewhat by the difficulty in reading my handwriting. I guess I was fortunate not to be detained as a spy.

From Cape Town, the *Africa Maru* took us across the South Atlantic to Buenos Aires. The sailing was made somewhat exciting by the fact that, on New Year's Day 1941, a good number of the Japanese crew, including the ship's doctor, were incapacitated by an excess of sake. The Second Officer asked fellow passenger Paul Nordby and me to help steer the ship.

I said farewell to the *Africa Maru* after over a month on board. She was an old but steady ship, but she had some problems. One passenger laid out two in verse:

And no one should recoil at
Only getting to the toilet
When the water on the floor is at low tide.
And after saying Buenos Noches
We must first appease the roaches
Who, with liberty, upon our clothes have fed
Though the ugly little creatures
May have redeeming features
We cannot see them when we sweep them from our bed.

Argentina, in 1941, was a beautiful land with fantastic food, not yet fractured politically by the later juntas. British influence was noticeable, although another friend from Columbia and I wandered into a restaurant one night that turned out to be a Nazi club.

My stay in Argentina and a subsequent trip over the Andes to Chile were largely touristic. The war and the threats to imperial rule seemed farther away. But the politics of Richmond, California, did once more appear.

I was invited one evening to lunch at the home of the U.S. ambassador to Argentina, Norman Armour. One of the other guests was James Farley, at one time Roosevelt's Postmaster General and now an executive with Coca-Cola. He was famous for his recollection of names.

The janitor in the Richmond post office was a Scot named George Sanderson. He used to boast to a skeptical community that he was a friend of Jim Farley. When I met Mr. Farley, he asked where I was from. I told him Richmond, California. "Oh yes," he replied, "I know Richmond. You know George Sanderson there? He's a good friend of mine. Gave me a big black dog, which is my pride and joy. Also, the postmaster, Les Thomas. Give them my regards when you get home." When I left him after lunch, he said, "If you ever see me in a crowd, don't fail to come up and say hello." I had met a consummate politician.

The voyage home on another Japanese freighter was uneventful except for three days docked in Rio de Janeiro during Carnival.

I arrived in San Francisco in early April, more than ever aware of a world in turmoil and convinced that the United States would eventually be drawn into the global conflict. I sought a way to become a part of the nation's effort.

5

SPIES WITH SCISSORS

During the war years I was introduced to the practice of intelligence, an essential tool in the world of diplomacy. These were also, for me, years of both joy and tragedy.

I returned to San Francisco in March 1941. My views about the war and the U.S. position had changed radically. Our involvement in the war was not only inevitable but necessary. We were, in fact, already engaged. President Franklin D. Roosevelt had approved the Destroyers for Britain deal in September 1940, sending forty overage vessels to that beleaguered country. The same month, Congress had passed the Selective Service Act. The month I arrived home, Congress had approved Lend-Lease legislation.

Believing, upon my return, that our participation in the war was inescapable, I sought a way to become involved. A friend from college was the recruiting officer for Naval Intelligence in San Francisco. Through him, I applied and was accepted for a civilian position, pending my commissioning. I notified my draft board and entered on duty as a civilian in the Twelfth Naval District Intelligence Office in San Francisco in January 1942. That June I was commissioned as an ensign and, in August, was sent for training. The ways of bureaucracy ground slowly, even in wartime.

Basic training for new Naval Reserve officers was at Dartmouth College in Hanover, New Hampshire. I traveled there in July 1942 on the Boston and Maine Railroad, known locally as the Broken and Maimed, in carriages that seemed left over from the Civil War.

In seven weeks a group of recent Annapolis graduates and veteran petty officers sought to make a motley group of civilians into respectable representatives of the Navy. We had courses in the

Bluejackets' Manual, Navy Regulations, Correspondence and Communications, Navy Phraseology, United States Fleets, and Naval History. And we did two hours of marching and calisthenics daily. On the hallowed grounds of Dartmouth College we were more resented than revered. As we marched beneath the windows of the dorms, we were sometimes bombarded with bags of water.

Training was supplemented by several weeks at the FBI training center in Quantico, Virginia, outside Washington, where we learned such things as the fine art of "tailing" a suspect through a crowd without being detected. On one occasion we were dispatched into the crowded lobby of the Mayflower Hotel to "tail" one of us appointed as a suspect.

Upon completion of training, I was assigned back to the Twelfth Naval District in San Francisco, where I remained until January 1945. In wartime the objectives and the tasks are relatively clear. In later years in different circumstances, I was to learn about the vulnerability of intelligence to questionable sources, political pressures, and the complex challenges of penetrating impenetrable societies.

The Intelligence Office of the Twelfth Naval District was on Market Street in San Francisco. Reserve officers from a variety of professions—lawyers, private detectives, collection agents, police officers, and journalists—composed the corps. We even had one man proficient in safe-cracking; I never inquired as to his previous profession.

Our work at that time was essentially counterintelligence, seeking to determine the existing threat from enemy (primarily Japanese) sympathizers and agents in Northern California. The office kept files on enemy nationals and on Americans in some way associated with them. Such files were, in the days before computers, mainly on 3x5 slips of paper—"flimsies" we called them. We even had a song, "Keep the Flimsies Flying," to the tune of "Keep the Home Fires Burning." We also did background checks on applicants for Naval Intelligence positions. Although I do not remember checking, my name was probably in the files. The FBI had seized the files of Japanese-owned hotels, including the Yamato Hotel at the edge of Chinatown. A cousin of mine and I had once stayed there for a night.

To some extent, our task was to close the barn door after the horse had left. We were interested in the names of individuals who might have worked closely with Japanese intelligence and might therefore still be suspect. At one point I was sent to the Japanese Relocation Center at Tule Lake in Northern California to interview some of the Japanese-American internees who had worked for the major Japanese companies.

The files of major Japanese companies operating in San Francisco had been seized, including those of the Mitsubishi and Mitsui trading companies and the Yokohama Specie Bank. I was assigned to search the files of these companies for possible useful information about Japan. I found little information about Japan but a great deal about the United States.

Before 1941, the United States was a virtual open book for potential enemies, even regarding military information. In September 1944, I prepared a report entitled "American Publications as a Source of Espionage Information," demonstrating how much military information, even in wartime, was available through public sources. Much of what we found related to what the Japanese had done before the war, to a great extent through the extensive use of American publications. The last Japanese Navy language officer to operate on the Pacific Coast before the outbreak of war was Lieutenant Commander Itaru Tachibana, who covered the state of California and was arrested and deported from Los Angeles in June 1941. Seventy per cent of the material he gathered came from newspapers, periodicals, books, and maps.

The information forwarded to Japan by military espionage agents concerning military matters was supplemented by information sent from Japanese commercial firms in the United States. These commercial firms relied upon publications to an even greater extent. The Mitsubishi Trading Company office in San Francisco, for example, subscribed to ninety-one journals and magazines. Through their use these firms were able to transmit to Japan details on Army and Navy bases, the progress of Selective Service in the United States, manpower mobilization moves, developments in aircraft and shipbuilding industries, details of individual planes such as P-38s and B-17s, ship movements, American industry and natural resources, political information, the diplomatic and political power of American churches, stockpiles of strategic materials, and complete details on the petroleum industry. German firms and agents demonstrated comparable interest in American publications. One report from Portugal reported how agents there were paying significant sums to sailors on ships sailing to America to bring back publications.

The Japanese firms paid considerable attention to social unrest marked by race and labor problems in America, perhaps to feed the presumptions of their superiors in Tokyo—even if such presumptions were wrong. If the Japanese and German governments of the time took these seriously, it is not surprising that they underestimated American strength.

The files also revealed some problems within the businesses themselves. A letter from a Japanese businessman in Mexico to the Yokohama Specie Bank in San Francisco complains: "The commission that I receive from the shipper was absolutely confidential. Beside, I was charging 5% more and on account of your error, Mr. Higelin discover my combinations and the damage and loss that your fault will cause me are indescribable for the future."

These revelations reveal a central fact about intelligence in general. Some of it may resemble the "cloak and dagger" activities of fiction, but much of it, whether in war or peace, involves the drudgery of poring through papers.

During these war years I was not only absorbed in tracing Japanese espionage. Two significant events in my life occurred.

In 1940, before I set out on my world trip, I was the adviser to a youth group at the First Presbyterian Church in Richmond. Among the group was a high school senior named Jean Frances Craig. I was rather attracted to her and sent her two postcards while on my trip. When I returned she had entered the University of California as a freshman, and I renewed the pursuit. We found that we enjoyed each other's company, and I proposed to her in December 1941. We were married in Richmond in November 1942, surrounded by my naval colleagues. Our wedding was a happy affair, despite the fact that I had a temperature of 101° during the ceremony.

Jean has been a wonderful partner and companion during the more than six decades of our marriage, going willingly to difficult places in the world and in each place capturing the admiration and affection of our friends and colleagues. She contributed every bit as much to our success in diplomacy as I. In the intervening years, she has also been an understanding mother to our three sons and two daughters as they faced the particular stresses of Foreign Service life, the tensions of the sixties, and the challenges of frequent upheavals and separations.

My father during these years, in addition to his work on the *Richmond Independent*, became heavily involved in the problems of housing the many who flowed into Richmond to work in the Kaiser shipyards building Liberty ships for the war. He began to show increasing signs of what today would be recognized as serious depression and became increasingly withdrawn and fatigued. He complained more and more of discomforts that could not be medically diagnosed.

In the 1940s, mental illness carried a stigma. When I suggested to my mother that we should consult a psychiatrist, she reacted with horror. "Your father is not crazy," she said.

My aunt Dolly, the nurse, and her son, Richard, who was at that time studying psychiatry, were of little help. "Fred is just tired and needs a good rest" was the frequent refrain.

My wife and I were living in Berkeley at the time, twenty minutes away from my parents in Richmond. On the morning of August 13, 1943, my mother called to say that my father had driven out early in the morning and was missing. We left immediately for Richmond. By the time we reached the house, my father's car and body had been found. He left my mother a note explaining his sense of hopelessness about his illness and its impact on the family and lovingly thanking her for her loyalty.

No event in my life has touched me more deeply than my father's suicide. I continually ask whether there was more that might have been done. I have reviewed with psychiatrists possible reasons for the depression, including my absences, my marriage, or aspects of my father's difficult early life. There have been no clear answers.

The world in 1943 was not prepared to recognize depression, nor did it have the medications developed in later years. My father was only 55 when he died. I was deeply wounded by his passing, but I recognize that God may have been working in a mysterious way. It is likely that I would have continued in the newspaper world, and that such contribution to diplomacy as I may have made would not have been made. Had I, nevertheless, followed the diplomatic path, how he would have enjoyed the travel to places about which he used to read.

After the war, the *Richmond Independent* was sold to a Texas group, which, within a few short years, shut down the paper altogether. When the *Independent* ceased publication, I felt that still another friend and relative had passed from the scene.

In January 1945 I was transferred to New York for additional intelligence training prior to an overseas assignment. During the ten weeks in New York my wife and I were billeted in the Henry Hudson Hotel on East 59th Street. Until then, it had been a hotel exclusively for women. A hotel newsletter described the change:

> The Henry Hudson's management recently inaugurated a complete change in policy that transformed their former "women's hotel" into the present house known as the Henry Hudson. The transition was a gradual one, made over the plaintive and plentiful protests of female patrons.
>
> Exclusively a feminine retreat originally, with only an occasional male relative permitted to intrude into the hallowed halls, the initial step in overcoming opposition was to throw open the first two floors for masculine occupancy. This hurdle was finally taken, with male guests not permitted above the second floor.
>
> Time and human gregariousness combined to form a valuable ally in the next step toward social (and economic) progress. Permission was obtained by males to visit above the two-floor Coventry—with a pass from the room clerk, of course. In time, the latter formality became superfluous and was discarded entirely when admission to the 18th and 20th floors was sought. Male guests could not only invade these sacred precincts without a pass, but in short order they were occupying rooms on these floors, too. A new ruling was obviously due and eventually the "For Women Only" edict above the 15th Floor was removed.

> And so it has come to pass that the Henry Hudson has no restrictions at all regarding a guest's gender. There are, too, such additional innovations as razor blade cuts in towels, complaints of cafeteria chairs being too low, and shoe polish on bedspreads. An odor of shaving cream and cigars pervades corridors where formerly feminine perfumes wafted—and there is also a house officer.

During that stay in the Henry Hudson, Jean answered the phone one morning, and a woman's voice asked whether Lieutenant Newsom was there.

Jean replied, "This is his wife. Can I help you?" The person at the other end hung up.

Before my wife could hang up, the telephone operator came on and said, "Don't worry, honey. It happens all the time."

In April 1945, after completing the course in New York, I was transferred to the Joint Intelligence Center attached to the headquarters of Admiral Chester Nimitz at Pearl Harbor. He and his staff worked closely, sometimes contentiously, with General Douglas MacArthur and his staff in the pursuit of the Pacific war. In Pearl Harbor, I was assigned as an editor for the *Joint Intelligence Bulletin*, digesting information for the fleet. In so doing, I moved from counterintelligence to the active collection of information on the enemy.

That information came from many sources: our own archival resources, captured documents, operational reports, enemy prisoners, and aerial photography. If American agents were operating in Japan or behind the lines, knowledge of their activities was closely held.

Our archival material was obviously inadequate. The center was charged with preparing information on Japanese-held Pacific islands, such as Tarawa, that were central to the war plans. The Japanese were not free with information on these islands, and much data had to be obtained from old atlases and guidebooks. Many prewar observations on these islands spoke of their numerous snakes. In the Navy's advice to the forces destined to invade such an island, much emphasis was therefore placed on avoiding the snakes. Few snakes were ever found; perhaps the initial bombardment killed them or led them to flee. At the Joint Intelligence

Center, we endured much ridicule from those returning from the campaign over our reports on the nonexistent snakes.

As an editor of the intelligence bulletin, I was to review the translation of captured documents, operations reports, and reports of prisoner-of-war interrogations for information useful to the fleet.

Documents captured on the battlefield disclosed information on military organization and, occasionally, on conditions on the Japanese mainland. Most numerous were the diaries kept by Japanese soldiers and recovered from their bodies during the Pacific islands campaign. These were frequently moving personal accounts, some written up to the very hour of their death. The diaries were less useful as intelligence sources than as reflections of the morale of the troops and as compelling human documents revealing the enemy's determination.

The submarine reports were the most thrilling. The exploits of our submariners in the Pacific—and especially one Commander (later Rear Admiral) Eugene Fluckey—included such adventures as entering and cruising around Tokyo Bay. I had a personal interest in the submarine reports as I noted the sinking of several of the Japanese ships on which I had so recently traveled.

A group of Japanese naval prisoners of war were held at a nearby camp. At least some of the prisoners believed that, having been captured, they were permanently disgraced. They thus felt no compulsion about cooperating with us, including various experts we identified among them. When we needed to understand some technical aspect of a weapon or vessel, for example, we could find an expert in the camp to help us.

In the presatellite era, aerial photography did not have the dramatic resolution it does today, but it was a useful source in determining battle damage and troop concentrations. On one dramatic day, August 6, 1945, aerial photography brought us pictures of Hiroshima and the chilling evidence of the first use of the atomic bomb. The atomic age had begun. The shock of the pictures was softened only by the hope that the end of the war was nearer. Our unit had been designated to join Operation Olympic, the planned invasion of Japan.

In October, I was assigned to return to the United States on the hospital ship USS *Tryon*. The ship had picked up Australian and New Zealand troops in Japan; they had been prisoners of the Japanese since the capture of Singapore in 1942. We were asked to interview them for information that might be useful in war crimes trials. They were a brave group, remarkable in how they distinguished between the good and the bad among their captors.

With the end of the war, my involvement in official intelligence was over for the moment. It would be three years—after a further interlude in journalism—before I returned to such activities.

6

DON'T BOTHER ME WITH WORLD NEWS

I was discharged from the Navy on January 1, 1946. The immediate postwar years were for my wife and me years of transition—from the Navy, to journalism, to the Foreign Service.

Businessmen often denigrate the bureaucrat, saying, "You've never had to meet a payroll." For a year and a half, Jean and I did meet payrolls—even if occasionally by the skin of our teeth.

With my father's death during the war, the prospect of returning to the *Richmond Independent* disappeared, but I still seemed destined to work with a newspaper. My mother and I decided to buy one.

Many newspaper men and women have dreamed of owning a newspaper. What they leave out of the dream is the harsh truth that owners of newspapers who are not independently wealthy must make them pay. In this respect, newspapers are something like farms.

Not far from Richmond was the small community of Walnut Creek, separated from the San Francisco Bay area by a range of hills. The town had two weekly newspapers, the *Walnut Creek Courier-Journal* and the *Walnut Kernel*. The *Courier-Journal*, owned by the widow of its longtime owner, John Silver, was for sale. We decided to make a bid.

The *Courier-Journal* was a weekly, with a circulation of 600; many of the subscriptions were in exchange for goods such as eggs and vegetables. The paper's commercial printing operations paid many of the bills. A proposed tunnel through the hills would transform this quiet agricultural community into a bedroom suburb for the Bay Area. There was room for growth.

Our bid was successful, and we became the proud owners of the weekly *Walnut Creek Courier-Journal*. Our equipment consisted of one Linotype machine, two hand-fed platen presses for commercial work, and an antique hand-fed cylinder press for the newspaper. The cylinder press belonged in a museum; the latest patent date on the machine was 1885.

Initially we had two employees, a Linotype operator named Joe and a printer named Donald, who also fed the press. It was contemplated that my wife would do the copyediting, the bookkeeping, and the commercial printing. This meant printing business cards, letterheads, advertising circulars, and event programs on a small press—until she became too pregnant, unable easily to reach the press. Both employees were reasonable workers. Donald worked best when he prepared himself with a bottle of Southern Comfort. He would sing gospel hymns as he fed the press. Joe also made up the pages.

My job was to prepare the news and sell the advertising. We had two long-term advertising contracts, one with the Pacific Gas and Electric Company, the other with Safeway stores. The Safeway contract required that we travel to San Francisco once a week to pick up the mat used to cast the ad.

We learned much about the private sector in the year and a half that we ran the newspaper. We were dependent upon our ability to persuade small-town merchants that it was in their interest to advertise with our newspaper. Many were working on a very thin margin and depended less on advertising than on the continuing goodwill of longtime customers. All of them faced competition from larger stores in the metropolitan area and the threat that those stores would move to Walnut Creek as it became suburban. Some advertised not so much for the benefits gained, but as a gesture of goodwill to us as individuals.

It was therefore important for the publisher to be active in the community. I was a member of the Chamber of Commerce and the Lions Club and attended community functions both as a reporter and as a supporter.

Our newspaper operated under a countywide contract with the International Typographical Union. This meant that our two employees were members of the Union and that we operated under union rules. We were thereby introduced to the basic problems of labor-management relations.

To the printers the union card was their ticket to independence and to the prospects for greater pay. They would do nothing that jeopardized that card. We understood their position, but that did not make it any easier to run a small business within their rules.

Joe, our foreman, had once owned a print shop and understood problems of ownership. He did all he could to help us without breaking any union rules. When he described the importance to him of the union card, it was with almost religious fervor. In his first job, he had received two dollars a week for 48 hours. He was now receiving $80 a week for 40 hours. That card represented the organization that had gained him the difference.

Relations with one's employees, in the final analysis, depend upon the results of negotiations. Being the smallest of the five newspapers under a countywide contract made our position particularly difficult. Other publishers had greater flexibility to meet employees' demands than we did. We were subject to the results of negotiations between the union and the larger newspapers. Most of the union members had neither knowledge of nor sympathy for the problems of the publisher.

One day I got into an argument with the union president during one of his periodic visits to our shop. Union scale negotiations were then in progress, and they were making what we considered exorbitant demands.

"Right now," I said, "we are paying $1500 in salaries out of a monthly gross of $3000."

"You can't complain about that," he replied. "One hundred per cent profit."

It was useless to explain to him that at least $1000 of the remaining $3000 went to other necessary expenses or to tell him that in the preceding year our total earnings had been $3600, while our two printers had earned over $4000. He would either not understand or refuse to believe our figures.

Many of the union regulations were difficult to accept. We were not allowed to operate much of the equipment in our own shop, nor were we permitted to learn how. Only the menial tasks such as feeding the presses and inserting and folding papers were left to us. The printers' feeling of independence gave us frequent doubts about who actually owned the plant.

One day Jean was in the back shop inserting the second section of the paper into the first. Our foreman resented women in the back shop, so he sent the other printer to take over the job. My wife could not see having a man folding papers at $1.81 an hour and told him to go back to what he was doing. The foreman said nothing then, but on Saturday he came in to quit. The other printer was taken sick, and no others were available in the jurisdiction.

His reply when I asked him why he wanted to quit was, "When I tell a man to do something in the back shop, that's what he's supposed to do. No one else can countermand that order. Your jurisdiction stops at the door to the back office; either I'm foreman in reality or I quit."

The inequality of pay rankles the employer. The best we could afford to pay our college-graduate advertising man was $35 a week, while the printers were getting $80 a week. The printers justified the difference by saying they were at the top of their career ladder and few of them would ever make more than the union scale, while the college graduate was just beginning and had a greater earning potential.

This was more logical than another explanation given to us: since it took three people in the front office to produce the advertisements and the copy that was set on one Linotype machine, the Linotype operator should get as much as the three in the front office combined.

Few of our union employees understood the anxiety of the moment when there is not sufficient money in the bank to meet a payroll or the race to the bank with the check that comes in a later mail to cover the account. Few realized that our freedom to come and go as we pleased was largely negated by the 24-hour-a-day responsibility of running a small business.

We considered various ways to remedy our situation. We looked into new machinery that we might operate ourselves and new adaptations to the old machinery. Given the schedule we were already on, it was impossible for us to consider taking on any greater measure of work. We considered the possibility of nonunion labor, but investigation showed the quality and dependability of such labor were below our standards. We were offered the opportunity to enter into a strike-breaking scheme but rejected the idea.

Had not another window opened for us, we probably would have continued to work on the *Courier-Journal*, benefiting, as our successor did, from the postwar expansion of the region and from new developments in printing technology. But I have been a great believer that some force guides my destiny, and serendipity again entered to change the course of my life.

My interest in the wider world had never disappeared. For many in the Walnut Creek community, the wider world was of little interest. We changed the weekly to twice weekly, and I started a column of comment on the world situation, causing one subscriber to cancel his subscription. He told me he took our paper precisely because it did not bother him with such matters.

Then one evening at a party in Berkeley, I met a friend from college who said he was going to take a special examination offered to war veterans for entry into the Foreign Service of the United States, the diplomatic arm of the Department of State. I was intrigued, even though I had not, as he had, studied international relations at Berkeley. So I took the two exams, a written one and an oral, and passed. Sadly, he did not.

The oral exam came on the day our first son was born. Going from the hospital to the exam appointment, I brought cigars to pass out to the examining board. I like to think that gesture did not influence their decision.

While still in Walnut Creek, I noticed an item in our paper that Mr. Elbert G. Mathews, the American consul general in Calcutta, India, and Mrs. Mathews were visiting family in the nearby town of Lafayette. I had not spoken with any Foreign Service officers since taking the exam and my wife had never met any, so we called and arranged to visit them. That visit established a lifetime friendship and played a significant role in my career. Bert Mathews returned shortly thereafter from Calcutta to become the director of South Asian affairs in the Department of State. He knew of my previous visit to India and asked whether I wished to serve in the subcontinent. I enthusiastically agreed and was assigned, as my first post, to Karachi in the new state of Pakistan.

We sold the paper, with a slight profit, to Dean Lesher, the enterprising publisher of two newspapers in the San Joaquin Valley. Within a short time, he had made the newspaper daily, changed the name to *Contra Costa Times,* and built the business into a million-dollar enterprise.

It was not easy to explain to friends in Walnut Creek why I was abandoning the opportunities in a community on the verge of great progress to go to foreign lands. When I told one woman in Walnut Creek that I was going to work for the State Department, she replied, "How nice. You may run into my brother-in-law. He works for the State Highway Department." Many did not understand what the Foreign Service was all about. Though I might have remained in Walnut Creek and become a millionaire, I never had any doubt about the choice I made.

So, with our four-month-old son, we moved to Washington in September 1947 for three months of training. Housing was difficult in immediate postwar Washington, but we were able to rent a house in Falls Church, Virginia, from a chiropractor. His only stipulation was that he be able to come back to the house every Saturday night for a bath.

I was sworn in as a Foreign Service officer in September upon my arrival in Washington. I joined forty-four others in the introductory training course, held in temporary structures near the old State Department building. Our course began on October 6, 1947.

Those of us who entered the Foreign Service in 1947 were joining a service in transition. Seven hundred officers, almost entirely men, had staffed the prewar service. In the years immediately after the war it would grow to more than three thousand.

The international role of the United States had expanded greatly. New nations were being formed; new Foreign Service posts were being opened. New languages would be required. New functions relating to foreign aid and information were being added.

The three months of basic training concentrated on the administrative and fiscal responsibilities we would assume. We were introduced to the consular functions—visas, passports, citizen protection, and document authentication. Our introduction to diplomatic communications included learning to write a "despatch" in a nineteenth-century form. Addressed to the Honorable, the Secretary of State, the despatch concluded, "Sir, I have the honor to be your obedient servant." E-mail was decades away.

We learned protocol: Which corner of our calling card to turn down if we were leaving the card in person; the precedence of calling; how to arrange proper seating at an official dinner; the responsibilities of diplomatic wives. Before the war, Foreign Service officers used to leave their cards at the White House. Our class was invited to a Christmas party on the White House lawn. President Truman appeared, but we did not shake his hand—or leave a card.

We were admonished on proper dress and were encouraged, from our relatively meager salaries, to purchase formal dress: tuxedos, tailcoats, morning coats, and striped trousers. I believe I wore the morning coat only once—when calling on the emperor of Ethiopia. The more formal garments still hang in my closet in mint condition. Much of this pattern has been abandoned in recent years. Because some countries still followed rigid protocol customs, however, it was important then for an American diplomat to dress properly and know the rules.

Not all of the previous generation's Foreign Service officers were comfortable with the postwar changes. Their world was Eurocentered. Even when assigned to a post in Asia, they had been dealing with European colonial officials. The emergence of new independent nations often meant adapting to new cultures, new languages.

Some years later when I was responsible for our relations with North Africa, we sent an ambassador to a North African country who had previously always served in Europe. He was accustomed to giving formal, black-tie, sit-down diplomatic dinners. In Africa one must be prepared for a less formal approach. Sometimes guests may not be able to come at the last minute. Or guests may bring along a friend or relative who suddenly drops in for a visit.

The ambassador was much disturbed by the vacant chairs at the table or by the need to rearrange seating for an uninvited guest. He began, after such dinner occasions, sending a note to the Foreign Office giving the names of those who had thus violated his view of protocol. He was, after several notes, called in and informed that things were done differently in the country to which he was now accredited.

There were exceptions. One of my first chiefs in the Foreign Service was a man named Hooker Doolittle. As consul general in Tunis during World War II, he saw the handwriting on the wall for the colonial powers. He had risked his job and reputation and angered the French by assisting Habib Bourguiba, then a nationalist leader and later president of Tunisia. Doolittle had lost his household effects three times in his career: in Tiflis at the time of the Russian Revolution; in Bilbao during the Spanish Civil War; and in Tunis. His effects were threatened again when, as consul general in Lahore, he was threatened by the disorders that accompanied the partition of India. I asked him once whether he had any regrets in his career. "No, not at all, "he replied, "I have been a witness to the making of history."

New diplomatic functions such as economic assistance and information services became part of America's diplomatic arsenal. These functions required contacts beyond those with traditional State Department counterparts abroad, including contacts with foreign publics. Not all of our older American colleagues saw this as appropriate.

What was less prominent in our early training were the basic functions of international relations—how to negotiate, how to assess a foreign political scene, or understanding the relationships between force and diplomacy. We received guidance on the forms of diplomacy more than on the substance. That we were required to learn on the job as the years passed.

Finally, in January 1948, after various housing adventures in postwar Washington, my wife and my infant son and I set out for Karachi. At that time, Foreign Service officers not only could travel by sea, but they could do so on foreign-flag vessels. We chose to sail on a Norwegian freighter, the *Hoegh Silver Moon*. Another Foreign Service family, Paul and Elizabeth Geren and their infant daughter Natasha, en route to Bombay, were fellow passengers.

In early January 1948, a major blizzard hit the east coast of the United States. To reach the boat in time, I drove our Nash sedan from Washington to the dock in Brooklyn over mainly icy roads. When I finally skidded down into the dock, the longshoremen said they could not yet take the car. I told them I was not about to try to drive back up the icy ramp, and I left the car with the unhappy dock workers. It was eventually loaded onto the ship and reappeared on the ice-free docks of Karachi.

The 25-day trip via Alexandria, Egypt, and the Suez Canal was uneventful, except for a minor problem in Alexandria. The two infants on board, quite naturally, produced daily diapers for washing. My wife and Elizabeth Geren hung them out to dry on the afterdeck. When we approached Alexandria, the bos'n came to me and asked that they not hang out the diapers while in port. He explained, "I must go ashore here."

On the night of January 30, one day out of Karachi, we were listening to the BBC radio on the ship. Suddenly I heard the voice of Robert Stimson, the man who had been my host in Bombay seven years before and who had arranged for me to meet Mahatma Gandhi. His voice, calm and solemn, was reporting that a short time before, while leading followers to prayer in the gardens of Birla House in New Delhi, Gandhi had been shot and killed by a Hindu extremist. Against that shocking background, we arrived next morning at a troubled and crowded Karachi to begin our diplomatic career.

7

A NEW NATION

In January 1948, seven years after I had first visited the Indian subcontinent, I landed with my wife and our infant son, John, in Karachi. This time I was arriving as a commissioned third secretary and vice consul in the Foreign Service of the United States.

If the training at the Foreign Service Institute had been elementary education, the twenty-six months in Karachi, Pakistan, constituted a graduate course. Nearly every issue I was to encounter in later years was present in that initial assignment: refugees, ethnic and religious violence, Islam, the Israeli-Palestinian dispute, nation building, dealing with deposed rulers, congressional visits, and how to tell America's story. It was also our introduction to protocol, official visits, and servants.

The subcontinent had now become the Indo-Pakistan subcontinent; two new independent nations had been born out of British India. When the partition of India occurred in 1947, Pakistan was created out of four western provinces, Sind, Punjab, Baluchistan, and the Northwest Frontier, and one eastern, East Bengal. To the west were the tribal territories that had always had a special autonomy in British India and to the north were a series of small, princely states. The largest city and logical capital for the new state would have been Lahore in the Punjab, but it was considered too close to the Indian border. Instead, the seaport of Karachi, in Sind, was chosen as the capital.

In Karachi in 1947, the previous population of 600,000 had risen by at least half a million refugees—Muslims from India, seeking safety in the new Muslim state from the communal killings that had convulsed the region. Those who had not found housing slept on the sidewalks of the city with their meager possessions. Damage and casualties from Sikh-Muslim skirmishes of the day before were still visible on the streets.

On arrival at the port, my wife, Jean, who had not previously been out of North America, found the scenes of chaos in Karachi initially overwhelming. She asked if we could spend another night on the ship. We did, and the next day she faced courageously the circumstances of her new home. It was not long before she was guiding visitors to some of the more distressing sites of Karachi that had so affected her at first.

In the early days of Pakistan, there were those who questioned whether partition had been necessary. Yet the view of the majority as we heard it was that the final years of the British Raj had convinced at least the Muslim elite that they could not live together with the Hindus in a united India. They often referred back to an election in East Bengal won by a Hindu party after which, in a communal spoils system, Muslims were summarily replaced by Hindus in key positions. But whatever the facts or the justifications, the results were tragic. Not only did Hindus turn against Muslims, but Sikhs sought to carve out a separate state in East Punjab.

In the upheavals and massacres that accompanied the partition, an estimated twelve million Muslims, Hindus, and Sikhs were displaced. From Karachi, the Hindu third of the population left for India, and more than half a million refugees from India descended on the city. An excerpt from a letter to my family on February 11, 1948, describes my initial reactions:

> The first impression would undoubtedly be that of a drab, brown, hot, desert village. It is only on longer acquaintance that one discovers that it is a bustling, sociable, quite livable capital city. It spreads over a wide area; there are really several cities in one. There is the port city; the native city; the European city; the Hindu city; and a wealthy residential suburb near the beach called Clifton. Where we live in the Cantonment, or European area, there are attractive gardens, spacious houses, paved streets, and at least one pleasant park. In some parts there are even sidewalks, but there might as well not be. No one walks on them. It is a city desperately overcrowded. At

> night the main streets of the business district are lined with people sleeping on the sidewalks because they have no place else to go. Where they eat is a mystery. There are far pleasanter places than Karachi, but I am sure there are worse. If, as I do, one likes the haunting music, the rhythmic crowds, the bright colors, and is amused by the animals wandering aimlessly about the streets, the constant battle against being cheated, the magicians, chiropodists, barbers and other tradesmen wandering around and is interested in the basic problems of this everlasting struggle for existence, then you can forget the lack of comforts, the distance, the heat, and all the rest and remain completely satisfied by the thrills of this new experience. The climate here is pleasant (in April)—quite a bit like Honolulu was. The only thing that really bothers us at times is the noise. This is only because we are conscious of noises that will awaken the baby. But at night there is a constant din of bells from the camel carts and gharrys (a kind of horse-drawn vehicle); drums from the nearby home of the commanding general; native orchestras playing in the servants' compounds; crows, goats, babies, arguments, and the inevitable squeaking of the shutters in the wind.

In the early days of Pakistan, given the conditions in Karachi, health was a constant concern. I was out of commission for some weeks with hepatitis. Jean was the victim of several tropical diseases. Amoebic dysentery was a constant threat and infected so many that we had an organization we called "Saludas Amoebas" with a song, "Every little movement has amoeba all its own." We benefited from the skill of a Dutch doctor, Dr. P. W. Van den Broek, who had spent the war as a doctor in a Japanese concentration camp in Singapore, caring for European women evacuees from Java, and from the Catholic nurses from New Jersey at the Holy Family Hospital, where our son Daniel was born in May 1949.

The following excerpt from a letter to the Foreign Service Protective Association dated October 10, 1948, regarding Jean's treatment for amoebic dysentery illustrates the problem: "Under normal circumstances this treatment would have been given in a hospital, but the lack of adequate hospital facilities in Karachi made this impossible. There are two hospitals here, but neither, by any stretch of the imagination, is satisfactory for the care of American patients. Symbolic of conditions is the statement made to Dr. Van den Broek by a local patient: 'Conditions at the Central Hospital are so much better since the British left. We have much more freedom. Patients can now spit anywhere they want to.'"

We had been warned beforehand that housing was extremely tight. With the movement from Delhi of Muslims who had been in government service, the demands for homes for senior officials took priority. Many homes of prominent Karachi residents were taken over by the government. Most diplomats were housed in the grandly named Palace Hotel. Those with children were given houses, usually to be shared with another family. For three months, we shared our first house in Karachi with another newly arrived couple, Sylvia and Harold Josif.

The Pakistan government requisitioned the home of Jamshed Nussarwanji, a prominent Parsi merchant. He made a deal with the government that stipulated he could keep his house if he would build three for diplomats on land behind his property. We were fortunate to receive one of these houses, a hastily built, two-story residence. Its unique features included a sloping upstairs floor that allowed rainwater to flow into the bedroom and a front door with a space at the bottom just large enough to accommodate the shrew that visited our kitchen every night. During our time, squeaky ceiling fans provided the only air-conditioning. The windows had no screens. Mosquito nets were a must.

Two other houses had been built on the same arrangement, but there had been insufficient plumbing fixtures for the three houses. Each house had "The Best Niagara," a toilet with an overhead pull chain. We also had the only bathtub, with only a cold-water faucet, while the other two houses had kitchen sinks. Outside in the courtyard, adjacent to the kitchen, hot water was prepared in a tin canister with a burner for charcoal in the center. We used to amuse ourselves by discussing with our neighbors the relative merits of each of the fixtures in good-natured efforts to determine which house was superior.

One of the first tasks in establishing a household is the hiring of servants. Potential candidates, each with a handful of "chits"—recommendations from former employers—lined up to be considered. Many of the chits, masterpieces of florid English addressed to "Respectable Sir," were prepared by professional typists in the bazaar.

Our complement of servants represented a spectrum of the religious and caste categories of Indian society. Even though Pakistan was now a Muslim country, the Hindu caste system persisted. We had a Muslim bearer (butler) named Abdul, a Christian cook named Jafaar, a Hindu ayah (nanny), Soni, and an untouchable Hindu, Lachme, as the sweeper who cleaned the floors, the toilet, and six inches up the legs of tables or chairs.

Jafaar, who asked that we post a sign on our gate with his name (Jafaar Ahmed) and the initials B.A.C.C. (standing for British and American civilian cook), performed miracles, cooking with charcoal in three cavities hollowed out of the cement block wall. He was also a member of the local Methodist church and proudly displayed a membership book that had his name in it. Not only did it have his name, but he pointed out to me that his name had a star after it. When I examined it, I saw that the mark was an asterisk; at the bottom of the page it was followed by the words "delinquent in dues." I never had the heart to tell Jafaar, whose English was limited, the true implications of the star by his name.

It was our introduction to the world of servants. We discovered that, while it would have been difficult to manage the household without them, they represented a new dimension of the family. Illnesses (feigned or otherwise), the births of their children, and their general welfare were our responsibility. While they generally worked well together, there were moments when their petty arguments illustrated the basic problem of maintaining peace in an intercommunal land.

Transportation, housing, and office space were problems even for diplomats. The first U.S. embassy chancery was on the second floor of a building, over an automobile salesroom. By April 1948, the American staff had grown from the three-person consular office to ten Americans. The staff included an Army attaché, a colonel who brought to the embassy the additional skills of his prior experience as a one-man band in vaudeville. The defense attaché office expanded later. When the Department of Defense was created in the Truman administration, the embassy received a message saying that as a result of the consolidation, the defense attaché staff would be reduced. But the accompanying roster listed one more position than then existed. The chargé d'affaires at that moment, Hooker Doolittle (who had a sense of humor not always appreciated in Washington), sent back a message, referring to the department's instruction, asking, "Where do we house the reduction?"

Prior to partition, the United States had been represented in Karachi by a consul, Gordon Minnegerode, who was somewhat overwhelmed by the new responsibilities that suddenly descended on his office. He was replaced as chargé d'affaires by a veteran Foreign Service officer, Charles W. Lewis.

We saw nation building at close hand. A remarkable group of Indians, now Pakistanis, who had served in the civil and political services of British India, came to Pakistan and assumed the responsibilities of government. They worked tirelessly and honestly to bring order out of chaos. Homes were built for the refugees. When we left two years later, many had been housed.

Most of the Pakistanis were Sunni Muslims, although many felt a close tie to Iran. One significant group, especially in Karachi, were the Ismailis, followers of the Agha Khan. The Agha Khan had been one of the founders of the Muslim League, the party that had worked for partition. He visited Karachi while we were there, and we attended a tea in his honor. When someone asked him about the current politics of Pakistan, he responded, "I gave up politics for horses long ago."

A functioning government was created, but it was not easy. When officials fled to Karachi after partition, no files existed other than the few papers the refugee officials were able to bring with them. Extensive negotiations were required before the files and resources of British India were ultimately divided. The Pakistan Foreign Ministry had, literally, to start from nothing. Two memorable officials molded the early diplomacy of Pakistan: Sir Zafrullah Khan, the eloquent foreign minister, and Mohammad Ikramullah, the dedicated foreign secretary.

Although files were eventually transferred from New Delhi, very little of the machinery of government went along with them. I was told when I arrived in Karachi that, initially, because of an absence of typewriters in the new ministry, our embassy staff would type Pakistan's replies to our notes on embassy typewriters.

What Pakistan did get in the partition was the viceroy's train, which just happened to be on Pakistan's side of the border. On New Year's Day 1949, Prime Minister Liaquat Ali Khan and Begum Liaquat invited the entire diplomatic corps on the train for a weekend trip to the ruins of the ancient city of Mohenjo Daro, 200 miles north of Karachi. The train stopped at several towns along the way where the Liaquats greeted the crowds. From the train, we could see people rushing the chairs and tables from one welcoming site to another in the next village. The train moved slowly.

I described the physical condition of the early Pakistani offices in a letter to the family written on February 18, 1948:

> There are three or four nice permanent buildings here, but the state of many of the offices in which the new government must work is one of unbelievable dilapidation. In one office I visited there were great gaps in the ceiling and pigeons roosted in the attic. Our conversations were frequently interrupted by whirring wings swooping low over our heads. Even in the office of so important an official as the Minister of Interior, partitions made of odd pieces of scrap lumber had been erected. With the countless handicaps, though, I have been impressed with the job this new government has done. It must be realized that, out of Karachi's population of 600,000, Hindus and Sikhs numbering about 400,000 have fled. These people were the clerical workers, the government clerks, the educators, representing a great mass of white-collar workers. The city's population has been replaced by a like number of Muslims, but they are, for the most part, poor peasants. In spite of this handicap, in spite of the difficulties with India, in spite of serious financial problems, the new government has resettled nearly 2,500,000 people (almost the population of Los Angeles) who have migrated from India.

Pakistan, from the beginning, was a troubled country. Because it was carved out of Muslim majority areas, as noted, it consisted of four provinces to the west of India and a fifth Muslim majority province, East Bengal. Not only was East Bengal separated by geography, but also by language. Religion was the only tie. The United States did not, at the beginning, open an office in the East. Officers from our embassy in Karachi visited Dacca, the provincial capital, on rotation to perform consular services and make observations about the politics. Few of us thought that this strange arrangement would last, and it did not. East Bengal became independent Bangladesh in 1971.

The tribal territories bordering Afghanistan were fiercely independent, as they remain today. We had an illustration of this independence in our first visit to the Northwest Frontier Province early in 1949. Jean and I, my mother, our two-year old son, and another couple from the embassy, Jean and Merritt Cootes, were guests of the last British governor of the province, Sir Ambrose Dundas, in the provincial capital, Peshawar. One afternoon, the three women, together with our son and the Hindu ayah, decided to check the road conditions and drive toward the Khyber Pass, which we planned to visit the following day. On the way north, they drove by an unmarked tribal checkpoint, but paid little attention to it. On the way back, however, armed Pushtu tribesmen stopped their car at a barrier placed across the road near the checkpoint's shack. They decided not to get out of the car and tried to explain in a mixture of languages that they were from the American Embassy and were staying with the governor of the province. Several anxious hours passed before the tribal guards were able to reach someone via a wind-up radio phone to check this story. They were released and returned to Peshawar. The most concerned of all during this episode, understandably, was the Hindu ayah.

That night at dinner at the governor-general's residence, Sir Ambrose, having heard of the incident at the checkpoint, spoke quietly to the two Jeans and cautioned them against driving alone through tribal territory. He commended them for staying in the car, because they were safe on a Pakistan government road. Had they got out of the car they would have been in tribal territory and most likely held for ransom. A lesson learned.

Much of diplomacy consists of ceremony. The most significant is the presentation by an ambassador of his or her official letter of appointment (credentials) to the head of state. Ambassadors cannot function officially until they have presented their credentials. In a carefully choreographed ceremony, the ambassador, in formal dress, with the embassy staff, stands and presents the letters of credence, reading a short formal statement to which the head of state responds.

I was a participant in the presentation by the first U.S. ambassador to Pakistan to the Governor-General (and founder) of Pakistan, Mohammad Ali Jinnah. The ambassador, Paul Alling, arrived February 17, 1949, and presented his credentials on February 27, a rare rainy day in Karachi. My letter of the day describes the event:

> After a lazy morning of reading, I began, about ten o'clock to assemble the various portions of my full dress regalia in preparation for the ceremony. (Some countries have elaborate diplomatic uniforms; we do not.) Abdul helped me with the shirt, white tie, waistcoat, and tailcoat. The high silk hat had already been borrowed. At ten-thirty, Mr. Lewis (the counselor of embassy) came by in his big Cadillac to pick me up. We then proceeded to the Palace Hotel, where we met the ambassador. Mrs. Ross (one of the embassy wives) made the best remark of the day when she said, as we were leaving for the hotel in our formal dress, "Now all you need is the corpse."
>
> The nearer we got to the Governor-General's House, the harder it rained. In Karachi it rains so seldom that no preparation is made. When we arrived at Government House, the ambassador was to review the Guard of Honor of the Pakistan Navy drawn up on the lawn before the house. Instead, the Guard of Honor was crammed into the covered driveway at the main entrance. Only the ambassador's car could thus get in and the rest of us had to make a rather unceremonial dash, with tails flying, from our cars to the shelter of the portico.
>
> The entire proceeding moved with the precision and formality of a society wedding. Promptly at eleven we formed

> a procession of twos according to our rank and proceeded up the staircase. We had previously been shown on a chart exactly where we were to stand as the ambassador gave his formal speech of presentation. . . .
>
> Jinnah was standing as we came in. His aide stepped forward and, as the newsreel cameras off to the side turned, his aide introduced Mr. Alling to the Governor-General. Mr. Alling stepped forward and shook hands, then stepped back. Col. Hosket (the U.S. Military Attache) stepped forward and handed the ambassador his letter of credence and message to the Governor-General, much as the best man hands over the ring. Col. Hosket stepped back, and the ambassador opened the fancy white envelope, closed with the Seal of the United States, and read about a five-minute message, "The President of the United States sends his greetings to the Governor-General," and Jinnah, in a low voice but in flawless English, read the reply. When he had finished, he then invited the ambassador to stand with him, and the ceremony proceeded with the introduction of the ambassador's staff. Then the ambassador and Mr. Jinnah retired to the Governor-General's office for an informal talk.

This was a ceremony in which I was to be a participant several more times, both in foreign capitals and at the White House in Washington.

Alling fell ill in 1949 and was replaced by U.S. ambassador to Finland Avra Warren. His arrival presented us with a public relations problem. His photograph had appeared earlier in *Life* magazine, undressed and ready for a sauna. This raised a number of eyebrows in conservative Muslim Pakistan.

Early on, one issue that arose concerned the future of Kashmir. It involved India, Pakistan, and the international community and is still with us today. The state of Kashmir, although ruled by a Hindu dynasty, was predominantly Muslim. Pakistanis had expected it would opt for the new Muslim state. But Kashmir was also the ancestral home of Jawaharlal Nehru and coveted by India. Pakistanis claimed that in the agreement negotiated by the British that defined the border between the two countries, the road to Kashmir had been improperly placed on the Indian side. The Hindu ruler of Kashmir opted for India, and the first of several wars between the two countries threatened. The United States initially sought to remain neutral.

Chargé Hooker Doolittle was not inclined to follow Washington's neutral stance on the issue. A devotee of doggerel verse, he had once composed an epic entitled, "Pandit, the Bandit," referring to Nehru, and showed it to several visitors.

Through the efforts of a United Nations–appointed mediator, Joseph Korbel (father of future Secretary of State Madeleine Albright), a cease-fire was arranged, but the basic problem remained unresolved. As embassy duty officer on Christmas Day 1948, I was called to the Pakistan Foreign Office to receive their note accepting the cease-fire. It was a step toward avoiding conflict, but it proved to be short-lived.

Because of my journalistic background, I was appointed the embassy's information officer and charged with organizing the new U.S. Information Service office. I found a ground-floor office in the same building as the embassy in which to establish our information services. From Washington, we received a supply of books; we also loaned a number of our own personal books, films, and printed material about the United States. Soon we began to receive by radio the daily Wireless File with news and relevant statements.

These activities required the hiring of necessary staff. There was much talent among the refugees who had come from India, so the hiring of a staff presented few difficulties. English was not a problem because most of the applicants had been educated in English. To prepare material in Urdu, the language of Pakistan, competent translators were necessary. Some required training in our ways. I hired a young woman as librarian who began by placing books on the shelf according to the color of their covers. A learning process followed, encompassing the skills of our staff, the reactions of our audience, and the issues that faced us.

Our film library was sent some short health films produced by Disney. The subject of one was malaria and began with a full screen blow-up of a mosquito. We asked the projectionist of our mobile film van to bring us back reactions to the film. After one showing, he reported a villager telling him, "That film does not apply to us. Our mosquitoes are not that big."

The principal Karachi newspaper was *DAWN*. I was able quite quickly to establish a friendship with its editor, Altaf Husain, a somewhat acerbic individual with a bit of a chip on his shoulder about the United States. Like many Indians, he had strongly favored independence from Britain, but he was influenced by the anti-American trends of the British left. Misconceptions about the United States were common.

Throughout my diplomatic career I gained a great appreciation for the foreign nationals whom we employed. Nowhere was this more true than in Karachi, where they not only helped immeasurably in the creation of our work, but often gravely withstood taunts from their fellow citizens who were unhappy with American policy. In many places their lives were threatened; it took courage to work for the Americans.

The misconceptions about the United States were often substantial. In an article I wrote for the University of California alumni magazine, I described some of the problems:

> Pakistan is a friendly country. Despite sharp differences over Western policies in the Middle East, its people are hospitable and extremely interested in the United States. Yet, even here, great misunderstandings prevail.
>
> Some are easily corrected, such as the question put to me by the principal of a high school in Karachi: "What do the pound notes look like that are used in the United States?"
>
> Some reveal a lack of realization of the magnitude and complexity of our country. A university official once sent a note to our office: "Please send me complete statistics on the financing of education in the United States. The messenger will wait."
>
> Those that put us to the test are the malicious misconceptions resulting from the deliberate propaganda of other nations: "America is a land of monopolies where all wealth and privilege are concentrated in a few hands." "America is an imperialist nation interested only in exploiting the less developed nations of Asia." "The European Recovery Program (the Marshall Plan) is merely a device through which America seeks to rule the world."[1]

Two other events added to the challenge of "telling America's story" in the new state of Pakistan. Pakistan was founded as a Muslim state and believed it had a mission to "purify Islam" in the rest of the world. A special emissary, Chaudri Qaliquzaman, was sent through the Arab world to spread this word—creating some amusement among the Arabs. When, some years later, I was assigned to Baghdad, an Iraqi said to me, "You must be a good Muslim. You served in Pakistan."

As Muslims, Pakistanis shared with Arabs resentment at the establishment of the State of Israel. When the United States recognized the new State of Israel in May 1948, Pakistanis mounted a demonstration in front of the U.S. Embassy. I wrote to the family at the time: "Friday afternoon, after prayers at the mosque, two thousand Pakistanis held a mass meeting protesting against the recognition of the State of Israel by the United States and Russia and then marched on our embassy to stage a demonstration. I had gotten wind of their plans the afternoon before and helped arrange for their reception. When they approached I went down on the street and greeted the mob and invited the leaders to come up and present their complaints to Mr. Alling. They did and, after a brief talk with the ambassador, he and the leaders of the mob went out on the balcony and spoke to the two thousand people assembled below. When Mr. Alling and the others went out on the balcony, the crowd was shouting to take down the American flag which flies over the Embassy. Their leaders, however, were able to quiet them down by having a maulana (a Muslim religious leader) chant a few verses of the Koran. One of their leaders spoke and Mr. Alling spoke and the crowd, satisfied, moved away." The whole event ended peacefully. I doubt it would today.

Embassy security was not the preoccupation then that it has become today. No U.S. Marines were initially assigned to Karachi. An American security officer was posted, but the guarding of the embassy chancery was in the hands of paid local night watchmen (chokadars), with Pakistan military guards at the residence.

One night the security officer, making his rounds, found the guards on duty asleep. Chokadars had the practice of sleeping but training themselves to cough periodically to frighten intruders. The security officer admonished them, telling them that they had to stay awake. The next time he visited the chancery, the guards were awake at the entrance. They had hired local musicians to play through the night to keep them awake.

When Jinnah died in September 1948, the U.S. press largely pictured him as an uncompromising militant responsible for much of the bloodshed that surrounded the partition. The coverage was in contrast to the highly respectful American media treatment of the death of Mahatma Gandhi eight months earlier, creating one more spark of tension between the United States and the sensitive new nation.

In a letter home dated September 26, 1948, I mentioned a *Time* article on Jinnah's death: "*Time* Magazine printed a story of Jinnah's death which was just terrible and which was bitterly resented by the people here—and with due reason. It referred to him as a 'man of hate' and called Pakistan bankrupt and disorganized; it is neither. Saturday noon, the editor of *DAWN* called to say he was going to write an editorial on it and did I have any comment to make. I told him it would serve no useful purpose for him to write an editorial on this matter since so few had seen it in Pakistan. Much to my relief this morning I picked up *DAWN* and found no editorial. Whether my arguments carried any weight, I do not know, but it was satisfying to have had a part in heading off something that could have been very disastrous to our position here."[2]

From its establishment Pakistan has had a troubled history. Ethnic, tribal, and geographic differences have stood in the way of agreement on a permanent constitution. Although there have been brief periods of unstable democracy, power has rested primarily with the military, backed up by an oligarchy of landowners. During the Cold War, and more recently in the war on terror, the United States has frequently regarded Pakistan as an ally. It was formally an ally in the ill-fated Baghdad Pact. But the absence of true democracy and frequent military coups have made the Pakistan-U.S. relationship a difficult one.

Curiosity about the new nation resulted in early visits by prominent Americans, including members of Congress. The Foreign Service has, understandably, been very discreet in its descriptions of congressional activities abroad. I was introduced to the mixture of genuine interest, insensitivity, and personal agendas that so often accompany such visits. The social events that were part of congressional visits, however, were always useful in expanding embassy contacts.

Our first congressional visit in November 1949, brought us four senators—Theodore Green of Rhode Island, Homer Ferguson of Michigan, Allen Ellender of Louisiana, and William Jenner of Indiana. Members of a special Senate Subcommittee on Appropriations, the senators were examining American civilian agency offices abroad. Senator Green, then in his eighties (he stayed in the Senate until his nineties), was a welcome visitor. He said to me, "This is a new country where they probably do not know much about us. How can I be helpful to you in educating them?" At my request he gave a helpful lecture on the role of the Congress in U.S. policy. Others represented a different aspect of such visits. They were more interested in shopping and hunting. One of them, entering a reception where prominent Pakistanis were present, said to his American escort in a loud voice, "Hey, haven't you got any good-looking women in Pakistan?"

Other visitors at the time included columnists Dorothy Thompson, Walter Lippman, and a group from the *Town Meeting of the Air*.

In August 1948, Pakistan received its first U.S. naval visit—the cruiser *Toledo* and two destroyers. I have always had a weakness for naval visits, especially for that moment when an American warship, its flag flying, first pulls into a foreign port. The Navy, in my experience, has always done an excellent job in "showing the flag." And, in distant posts far removed from America, meals in the ship's wardroom provided a taste of home. But each visit was a learning experience. In Karachi, we arranged a visiting day for Pakistani officials and their families. The reaction of one Pakistani officer was, "We want one of these." Only too late did we become aware that "family" in Pakistan meant an extended family: in-laws, aunts, uncles, and cousins. We were overwhelmed with visitors.

In March 1950, Pakistan entertained the young Shah Reza Pahlevi of Iran. It coincided with the visit of another prominent American, Colonel Robert McCormick of the *Chicago Tribune*. The Pakistanis did their best, despite often inadequate facilities, to provide the young monarch with suitable hospitality. Arches honoring the shah with Urdu words of welcome were erected at intervals along the road from the airport to the city.

These arches were up in advance of the visit when I went to the airport to meet Percy Woods, the *Tribune*'s South Asia correspondent. On the way back to the city, I explained to Mr. Woods that these arches were erected for the visit of the shah.

"Don't tell Colonel McCormick that," Percy Woods said, "He'll think they were erected for him."

The two visits came together when, after some effort, I arranged for an invitation for Colonel McCormick to the reception given for the shah by the Pakistani governor-general. At the reception, the shah was seated on a sofa at one end of the garden and guests were invited, one by one, to join the monarch for a short conversation. Somehow Colonel McCormick arranged to get into the line and sat himself down by the shah. After a few minutes, it was clear that the colonel was not ready to leave. The wife of our chargé d'affaires intervened and successfully ended the interview. When the colonel returned to Chicago, he wrote a little book on his world trip in which he noted that, "While in Pakistan, I had a visit with the Shah of Iran in which I explained to him my views on military strategy that should be pursued in his area."

I saw visits from a different perspective when I was assigned to accompany Prime Minister Liaquat Ali Khan and his wife, Begum Liaquat, on an official visit to the United States in May 1950. Even though I was relatively junior, because of the small size of the embassy Jean and I had numerous occasions to become acquainted with Liaquat and Begum Liaquat. We were frequently invited to functions at the prime minister's residence and asked to stay after dinner. Begum Liaquat had been educated at an American school in Calcutta and was fond of American songs. Our defense attaché, Colonel Harry Meyers, played the accordion. He and his accordion were frequently invited to stay after dinner, and a small group of special friends of Begum Liaquat would gather around the accordion and sing the melodies of Stephen Foster, Jerome Kern, and other American songwriters.

Official visits are always preceded by negotiations. Which cities will be visited? How many will be in the party? How long will they stay? Who will pay for hotels, transportation, and incidentals? Will the president meet the visitor at the airport? Unless the rules have changed, American hospitality is not open ended. Visits were to last no longer than three days. Official parties were limited to twelve.

The Pakistanis and the Americans shared an interest in introducing the new country to American business and potential investors. President Harry Truman met Prime Minister Liaquat's party at Washington National Airport and, that evening, hosted a state dinner at the White House. The next day was filled with ceremonial visits to Mount Vernon and the Arlington Cemetery, with speeches to Congress and the National Press Club, and with various radio and TV press conferences. The following day was occupied with calls on various cabinet members and dinners by local business groups. On the last day, the ambassador of Pakistan gave a reception in honor of his prime minister. State visits are nothing if not an endurance contest for everyone.

From Washington, the party proceeded to New York. The program there included an appearance on a television program with Eleanor Roosevelt and a dinner at the Tarrytown estate of David Rockefeller. The party proceeded from the Waldorf-Astoria hotel in a motorcade through New York afternoon traffic. For a thrill I recommend riding in the last car of such a motorcade.

Other cities visited included Chicago, Kansas City, San Francisco, Los Angeles, Houston, New Orleans, Schenectady, and Boston. One problem arose in making the arrangements related to Hollywood. The embassy received word from the prime minister's office that they did not wish to visit Hollywood. The young shah of Iran had earlier visited Hollywood and been embarrassed by published photos of a Hollywood event featuring starlets with low-cut necklines. The Pakistanis wanted none of that, and we so informed Hollywood.

The Motion Picture Producers Association is a powerful group, sensitive to its international market. They sent a representative to Karachi to convince the prime minister and his wife that they should visit the movie capital of the world. They were assured that no events or photographs would embarrass the Pakistani couple.

They did decide to visit Hollywood, where a suitable program was carefully arranged that included the set of a family film, James Stewart in *Harvey,* and no low necklines. However, as we were making our way to the set of *Harvey,* a man suddenly emerged from a side street and spoke to Begum Liaquat. She turned and followed him. I felt that my public affairs responsibilities required that I follow her. She had somehow made known that two of her favorite stars were the comedians Abbott and Costello. I turned the corner just in time to see her posing for a picture between Abbott and Costello, both of whom were dressed in French Foreign Legion uniforms. The French war against the Algerians was a highly sensitive subject in the Muslim world. I spoke to Begum Liaquat and asked her what the reaction might be if this photograph appeared in *DAWN*.

"Oh, David," she said in alarm, "You must try to recover the film." Fortunately I was able to do so, and a possible crisis relating to the visit was averted.

Escorting an official visitor to the United States also reveals something about our own country. Visits to eastern cities were marked by hospitality and appropriate politeness, but little exuberance. Liaquat and his wife were gregarious, outgoing people. They finally found a response to their personalities in Texas, where Liaquat, was made an Honorary Colonel in the Texas Rangers. He was so delighted by this that he told the audience, "When I retire, I want to retire in Texas." Fearing that such a response would not be helpful to the prime minister in Pakistan, I asked the Voice of America not to report that particular statement.

Our tour had ended in March 1950 at the time I was ordered back to the State Department to help prepare for the prime minister's visit. I did not yet have an onward assignment after that. Our time in Karachi had been an exciting one, made particularly pleasant by the friendship of many Pakistanis. Nevertheless we agreed with the personnel people in the department that the time for change had come and that I should consider a healthier post and different work, work that would broaden my Foreign Service experience.

We sailed home, again on a Norwegian freighter, the *Hoegh Silverwave*. As freighters do, it made unscheduled stops, including one in Massawa in Eritrea to pick up fish meal. In a second stop at Haifa, we were delayed for a week by Passover observances. Tied up next to a ship that had just arrived from Constanza in Romania, we were given another reminder of the tragedies of the Jews. The ship was carrying gaunt refugees from the European camps, marked by numbers tattooed on their arms. On the docks were a host of relatives vainly looking for kinfolk disembarking from the ship. There were unforgettable, touching moments when relatives were recognized and cries of joy were shouted on ship and dock.

Because of the delays, the voyage took longer than planned, and I was required to leave the ship and fly home from Haifa. My family remained on board for another ten days. They told me they had become increasingly tired of the Norwegian diet of codfish balls.

So, what happened? I met them in New York with the news that we had a new assignment—to Oslo, Norway.

8

BANANAS IN GÖTEBORG

In an essay entitled "Traveling with Children," Robert Benchley called the experience "like traveling third class in Bulgaria." Jean and I never traveled in Bulgaria, not even in third class. We have, however, traveled with children.

When we moved to our new post in Oslo, Norway, in August 1950 with our boys John, three, and Danny, one, we decided to do it in the most comfortable way possible for all of us. We booked a flight on a Pan American Stratocruiser, the kind that had bunks. On the advice of our pediatrician, we gave each boy a small dose of Phenobarbital so that, we hoped, they would sleep through the night flight.

We settled them into their berths and took our comfortable seats nearby. The whole idea of bunks on an airplane excited them. It took them a long time to settle down. We had just begun to enjoy our Pan Am meal when a child's voice shouted over the noise of the engines, "Daddy, Mommy, come look at the moon."

If the Phenobarbital had any effect, it seemed only to stimulate the boys further. There was very little sleep for any of us. Then, as we landed and the plane rolled to a stop at the gate, John vomited.

After that beginning, everything during our fifteen months in Norway was positive. Although we occasionally missed the unpredictable excitement and exotic scenes of Asia, we found welcome—if temporary—relief among friendly people in a beautiful country.

We arrived in Norway five years after the end of World War II, but in that country the memory of the effects of the war and the occupation were still fresh. The Norwegians were adjusting to the realities of rebuilding and of the emerging Cold War. The Marshall

Plan was underway to assist in the economic recovery. Norway had already decided to abandon traditional neutrality and join the North Atlantic Treaty Organization (NATO). General Dwight Eisenhower, then head of Supreme Headquarters Allied Powers in Europe (SHAPE), visited Oslo in January 1951.

Many of the basic requirements of life, such as housing, were still scarce. Imported foodstuffs were hard to find. As diplomats, we were fortunate; we could travel to Göteborg in Sweden to get bananas and oranges. Norwegians benefited from the neutrality of Sweden, but Stockholm's policy of neutrality still rankled them.

The courageous exploits of the Resistance illuminated many conversations. We spent one evening with the young men who had blown up the heavy water plant at Vermark on February 28, 1943, in one of the great exploits of the war. In their modest way they described the delicate details of an operation that profoundly affected the course of the war.

My initial assignment in Oslo was as a vice consul, my first experience in this ancient role. I found the consul's role to be a combination of city clerk, parish priest, and diplomat. In Europe, with its tradition of city states, my title as vice consul often elicited more respect than that of a third secretary of embassy. No phase of diplomatic work takes one more deeply into personal problems; and in Norway in the immediate postwar era, such problems abounded.

Feelings against the Germans still ran high. The story of the disappearance of the ABC Berlin correspondent Lyford Moore provides one example. Moore was part of a group of journalists covering the annual trip by representatives of the U.S. Armed Forces to purchase Christmas trees in Norway in December 1950. On a snowy night shortly after his arrival, Moore disappeared.

Interest in the case in Washington was high. Not only was a well-known journalist involved, but Moore was also related to Mrs. Eisenhower. When days passed without finding him, the family sent Daniel O'Conner, a former FBI man, then a lawyer in New York, to work with the embassy and the Norwegian police.

As a consular officer, I was assigned to follow the case. The police determined that Moore had last been seen in one of the bars along the Oslo waterfront. Further investigation developed that Moore had fallen asleep in one of the bars. Witnesses in the bar said that Moore was awakened by one of the Norwegian bouncers. Thinking he was still in Berlin, Moore said something to the effect that "No God damned Hun is going to lay hands on me." At that point, he was hustled out of the bar into the snowy night. The entrance to the bar was not far from a pier that jutted out into the fjord. The conclusion of the investigation was that he had wandered out onto the pier and fallen into the fjord. When his body surfaced after the spring thaw, that conclusion proved to be correct. I was invited by the Norwegian police to witness the autopsy—my first.

Those of us who worked on the case were also introduced to the Norwegian fascination with the occult. Stories were common about sessions with the Ouija board or with mediums speaking to the dead on long winter nights in isolated valleys. Not long after Moore's disappearance became known, we began to hear of the special powers of a man in Lillehammer named Einar Haugen. We heard stories of how Haugen would pinpoint accurately the location of lost jewelry in houses he did not know and describe correctly where lost skiers could be found. We did not pay too much attention until one evening at a diplomatic reception a member of the Norwegian High Court suggested to me that we should not dismiss the possibility that Haugen might be helpful. Our Irish lawyer from New York was intrigued and asked the police to check with Haugen. They did, but without results.

One enterprising correspondent from a town in the far north of Norway, hearing of the Moore case at a time when Scotch whiskey was extremely hard to get, wrote that he had special powers to find lost sheep, and if we could send two bottles of Scotch, he could probably be of help.

Another reminder of the war was the presence in Norway of a number of young men, mainly Poles, who had taken refuge in Norway. They had been drafted by the Germans to work as slave labor in the mines of Scandinavia. In recognition of the plight of such individuals, the U.S. Congress had enacted the Displaced Persons Act of 1948. The legislation permitted those who could establish a sponsorship in the United States to apply for an immigration visa.

Much of my work in Oslo involved determining the eligibility of such persons for entry into the United States. The American visa was highly prized and it was not surprising that traffic in forged documents had developed. The review process, therefore, required determining the authenticity of letters of sponsorship and of an individual's status as a refugee. The drama in my office ranged from outbursts of joy from applicants ultimately determined to be eligible to expressions of bitter disappointment by those who for one or another reason would not be able to go. One young Pole, when informed that he was eligible for the visa, jumped over my desk and embraced me, knocking over a vase of flowers in the process.

One of the saddest cases in my memory was of a young family with three children. A medical examination showed that one of the children had tuberculosis and was therefore ineligible to enter the United States. The family wrestled with the dilemma of whether to leave one child behind. I never saw them again and never learned the outcome of their difficult deliberations. I thought often of Menotti's opera *The Consul.*

Adoptions were another source of human emotions. A number of Americans sought to adopt Norwegian orphans after the war. The process of certifying a child for an American visa was time consuming. The impatience of prospective parents led to pressures in Washington, including in the Congress. On one occasion, when I learned that a member of Congress had a special bill passed for his adopted child, I took the risk of expediting an adoption case involving a deserving couple in the Middle West.

We were continually on the lookout for fraudulent or altered U.S. passports. For the Norwegians, a passport was simply an identity document, and they could not always understand how seriously we took its misuse.

On one occasion, we received word from Washington that a young American wanted by authorities had altered his passport and was traveling in Scandinavia. We persuaded the Norwegians to be on the lookout, and he was apprehended at the Swedish border. The Norwegians felt they had no basis for holding him since no charges had been filed against him that would form the basis for extradition and he had not violated any Norwegian laws. We persuaded the Norwegians to hold him until we could arrange for his escorted return on an American vessel. Within a few days, he was placed in the custody of the captain of an American ship and returned to the United States. On the voyage, he apparently had free rein of the ship, but was locked up at night. The daughter of one of our embassy officers who had returned on the same ship wrote that she had met a most entertaining young man, but for some reason he mysteriously disappeared at night.

The substantial earlier emigration from Norway to the United States established close family ties and led to constant travel by family members. Virtually whole villages had moved back and forth between Norway and America. Many of those who emigrated—particularly to the states of Minnesota and Wisconsin—never became U.S. citizens. Consequently, much of the work of the consulate was to issue visas to Norwegians returning to communities in the United States. Very often, they were men working in the lumber camps who were returning to Norway after the death of a first wife to claim another bride.

One prominent citizen of Norwegian heritage was Senator Hubert Humphrey of Minnesota. While in Paris in November 1950 attending a meeting of members of the U.S. Congress and the European Parliament, he took the occasion to visit his mother's birthplace in southern Norway. I was sent to meet him in Kristiansand and accompany him to the village where his relatives lived. On the train en route to the village, I got a sense of senatorial sensitivities. The senator expressed his unhappiness that when he arrived in Paris, he had been met not by an American embassy officer but by one of the embassy's French employees.

He said to me, "I know the State Department gives instructions to embassies on how to treat senators. I am only a junior senator and obviously do not rate. I assure you that I will not always be a junior senator and that, one of these days, the State Department will instruct the ambassador to meet me." He was right.

This was also the period of Senator Joseph McCarthy's campaign against alleged Communists in the State Department. Humphrey's aide told me privately that he was worried about the senator's future because he openly expressed his opposition to Senator McCarthy's views. My letter home of December 2, 1951, describes the Humphrey visit: "The senator was coming to Kristiansand to see the birthplace of his mother and to visit a host of relatives he had never seen. Only one of his relatives spoke English and that not too adequately, so I had to act as interpreter at the family reunion.

The day was most memorable, however, for the senator's relatives gave him a real heart-warming country reception with special cakes baked for the occasion, gifts, and all the children dressed in the national costume. We had to visit two different sets; I never drank so much coffee or ate so many rich cakes in one day in my life. Then to top it off, we had a big dinner given that night by the city fathers."

Accompanying Senator Humphrey on a visit to a small Norwegian town was a memorable experience. I was able to speak some Norwegian and to interpret in uncomplicated situations, but my Norwegian was tested by the senator's gregarious political approach to Norwegians on the street. He would approach a somewhat puzzled villager, extend his hand and say in English in a Scandinavian accent, "I am Hubert Humphrey from Minnesota in America. How are you?" Many in the town had themselves lived in the United States and understood the senator, but in some cases, I had to explain the senator's keen interest in meeting the citizens of this Norwegian town.

When I related to a friend at the U.S. Embassy in Paris Senator Humphrey's comment about being met by a French employee, he explained that in that particular week, 186 members of the U.S. Congress were in Paris. The senator was perhaps fortunate to be met at all.

Later, while assigned to the embassy in London, I discovered that attention to congressional sensitivities was a constant problem in embassies in both London and Paris. On one occasion, a member of the House of Representatives complained that Ambassador David Bruce had not met him upon his arrival in London. The department forwarded the congressman's complaint to Ambassador Bruce in London. Ambassador Bruce wrote a telegram to the department explaining the transit time from the Embassy to Heathrow Airport, the average time required to wait for and meet an aircraft, and the number of members of Congress who visited London, and inquired of the department if they wished him to set aside all other duties to meet this requirement.

In 1950, American consular officers were also charged with verifying crew lists from American flag vessels. Sailors signing off of such lists had to appear at the American Consulate and sometimes became a burden to the embassy. Consequently, there was a tendency for those of us in Oslo to persuade sailors that Copenhagen was a much more interesting place than Oslo and they should sign off in Denmark, rather than in Norway. One letter home of November 25, 1950, described a day in the consular section in Oslo:

> Friday was a fairly typical day. It started off with a visit from an American citizen who had married a Norwegian lady and had tickets to sail on a ship leaving Friday. The procedure, however, for getting a non-quota visa for the wife of a citizen takes about two months in Washington. I had to tell him that he could not take the ship and that he would have to wait at least another month. Then another man entered in just the same situation; he had already missed two ships and had hoped to get on Friday's but no word came from Washington and we could not issue the visa. Then I had a visit from a boy who suffered from multiple sclerosis, a disease of paralysis. He wanted to suggest ways in which we might help another American suffering from the disease who is presently in Oslo and whom we are trying to get admitted to a proper hospital in the United States. This is a sad case because we had also hoped that he might have been admitted to the hospital so that he could leave on Friday. But no luck.
>
> Then a visit from an American freighter captain. Then a call from a student who is going to school in Paris under the GI Bill of Rights. He had been touring Scandinavia on a motorized bicycle and the bicycle had broken down in Oslo. He had only $15 and no way to get back to Paris. We had to help him by making a deal with a local steamship company to take him and his bicycle at a very low rate.
>
> All these visits were interspersed with regular immigration cases. Even these cases can be difficult. Sometimes evidence of tuberculosis appears on the medical examination they must take, and I have to tell them that they cannot go to the United States after they have made all preparations to do so. Then I have many displaced persons, many of whom now appear to be ineligible on a technicality. I spent a lot of time Friday afternoon discussing this problem with a

representative of the American Joint Distribution Committee here.

Some who could not immediately enter the United States applied for visas to Canada. Once when discussing such a case with Shirley Burwash, a Canadian consular officer, she expressed some annoyance at this practice. "Canada is not a vestibule for the United States," she said.

Our tour in Norway introduced us to the noncareer ambassador. Particularly in pleasant posts where English is spoken, ambassadorships have frequently in American history been given to political figures and to private individuals who have made contributions to political campaigns. Officers in the career Foreign Service who have worked their way up through the ranks complain about the system and about some of the less-qualified diplomats appointed ambassador. After my retirement, I became involved in the organization of the American Academy of Diplomacy. One of the early objectives of the Academy was to stress the importance of adequate qualifications for American representatives abroad. I learned from this experience that ambassadorial appointments are one of the last unchallenged forms of political patronage in the United States. Members of the Senate Foreign Relations Committee, and those in politics generally, are most reluctant to challenge a president's prerogative and "the system."

Our ambassador in Norway was Charles Ulrich Bay, an executive of the American Export Lines and a contributor to the Truman campaign. He apparently wanted to be ambassador to Norway because his ancestors came from that country. He was fond of sailing and owned a 12-meter yacht. When he appeared in Norway, usually in the summer, he spent the time, not in Oslo, but in Hanko, south of Oslo, where he could race his 12-meter yacht against that of Crown Prince Olav. In February 1951, in the middle of the Norwegian winter, he suddenly returned to Oslo. He made every effort to appear never to have been away, but he could not remember the names of most of the officers on the staff. We were all puzzled about his sudden return, for which the ambassador gave no explanation, until someone sent us an article from the New York *Journal American*. The item reported that when General Dwight

Eisenhower completed his tour of NATO countries, he reported to President Truman that Ambassador Bay was not present in Oslo. Truman phoned Bay at his Florida home and ordered him to return.

Perhaps in Oslo, where a good professional staff manned the embassy, the absence of an ambassador made little difference. When critical issues arise, however, ambassadors are likely to have greater access to a country's senior officials, and the word of a knowledgeable ambassador can carry greater weight in Washington.

Oslo gave us the opportunity to meet several prominent Americans who passed through Norway. We were at a luncheon Ambassador Bay gave for Metropolitan Opera star Lily Pons and her husband, the popular conductor Andre Kostelanetz. We attended concerts by violinist Yehudi Menuhin and sopranos Dorothy Maynor and Kirstin Flagstad (Flagstad was under a cloud in Norway because of allegations that she had collaborated with the Nazis).

We were in Oslo when Ralph Bunche was awarded the Nobel Peace Prize at a ceremony held in Oslo University's auditorium. The ceremony was attended by King Haakon and members of the royal family, the Norwegian government, and the diplomatic corps. Twenty-two African-American troops from Germany were also invited to the event. I noted in my letter about his visit that "some of the Southern members of the embassy staff demurred at the generous hospitality accorded to Dr. Bunche, but they were outnumbered." (This was 1950!)

I received one unusual request from Ambassador Bay. Zinka Milanov, a soprano at the Metropolitan Opera of New York, was married to the Yugoslav ambassador in Oslo. One day Ambassador Bay phoned me to report that Madame Milanov had called him with a problem. She was coming to visit her husband and was bringing her small pet dog. Like many countries in Europe, the Norwegians had strict rules about dogs from outside Europe, requiring that they be put in quarantine for a number of days before being admitted to the country. Ambassador Bay asked me whether there was some way we could get the Norwegian authorities to waive this requirement for Madame Milanov. I consulted with a Norwegian employee in the consulate, who said that this was highly unlikely. However, he had a suggestion. He had a friend who was captain of a Norwegian freighter that traveled back and forth between Oslo and Antwerp. "Would Madame Milanov entrust the dog to the captain for the time that she was in Norway?" This solution proved workable. It was the first and only time that I was required to arrange a visa for a dog.

In November 1951, I received a telephone call from Washington asking whether I would be interested in an assignment as public affairs officer in Baghdad. I was tempted to decline, even though the offer was an interesting one. The Winter Olympics were scheduled to begin in Norway in a few weeks, and Jean and I and our boys were enjoying life in Oslo, including the bright winter and the skiing on the lighted ski trail above Oslo. But the position and Baghdad represented true challenges, and I decided to accept.

A Foreign Service inspector was visiting us at the time and was in my office when I telephoned Jean to tell her we were on our way back to the Middle East. Her first comments were, "Where's Baghdad?" and "What about the Olympics?" Then to forestall any unexpected outbursts, I mentioned that the inspector was standing near me as I telephoned. The transfer was authorized, and we left Oslo in December 1951.

We arranged to travel by air from Oslo to Baghdad, via Damascus, on what was supposed to be a twenty-four-hour journey. Because of weather in Europe and canceled flights, the journey took us three days. We arrived in Baghdad on Christmas Eve 1951. This time, the boys were superb, even under those trying circumstances, and we no longer felt that traveling with children was necessarily like third class in Bulgaria.

1. Fred Newsom with his six-year-old son, David, in the family's garden in Richmond, California, about 1924.

2. Teenaged David, a student at Richmond Union High School, where he edited the school newspaper. Later, at the University of California, he was a reporter for the *Daily Californian*, the UC Berkeley student newspaper.

3. Ensign Newsom joined the U.S. Navy in 1941 and within a few years was commissioned a lieutenant. He served first in San Francisco in the Office of Naval Intelligence and the last year of the war at Pearl Harbor.

4. David and Jean in the garden of their house in Karachi in early winter 1949. David holds Dan, 6 months old, and John, two years older, is on Jean's lap.

5. The local staff of the Information Office of the U.S. Embassy in Karachi in 1948. In the front row sit a few spouses and officers (from left): Jean Cootes; Mrs. Hooker Doolittle, wife of the chargé d'affaires; Deputy Chief of Mission Meritt Cootes; David and Jean with John. The local staff provided the frangipani garlands.

6. On their second Foreign Service tour, in Oslo, Norway, 1950–51, David and Jean enjoyed the ski slopes at Holmenkollen and sometimes even just outside their front door.

7. During their years in Baghdad, December 1951–March 1955, when time permitted, the Newsom family sailed their boat, the *Peter Pan,* up and down the Tigris river, occasionally going ashore in the evening for a charcoal-grilled fish dinner with Iraqi friends. This photo shows the boat's exciting launch following its christening.

8. David, prior to participating in the presentation-of-credentials ceremony for the new U.S. ambassador, Waldemar Gallman, poses in the carport of the Newsom home in Baghdad with sons Dan and John, November 1954.

9. Mr. and Mrs. Diplomat strolling the hall in the Department of State on their way to a reception line for an event in the Benjamin Franklin Room.

10. David was sworn in as ambassador to Libya at a ceremony on the 8th floor of the State Department, August 1965. Shown here at the signing of credentials are (from left, rear) son John, Under Secretary for Political Affairs George Ball, son Daniel, Jean, and Chief of Protocol Lloyd Hand; (below) David, with son David and daughters Katie and Nancy.

11. A favorite pursuit of the American ambassador in Libya was driving Land Rovers into the Sahara on expeditions mixing business with pleasure. Here, David is posing with one of the Tuareg guides.

12. Five Newsoms encounter a "homecoming" welcome at Wheelus Air Force Base near Tripoli, Libya, after a much-needed home leave to visit John and Dan.

13. A Tunisian reporter interviews Assistant Secretary for Africa Newsom during a visit, circa 1973. U.S. ambassador to Tunisia Talcott Seelye joins in the conversation.

14. President of Senegal Léopold Senghor escorts David on a tour of the city of St. Louis in March 1972, then celebrating its centennial.

15. With guest of honor Newsom are his hostess, Mme. Hamdi Ould Mouknass, wife of the Mauritanian foreign minister, and U.S. Ambassador to Mauritania Richard Murphy, in Nouakchott, early 1972.

16. On a 1970 visit to Guinea, David tours with President Ahmed Sekou Touré.

17. Emperor of Ethiopia Haile Selassie and one of his favorite Chihuahuas greet David on one of his visits to Addis Ababa.

18. On a visit to Nairobi, Assistant Secretary Newsom meets Kenyan President Jomo Kenyatta.

19. Meeting U.S. Olympic great Jesse Owens, winner of four gold medals at the 1936 Olympic Games in Berlin.

20. In West Africa David visits the famed Timbuktu in Mali, accompanied by Ambassador Robert Blake and a Tuareg guide, circa 1973.

9

UNGOVERNABLE

The first glimpse of Baghdad in December 1951 was of our hotel, the Zia, situated on the banks of the Tigris, a hotel made famous in the Agatha Christie novel *They Came to Baghdad*.[3] We awoke the next morning to a bustling city and walked out to the busy main thoroughfare, Rashid Street. We watched as Kurdish porters with extraordinary loads strapped to their backs made their way shouting "*Balik balik*" to warn the pedestrians that they were coming through. Camel and donkey carts jostled with automobiles and bicycles for space in the street. We strolled along the sidewalk, past coffee shops and kabob cafes, against a background of klick-klack noises coming from the ever-present backgammon games. Antique shops, grocery stores, and that venerable British institution, Spinney's Chemists, faced the street.

Initially, we could not relate what we saw that morning to the fabled Baghdad of T*he Arabian Nights*. As the days and weeks went by, we realized more and more, however, that we were in the land of Scheherazade and the Bible. We learned that during Ramadan, the Muslim month of fasting, storytellers still read out *Arabian Nights* tales as they sat on tall stools in the courtyard of the principal mosque. South of Baghdad lay the Old Testament cities of Ur, Nimrud, and Babylon. Babylon was a must-see antiquity for American visitors, particularly for members of Congress, and we traveled over the dusty road many times to see the mounds of Nebuchadnezzar II guarded by a solitary stork sitting on its nest on an abandoned tower.

To the north was the ruined city of Nineveh, capital of the Assyrian empire, then being excavated by Professor Max Mallowan of the British Museum, assisted by his wife, Agatha Christie. When we visited the site in 1953, she was the official photographer of the dig and guided visitors through the ruins as if the mounds of brick were alive. We recall her saying to us during one visit, "I'm sorry the throne room is a bit dusty today, but let's go there anyway."

We eventually moved into a new house in an area south of the city. The move was somewhat delayed because the contractor had mixed up the electrical circuits. When the light switch was turned on, it rang a bell for the servants, and the bell for the servants illuminated the room. We felt a correction was necessary so that one of us would not have to stand and hold the switch while the other read.

The house also had other inhabitants—yellow scorpions, stirred up by the construction work. Jean killed thirteen within a few days. We thought of painting scorpion symbols on the gate to dramatize our battle, but we were somewhat humbled when Jean's sister in Northern California replied to our account of scorpions by writing that she had killed fifteen rattlesnakes in her yard.

Upon our arrival in Baghdad, we were greeted with an invitation from Lispinard Crocker, the wife of our ambassador, Edward S. Crocker II, to come to the Embassy for a Christmas party. Not only did a welcome await us, but so did thoughtful gifts for the children. After our tiring journey, we were most grateful not to spend Christmas Eve in our hotel.

We continued our earlier protocol lessons with Mrs. Crocker, adding to those that our first ambassador's wife, Romaine Alling, had provided in Pakistan. Veterans of traditional diplomacy, they taught us much about the protocol of their era: where and when to leave cards, which corner of the card to turn down to indicate whether the card had been delivered or presented in person, where to sit—according to rank—on a sofa or in an automobile, and the proper attire for various occasions. Riding in a taxi in Istanbul with three ambassadors during a Chiefs of Mission conference, Mrs. Crocker stopped the vehicle in midtraffic because the seating was not according to the ranks of the passenger envoys.

It was expected by the Crockers that people would wear black tie for meals at the Residence: "dress for dinner" after six o'clock. On one occasion, a young officer stationed in Beirut joined his chief of mission, the U.S. minister in Lebanon, on a visit to Baghdad. I was at the airport to receive the party. When I returned to my office, Mrs. Crocker called and asked me to invite the young officer for dinner, "Eight o'clock, black tie."

When I called to extend the invitation, I learned that he had not brought a dinner jacket. I called Mrs. Crocker to tell her that he had accepted, and we would see if he could borrow a dinner jacket in Baghdad.

She replied, "You'll do no such thing. If he does not know how to travel properly as a Foreign Service officer, he can come and suffer."

I called the young man back and advised him to wear a dark suit. As he was leaving the Residence after dinner, he apologized to Mrs. Crocker for not having brought his dinner jacket. She looked at him coldly and said, "Well, I guess you think we don't eat dinner in Baghdad."

For the diplomatic corps and the elite Iraqis, life centered around the Alwiya club with its swimming pool and rooms for bridge and dancing. In the days before air-conditioning the pool provided welcome relief from the summer heat.

Our family found an additional way to escape the heat. We had a boat built for cruising on the Tigris River. Named by our son John, the *Peter Pan* was a story in itself.

In Oslo, I had just placed an order for a twenty-foot outboard motorboat but, sadly, had to cancel the order when we were transferred. I took the plans with me in the hope that there might be a boat builder in Baghdad. After all, there was a river.

Philip Hitti's *History of the Arabs* told of how Baghdad in the days of Harun al-Rashid was a thriving port.[4] Other books described a raft made from timber and inflated goatskins—the *guffa*, the world's oldest boat—that brought goods from Mosul to Baghdad.

When we arrived in Baghdad we discovered that the only boats on the river were the guffas, along with barges and tugboats built around tank engines salvaged from World War II—but no pleasure boats. As the winter rains subsided, I decided to see if I could have a boat built. I made contact with the builder of the tugboats. He came to my office one day, and I brought out the blueprints of the boat I had planned in Norway. Like all blueprints it had a deck view, a profile view, and a cutaway view. The builder studied the prints and then scratched his head. He turned to my interpreter and said, "Which one of these three boats do you want built?" Further conversation disclosed that his father had handed down the design for the tugboats and he had never seen a blueprint.

I ultimately resolved the problem through the cooperation of a young man in one of the oil companies, with whom I built a boat from templates in the furniture bazaar. One furniture maker moved all of his products into the narrow alley of the bazaar to make way for our construction. I spent several interesting afternoons sitting in the furniture bazaar practicing my Arabic and learning about another phase of Iraqi life. To get the boat out of his shop, the builders had to remove the entire front entrance. Thereafter, we enjoyed many pleasant evenings on the Tigris, dodging fishnets stretched across the river.

Iraq at that time was ruled by a monarchy installed by the British after World War I. The secret Sykes-Picot agreement of 1916 between Britain and France had established spheres of influence in west Asia. Faisal, the son of the ruler of the Hejaz, was initially proclaimed King of Syria. But the secret agreement had awarded that country to France, and the British thus moved Faisal to Iraq.

When we arrived, 18-year-old Faisal II, grandson of Faisal I, was on the throne, protected and guided by a Regent, his uncle Abdulillah. Faisal's father, Ghazi, had been killed in an auto accident in 1939. The core of the establishment was a group comprised mostly of Sunni Muslims, former officers in the Ottoman forces who had participated in the Arab revolt against the Turks in 1918. Some had worked directly with T. E. Lawrence (the famous Lawrence of Arabia) and, at evening parties, used to tell tales of their exploits. The most prominent was Nuri al-Said, who frequently served as prime minister when it suited him to do so, if it also suited the regent and the British advisors.

Iraq under the monarchy had the trappings of democracy without the reality: a parliament, political parties, and elections. But parties were carefully controlled reflections of ethnic and religious divisions. Elections were manifestations of the same control. In one election during my time, Nuri al-Said had all the opposition candidates arrested the night before the election and released the day after.

Shortly thereafter, when I was in Kurdistan, I was invited to tea with a district officer. The Kurds who had been arrested and released sat on one side and supporters of the government on the other. The two sides would speak to each other only through the district officer.

Iraqis are a proud, if divided, people. The divisions were apparent, even in 1950, although among the educated elite relations were generally cordial and intermarriage was not uncommon.

In the political world, candidates and parties were classified as Sunni, Shi'a, or Kurd. The Kurds in the north—inhabiting a beautiful land of mountains and rivers—were a people apart from the Arabs in customs, language, and history. One evening we were having a reception for officials of the Ministry of Education, all Arabs, in our home. Suddenly a group of Kurds with wide turbans and bandoliers appeared at the gate. I had met them in the North and welcomed them, but when they entered, the other guests all moved to another corner of the garden.

To those of us who had been in Iraq in the 1950s, the disorder following the U.S. invasion in 2003 came as no surprise. In a briefing I prepared in 1952 for visitors to Baghdad, I noted, "Beneath the current calm in Iraq there are seeds of cynicism, discontent, opportunism, and extremism which could destroy the dramatic possibilities of this country." Lord Salter, a prominent British economist who spent three months in Iraq during the period, described the country as "a seething cauldron."

Iraqis were intensely political. On one occasion, at a lunch I attended, the host said, "Today is Friday, and we do not discuss politics on Friday." There was dead silence until someone mentioned a revolution in 1922, and the conversation quickly went from past history to current history.

Iraq is the only country in which I served where I was denied a life insurance policy, and that was in 1955. Perhaps I had never raised the question of life insurance in other assignments.

The major fear of Iraqi leadership then—as now—was the disintegration of the country. In one meeting between our ambassador and Nuri at which I was present, I recall the prime minister saying, "This country consists of three major groups, Sunni, Shi'a, and Kurd. If the balance among these groups is ever destroyed, the country will become ungovernable." How prophetic.

During this time, Iraq was very much a British domain. The British exercised mandate authority through a 1922 treaty. Elite society, both expatriate and Iraqi, revolved around borrowed traditions from Britain—the hunt, the clubs, the royal protocol. British education was considered superior to any other. Under increasing Iraqi pressure for greater independence, the relationship with the British was revised in a 1930 treaty. Iraq later became a member of the League of Nations and its independence was acknowledged. Britain, however, retained a dominant position through the treaty, particularly in commerce and military sales and training; British military forces were stationed at an air base, Habbaniyah, west of Baghdad. With their long experience in the region and their language skills, the British possessed a capacity for indirect rule that others envied.

Britain was jealous of any other country that challenged its favored position, including the United States. Lucrative contracts with British firms offered opportunities for favors to Iraqi politicians and friends. The British embassy had the advantage of excellent language officers and close ties to Iraqi tribal and political leaders. Iraqi resentment of the British role, nevertheless, continued. Many Iraqi nationalists saw the monarchy as "an imperialist implant," not truly Iraqi. A commonly expressed view among the Iraqi elite was that Britain and the United States were manipulating events. When a cabinet change occurred, as it did frequently, discussions in the bazaar centered on whether the cabinet had been drafted in the American Embassy or the British Embassy.

Although I had previously served in a Muslim country, Pakistan, Iraq was my first tour in an Arab country. I was exposed for the first time to the tribes, the divisions, the complexes, the recollections of a glorious past, and the scars of humiliation that mark the Arab psyche.

I was assigned to Baghdad as public affairs officer (PAO), in charge of the United States Information Agency's work in Iraq. As a diplomatic officer I was number three in the embassy. On one occasion, when the ambassador and the deputy chief of mission were both away, I became chargé d'affaires. On this, my first time in charge of an embassy, my diplomatic duties and my information duties converged when the sergeant in charge of our Marine security detail, in a brawl at a local bar, took a poke at Reid Anderson, the anti-American editor of the local English language newspaper. The Marine guard involved was sent home; I wrote a letter of apology to the editor.

My principal task as PAO was to explain the United States and its policies. While attitudes toward the United States were not universally positive, we could claim important American accomplishments through our assistance programs, including dramatic help to the Iraqis in resisting a locust invasion in 1952.

I had a fine staff of Americans and Iraqis to assist in the work of the library, the film and lecture programs, exhibits, and educational exchange. Despite negative views of Washington policies, the United States had many friends among the Iraqis. Many students had been educated in the United States, and others had been educated at American institutions in the region, including the American University of Beirut and Baghdad College, a high school operated by a remarkable group of Jesuits from Boston.

However, an American education did not automatically create friends for the United States. Some students returned bitter over racial incidents and angered by what they saw as an anti-Arab tilt in American policy. The task was further complicated by cultural practices, preoccupation with the problem of Palestine, an undercurrent of sympathy with the Soviet Union, and our identification in the public mind with an unpopular Iraqi regime.

When I returned to Washington in 1955 after my service in Iraq, I wrote a paper entitled, "Elements of Political Instability in Iraq." Its focus was on the communist threat at the time, but if one substitutes the radical Islamists for the Communists, my conclusion may still be relevant: "The message of the United States has lost its appeal to an important segment of the intelligentsia in the Middle East. Many still respect our traditions, our history, and our institutions, but they reject our policies. Further, a militant minority makes any open expressions on our behalf unpopular. Paradoxically the effective intellectual leaders in these countries today admire and espouse political systems that represent the antithesis of true freedom of inquiry and freedom of thought."[5]

Differences in culture and practice required some acclimatization. We had officers fluent in Arabic, but Arabic is a language of studied ambiguity that does not always provide effective communication. Iraq, particularly in the tribal areas, was a society of frequent silences interrupted only by Arabic greetings as newcomers entered. An Iraqi once said to me, referring to one of our military attachés, "Colonel Murphy is a remarkable American. He can sit for half an hour and say nothing."

Private conversations in offices were a rarity—and looked upon with suspicion when they could be arranged. The offices of the average official, including ministers, were continuing conclaves. Men without any immediately apparent mission sat in chairs against the wall, kibitzing on the official's business and drinking glasses of tea. The minister obviously wanted to demonstrate that he was hiding nothing from the public. Little true transparency, however, existed in Iraq at that time, a circumstance that led to cynicism toward the government and assumptions of widespread corruption.

In all the developing countries in which I served, the belief in and reality of corruption were facts of political life that weakened and often undermined governments. Iraq was no exception. It was not easy for an outsider to establish the truth or falsity of claims of corruption. Few wanted to discuss the subject.

What was clear was the claim of many functionaries that they could not exist on their salaries without monetary supplements. Corruption reportedly ranged in form from bribes to the police or to nurses in hospitals to expectations of side payments or favors for contracts.

In Iraq, as in many a developing country, obligations by those in power to family, tribe, and followers led to expectations that the benefits of power would be shared. The sharing could take the form of official appointments, commissions, visits and villas abroad, or the suppression of unfavorable rumors. Controlling corruption was often inhibited by the assumptions of outsiders who believed that the only way to do business in a country was by offering extra inducements. In Iraq I encountered the rumors of corruption, Later, in Libya, I was to encounter the reality.

Iraq was then, and probably still is, a land of reciprocal obligations. Rewards were expected for favors. Editors, for example, who toned down anti-American diatribes at the request of the U.S. public affairs officer expected rewards. Other embassies were often suspected of paying to have something either printed or not printed.

Payment might be in the form of supplies of paper or equipment or a full-expense trip to a foreign capital.

Even an educational exchange grant posed problems. The U.S. Fulbright program, then in its infancy, was based on the principle of grantee selection by a commission that included both American and Iraqi members. In a land where visits abroad were favors to political followers or relatives, the concept of outsiders having a say in selection was hard to sell. Nor could one always be certain of the results. We selected a popular poet who occasionally wrote anti-American verse for a U.S.-funded trip to the United States, hoping to change his views of the United States. He clearly enjoyed his visit, but the end result was a series of articles in one of Baghdad's papers on the brothels of Texas.

We did have a remarkable group of American Fulbright scholars who brought both teaching and research skills to be shared with the Iraqis. One of the more remarkable was an entomologist, Neal Weber, who would go out into the desert and kneel down in the daytime heat to determine the highest temperature at which insects still moved. When he left we had the problem of disposing of a remarkable collection of scorpions and other desert specimens.

For the American diplomat, whether abroad or in Washington, the question of gifts was a constant problem. Regulations prohibited the acceptance of gifts of more than a certain value, and gifts over that amount had to be turned into the Office of Protocol. In countries such as Iraq, where the giving and the expectation of gifts was a part of the culture, the refusal of gifts was not always understood. What to give in return was also a problem. Outside of gifts of books or justifiable grants for educational exchange, the information officer abroad had little to give.

The exchange of gifts also represented, at times, a social hazard. One became wary of admiring jewelry or other items of value being worn or displayed by another, lest the item be suddenly thrust into your hands as "a gift." The unwritten understanding was that appreciation for the gift would be demonstrated by a reciprocal gift of comparable value. I once asked an Iraqi friend what to do if you inadvertently found yourself admiring an expensive object and realized it might be suddenly given to you. He replied, "Say, immediately, 'May it live in your family for a thousand years.'"

In Washington, the question arose frequently of how to respond to anticipated gifts from foreign rulers on official visits. The normal practice was to respond with a framed photo of the American president, not always equal in value to the foreign gift. On occasion efforts were made to discourage elaborate gifts in advance. During the Eisenhower administration, for example, a protocol official was sent to Morocco to dissuade the king of Morocco from sending the president a horse. Eisenhower, however, did accept two elephants for the National Zoo from Prime Minister Jawaharlal Nehru of India. As I will note, I was later involved in trying to discourage gifts of automobiles during a visit of the Saudi king to Washington.

In Iraq, no amount of gifts or favors could have eliminated the unpopularity of U.S. support for the creation of Israel, considered by the Iraqis a humiliation for all Arab peoples. References to the Balfour Declaration of 1917 that promised a home for the Jews in Palestine were frequent. We were there in 1951, only three years after the creation of the Jewish state and the prompt U.S. recognition. The unresolved conflict between Israel and the Arabs was a constant cloud over relations with the United States. Iraqi troops had been prominent in the abortive Arab efforts to invade the new state. Iraq's diplomats were prominent in United Nations efforts to protect the rights of Palestinians. Memories of the departure of the substantial and ancient Jewish community in Iraq were still fresh.

In November 1952 I was given a very close look at the Arab-Israeli dispute. I was assigned to accompany Senator Guy Gilette of Iowa on a trip through the region. With his high starched collars and black string ties, he represented another generation of politicians. The visit began in Cairo where we met the members of the new Revolutionary Council established in the revolution of July 1952, including Gamal Abdel Nasser. We then visited Beirut, Damascus, and Amman. In each of the Arab capitals the senator confronted emotional criticisms of the United States' support for Israel. He grew increasingly tired and unsympathetic with the Arab complaints.

We arrived at the King David Hotel in Jerusalem late in the evening. The next morning when we went to breakfast, we were greeted by a young man from the Israeli Foreign Ministry who welcomed the senator and informed him that there were twelve of his constituents from Iowa staying in the hotel and arrangements would be made for him to meet with them. The Arabs lost the war at that point as far as the senator was concerned.

In 1948 the office of my predecessor as public affairs officer had been ransacked by a Baghdad mob protesting the establishment of the Jewish state. My office, a three-story building on the main street of the city, was to suffer a similar fate in the year after my arrival, but with communist rather than Palestinian overtones.

On the morning of November 22, 1952, while I was on home leave in Berkeley, California, I turned on the radio and was met with the news that my office in Baghdad had been burned by a mob. A report at the time suggests that mob violence is not a new phenomenon in Iraq.

> On November 22, 1952, a group of students were parading outside a college in Baghdad, demanding the ouster of the dean. Their grievance was a rule that those failing one course would be required to repeat all courses of the year.
>
> The pattern of that November morning was a simple and not uncommon one in the Middle East. By eleven o'clock on that morning the placards demanding the dean's ouster had been replaced. The new ones read "Down with the Imperialists," "Peace," "Stalin," "Liberate South Korea." Two Communist-front organizations, the Partisans of Peace and the Union of Democratic Youth, both familiar with the art of demonstrations, had taken charge. . . .
>
> Many of the people of Baghdad regard riots as acts of God. Like storms, or floods, or plagues, they are something to be accepted and avoided. By Sunday morning, the 23rd, those who sensed the unrest kept to their houses. The police were unarmed and without orders to deal with the demonstrators.
>
> The mob's leaders had the targets clearly in mind. The first was USIS, the second the pro-Western anti-Communist English-language newspaper, the *Iraq Times*. . . . With tools they carried, they smashed through the steel doors and scaled the second-floor balcony. Kerosene was poured on stocks of paper and flames did the rest. Six thousand books

> in the library were dumped in the center of the floor and set on fire. From the two upper floors, every bit of furniture, stocks of pamphlets, files were thrown on a bonfire in the street. Projectors were not stolen; they were systematically smashed; so were radios, tape recorders, typewriters.
>
> What the demonstrators did not do in the three hours they spent in the building, looters finished.[6]

The Iraqi government was reluctant to pay the $100,000 in compensation we were requesting until I reminded a relative of the prime minister that Secretary of State John Foster Dulles would be visiting Baghdad later in the year, saying, "When he drives down Rashid street, past the shell of our building, how can I explain that the Iraqi government has not compensated us?" We had the check well before the secretary's visit.

Donald Maitland (later Sir Donald), Oriental secretary of the British embassy, was sitting in his garden across the river when USIS leaflets, tossed up by the draft of the fire, began to descend on his garden. "You Americans," he later told me, "go to great lengths to disseminate your propaganda."

One report I heard later was that the demonstrators were initially intent on attacking the British Embassy. That embassy, however, was located on the other side of the river, and the bridges were blocked. So, why not burn the Americans? It's all the same.

Turmoil in the Arab world arose at the very moment in history when the West, and the United States in particular, was becoming increasingly concerned over Soviet designs on the region. The question of which of the Arab nations would form the core of a Middle East defense was to dominate the politics of the region for the next decade.

Despite the outward insistence on Arab unity, that world has been constantly marked by rivalries among the nations created out of the Ottoman Empire in 1918. Syria claimed a special position by virtue of the history and prominence of its capital, Damascus. Iraq, the center of the most prominent of ancient Arab kingdoms, asserted its right to preeminence. And Egypt, the largest of the Arab countries, made its own claim. And that claim was asserted with greater force when Gamal Abdel Nasser, emerged as Egypt's leader.

During the early to mid 1950s, U.S. policy focused on enlisting Iraqi support for American efforts to contain the Soviet Union. But to approach a regime preoccupied with its own survival, the rivalry with its neighbors, and the reaction to the creation of Israel was not easy. Add to that a deep Arab resistance to treaties with the West at a time when nonalignment was becoming an increasingly popular idea in the developing world. Washington was continually frustrated that the Arab nations failed to see the ambitions of the Soviet Union in the same light.

In June 1953, dramatic events unfolded in Berlin. Berliners resisted efforts by the Soviets to put down labor demonstrations. Photos showed courageous young Germans standing in front of Soviet tanks. Believing these to be vivid, concrete evidence of the threats posed by Soviet power, I distributed the photos to local newspapers. None was used. When I inquired why, I was told that the Iraqi government had prohibited their use. They did not want any pictures that might encourage resistance to authority.

Iraq was one of those countries seen in Washington as friendly by policy makers who either ignored reality or declined to look beneath the surface. As a result they took initiatives that probably weakened the monarchy.

Against this background, the Eisenhower administration, and especially Secretary of State Dulles, conceived the idea of a pact of "northern tier" nations to oppose the Soviet Union. Dulles presented the concept in a speech after a tour of the region, including Baghdad, in the summer of 1953.[7] Britain supported the concept, seeing in it a way to revise its treaty with Iraq.

We had some indication of Iraqi attitudes when the United States signed a military assistance agreement with Iraq in April 1954. I was with our chargé d'affaires at the Foreign Office when Foreign Minister Fadhil Jamali signed the agreement and immediately announced to us that he opposed the agreement and was resigning. Our stock did not rise when the first shipment of trucks under the program arrived. The Iraqis had been promised new equipment, but the U.S. Army markings under the paint could still be distinguished.

The first step, taken in April 1954, was a pact between Turkey and Pakistan. Then in January 1955, Prime Minister Adnan Menderes of Turkey visited Iraq and in a late-night session with Nuri Said agreed to a pact with Iraq. Hermann Eilts, then political counselor at the embassy, and I were called out of a dinner party that night by our ambassador, Waldemar Gallman, to report the decision to Washington. We expressed our concern to each other at the time, but Ambassador Gallman was very much dedicated to the project and, as far as we know, raised no concerns himself.

The pact was announced in February 1955. Britain adhered to the treaty in April, Pakistan in September, and Iran in October. The Baghdad Pact, the northern tier alliance, was born. The United States strongly supported it, but never formally joined. Secretary Dulles was concerned over possible problems in securing Senate ratification. At each meeting of the pact, Washington sought alternatives to joining through other agreements and financial and military assistance. We used to say, "We were members of the social committee, the greens committee, and the finance committee, but not of the club."

The pact generated strong antagonism not only in Iraq but also in the rest of the Arab world. Washington hoped, naively, that an Arab focus on the Soviet threat would turn Iraqis away from their preoccupation with Israel. The Iraqis hoped, with equal naiveté, that signing the treaty would gain greater American support for the Arab cause. Scholars of Middle East history generally see the Baghdad Pact as a major factor in the ultimate overthrow of the monarchy.[8]

In 1956 Prime Minister Nuri visited Washington and met with Secretary Dulles. Nuri pleaded with him for the United States to take a more positive position on Palestine. When I accompanied the prime minister to Union Station, I noticed that he had a .45 automatic pistol in the pocket of his overcoat. He was clearly not confident of the future.[9] Two years later, the Baghdad Pact would collapse in the revolution of July 1958, and Nuri would be dragged to his death through the streets of Baghdad.

One positive gift of the Iraqi monarchy to the nation came through the development program. In what was considered a model for developing countries, primarily outside Iraq, the Iraqi government established a Development Board that included two eminent foreign engineers, one British and one American. The American was Wesley Nelson, who had worked on the Hoover Dam.

The development program concentrated on the taming of Iraq's two great rivers, the Tigris and the Euphrates, for flood control and irrigation. The centerpieces were three major dams in the north. Aerial photos revealed the outlines of canals constructed by the Abbasid dynasty in the thirteenth century. Those outlines, with their perfect gradients, became the routes of modern canals. But many Iraqis were skeptical of the program.

One newspaper editor wrote a series of anti-British and anti-American articles claiming that no dams were being built in the north and that the so-called development program was a cover for the construction of barracks to house British soldiers. I went to the editor and offered to fly him up north to show him what was happening. After hemming and hawing for a bit, he said, "I do not really want to know what is going on up there. My job as a journalist is to embarrass the government. I can't attack them directly so I attack those who are supporting them."

The need for flood control was demonstrated in the spring of 1954, when heavy rains and melting snows in the Kurdish mountains brought the rivers to flood levels that had not been seen since 626 A.D. The raging Tigris threatened Baghdad. Levees north of the city were hastily blasted and water diverted. Levees protected Baghdad, but the city became virtually isolated, and residents held their breath, hoping that the levees would hold. While it was still possible to cross the bridges to the western banks, many residents were evacuated.

Fortunately, the waters receded and Baghdad was saved. I wrote home at the time, "Two years from now, a new diversion channel being constructed by the Iraq Government Development Board will end the flood threat to Baghdad. But, not to be so challenged, this old river, which probably carried Noah, made one last effort to show its power."

In a demonstration of the tragic irony of Iraqi society, the offices of the Development Board were among the first targets of the mobs that took over the streets in the revolution of 1958. The young king, the regent, and Nuri were killed, and Iraq's long nightmare of military dictatorship began. In my paper "Elements of Political Instability in Iraq," I wrote prophetically: "Beneath this surface activity, there is discontent, frustration and impatience which provides easy opportunities for political extremists.... With any weakening of the central authority, this discontent could erupt and threaten the present fabric of Iraq's internal organization and international friendships." That was in 1955.

It is not within the scope of this memoir to relate the sad and tangled history of American relations with Iraq after 1958. In retirement in 2003, I viewed with dismay and some anger the U.S. decision to invade Iraq, a country about which we knew so little and about which, in the hubris of the Bush administration, we assumed so much.

In March 1955, I received orders to return to Washington to become officer-in-charge, Arabian Peninsula Affairs. My association with the Arab world was to continue.

10

TENTS IN BLAIR HOUSE GARDEN

From mid-1955 until 1959 I was assigned as officer-in-charge, Arabian Peninsula Affairs, in the Department of State. These were active years:

British and American rivalry in the region reached a critical point.

Revolutions in Iraq and Lebanon in 1958 changed the political map of the region.

Soviet and Chinese inroads into the region—marked by the Egyptian acceptance of Czech arms in 1955—further fueled the Cold War.

The nationalization of the Suez Canal by Nasser of Egypt in 1956 created an international crisis.

Two more Newsom children came into the world: Nancy in 1956 and Catherine in 1958.

The assignment was my first in the home office. Some of my Foreign Service colleagues tried to avoid Washington. But I loved the perpetual challenge of threading one's way through the egos and fiefdoms of bureaucracy to achieve a decision.

My duties primarily concerned the Arabian Peninsula, including Saudi Arabia, Yemen, and the principalities along the Persian Gulf, which included the so-called Trucial states—small Arab principalities that had been established under nineteenth century treaties with the British to control piracy. The principalities have since been incorporated into the United Arab Emirates. Britain also had treaties with other Gulf states, including Kuwait, Bahrain,

Oman, and Qatar. A British official resident in Bahrain maintained the treaty relationships and kept the sheikhdoms in line until the post was abolished in 1971.

Although my responsibilities dealt primarily with the Peninsula and the Gulf, the pressures were such that all of us in the Office of Near Eastern Affairs at that time were drawn into each crisis, regardless of our assigned responsibilities. Middle grade officers, like myself, frequently found themselves briefing Secretary of State John Foster Dulles directly. Because of my previous service in Baghdad, I also became involved in the problems of Iraq. Each of us gained new experiences in negotiation, military base affairs, congressional hearings, and state visits.

Early in my tenure on the Arabian Peninsula desk, I discovered that American involvement in the region went back to our early history. In 1953, the Cities Service Oil Company found oil in commercial quantities in the Dhofar province of the Sultanate of Muscat and Oman. The United States had signed a Treaty of Commerce with the Sultanate in 1833, a treaty that gave American citizens the right of extraterritoriality. In the ensuing decades, Congress had become opposed to such provisions, and because it was anticipated that a number of Americans would be living in Oman, it was necessary to renegotiate the treaty. Complicating the renegotiation were Saudi challenges to the sultan's sovereignty over Oman. Washington was advised that the treaty could be renegotiated without offense to the Saudi kingdom only if it could be shown that the United States did not depart from terms of address with which the sultan had been addressed in an earlier treaty. This requirement meant researching the earlier treaty.

The Treaty of 1833 had been negotiated with the sultan, then residing in Zanzibar on the East African coast, by an itinerant American consul and merchant, Edmund Q. Roberts. A search of the National Archives produced a series of foolscap-size, hand-written reports from Roberts. In these reports from Zanzibar paragraphs reporting conversations on the treaty alternated with information on the prices of dates, lumber, and other products being shipped from the region. In 1958, with this background, the American consul in Aden, Hermann F. Eilts, meeting with the Omanis, was able to satisfy all parties. A new treaty was signed in Salalah with Said bin Taimur bin Faisal, Sultan of Muscat and Oman Dependencies, in December 1958 and ratified by the U.S. Senate on April 28, 1959.

At the time I became officer-in-charge of Arabian Peninsula Affairs, the United States was in the midst of an Anglo-American dispute over a small group of villages in the Buraimi oasis in the southeastern corner of the peninsula. Until the discovery of oil, little attention had been paid to the demarcation of formal boundaries in the Arabian Peninsula. Tribal relationships with regional rulers were based on alliances and payment of the *zakat*, an Islamic tax.

The Buraimi oasis supplied water to much of the region and was a crossroads for traffic and commerce between Muscat and Oman and the Trucial sheikhdoms. The oasis was a key point in determining control of the area. The Emirate of Abu Dhabi claimed jurisdiction over seven of the villages in the oasis, and the Sultan of Muscat and Oman claimed authority over the other two. Saudi Arabia periodically asserted its sovereignty over the oasis on the basis of short-lived military occupations in the nineteenth century.

Although oil had not actually been discovered in the oasis, everyone assumed that oil lay under all the Arabian Peninsula sands. Determined to protect their future interests, the Saudis, in 1949, issued a "Unilateral Declaration of Frontier" that asserted their claim to the Buraimi oasis. The British protested on behalf of their protectorates, and efforts were begun to resolve the problem diplomatically. Frustrated by the slow pace of diplomacy, a Saudi governor in 1952 entered the oasis with forty armed men, claimed it for Saudi Arabia, and proclaimed himself the emir of Buraimi.

On paper, the dispute was between Saudi Arabia and the emir of Abu Dhabi, but in reality it was seen as one between surrogates of Britain and the United States. Although the United States initially sought to stay out of the dispute, it was inevitably drawn in because of its close ties to Saudi Arabia and the active interest of the Arabian American Oil Company (ARAMCO).

In 1954 the dispute was submitted to international arbitration, and an arbitration panel was convened in Geneva in September 1955. Throughout the process, however, each side accused the other of bribery, and the arbitration collapsed. In October 1955, British-led forces of the Sultan of Oman and Muscat invaded the oasis and took control for Sheikh Zaid of Abu Dhabi.

In my exposure to the Buraimi issue, I learned for the first time something about the politics of international oil and became acquainted with some of those involved. My previous post, Iraq, had been an "oil patch," but the oil interests there were largely in British hands and I was not exposed to some of the issues involved. As a boy in Richmond, California, I was aware of the links between the Standard Oil refinery in our town and the new discoveries in the Persian Gulf. But the experience on the Arabian Peninsula desk not only introduced me to oil politics but also to the delicate line between the interests of the U.S. government and those of the private oil companies.

One frequent visitor to my office during this period was James T. Duce, vice president for government relations of ARAMCO. He was a robust proponent of Saudi interests. Under his direction ARAMCO's impressive research department prepared the Buraimi case for Saudi Arabia.

ARAMCO, which became a Saudi company in 1980, was previously owned jointly by Standard Oil of California, Standard Oil of New Jersey, the Texas Company, and the Standard Oil Company of New York. Its sources of oil were entirely within Saudi Arabia, and "Terry" Duce saw to it that ARAMCO gave the Saudi kingdom whatever support it needed.

The issue was complicated by the fact that two of ARAMCO's corporate partners, Standard of New Jersey and Standard of New York, were also partners in the Iraq Petroleum Company with British Petroleum and France's Compagnie Française de Petroles (CFP), operating primarily in territory of British interests.

At one point, as the dispute raged, I received a phone call from a senior executive of Standard of New Jersey asking, "Has Terry Duce been in to see you?"

"Yes. I see many oil company representatives."

"Well, we just want you to know that he does not represent the views of this company."

The 1955 military takeover of the Buraimi oasis by British-led forces was a manifestation of the British suspicion of Saudi intentions and of London's determination to resist Pan-Arab threats to Britain's traditional position in the region. Many in Washington at this time saw the value of the continued British presence in the Gulf and were reluctant to undermine it. More determinant, however, were inherent American anti-colonialism and Washington's apprehension that the Soviet Union could exploit the continuing British presence to undermine Western interests. London believed, on the contrary, that Britain's network of alliances with the Gulf sheikhdoms was a firm barrier to Soviet inroads and considered American attitudes naïve and dangerous. The feeling in London was that Arab nationalists such as Nasser represented a greater threat to their interests than did the communists.

I was very much part of the dialogue with the British. Taylor Fain, a former student who had access to British archives, wrote his doctoral dissertation on British-American relations in the Gulf.[10] He describes some of the exchanges:

> Anglo-American cooperation in the Persian Gulf was also fraught with difficulties. The Foreign Office continually tried to "educate" American officials about the political and social climate in the Gulf and to affirm the importance of Britain's role in the region to the security of Western interests in the Middle East. Still, American policymakers expressed skepticism about the security of Britain's position in the Gulf, the wisdom of London's late imperial policies in the region, and the political stability of the area. This skepticism frequently created tensions between the allies. Typically, British Embassy counselor Willie Morris reported that David Newsom, the State Department's Officer in Charge of Arabian Peninsula–Iraq affairs, told him in February 1956 that "they [the Americans] for their part thought that we talked much too optimistically about the strength of our position in the Persian Gulf. Their information was that currents were already beginning to flow—dissatisfaction with old forms of administration, rising nationalism, and so on—all of which had developed, or could develop, an anti-British slant and which were going to create trouble for us."
>
> Morris shot back that "there might be some tendency on our part to slur over the difficulties in talking to the Americans; the reason was perhaps a fear that once we began to talk about the difficulties of the position, instead of getting

down to a discussion of what we should do about them, the Americans were liable to ask 'how soon do you think you can leave?'"

Newsom replied that it would be a great pity if we got the idea that the Americans wanted to see us go.

Upon reading Morris's account of his interview with Newsom, Derek Riches, head of the Foreign Office's Eastern Department, cabled the Washington embassy new instructions on how to treat the United States on Persian Gulf matters. The instructions reflect the anger and frustration he and his colleagues felt at what they considered the uncooperative US attitude toward Britain's position in the Gulf. He wrote: "We should continue to make clear that the special responsibilities which we exercise in the Gulf are ours alone; and that what we need is American understanding and even support but not American intervention. Our position depends upon the traditional relationship we have built up and maintain with the States. It can and certainly will diminish in time but I do not think it can be replaced or supplemented by other Western influence. If it goes, it will give place to Arab nationalism. In short there is a British position but there will not be an American or Anglo-American one."[11]

In another exchange, Under Secretary of State Herbert Hoover, Jr., raised with the British ambassador in Washington concerns about Communist-inspired propaganda and activity in Kuwait and suggested an exchange of information.

Fain writes: "The Foreign Office responded coolly to the Americans' concern, which it deemed 'a bit alarmist.' British Embassy counselor Willie Morris reiterated to David Newsom in April 1956 that while he and his colleagues were not 'overly sanguine' about their position in the Gulf, they did not think communism represented an immediate threat, particularly in Kuwait."[12]

The Anglo-American differences over the region were even more dramatically demonstrated in October 1956, when, in cooperation with the French and Israelis, British forces joined in an effort to seize the Suez Canal and topple the regime of Gamal Abdel

Nasser. President Eisenhower, angered by the unilateral British action and concerned that the action, particularly in cooperation with Israel, would seriously undermine the Western position in the region, put pressure on London and brought the invasion to a halt.

The Anglo-French-Israeli action came as a complete surprise to the U.S. government. Willie Morris, the British embassy officer who used to come daily to the State Department, suddenly in September stopped visiting us. Some years later, lunching with him in London, I asked why he had stopped coming. He replied, "The instructions we were receiving from London were so bizarre, we felt it would be embarrassing to share them."

In 1954, Egypt and Britain had agreed on the abrogation of the long-standing 1936 Anglo-Egyptian Treaty and the evacuation of British troops stationed in the Suez Canal. In 1955, angered by the conclusion of the Baghdad Pact, Egypt had agreed to accept arms from the Soviet Union through Czechoslovakia. In July 1956, Secretary of State Dulles, concerned about congressional opposition, had unexpectedly withdrawn a U.S. offer to assist Egypt in the construction of a dam at Aswan on the Nile. In retaliation for this act, Nasser ordered the nationalization of the Suez Canal, sending shock waves through the international community.

Secretary Dulles sought to forestall European military action against Egypt by organizing a Suez Canal Users Association (SCUA). (One disrespectful officer in the State Department referred to it as the Suez Canal Losers Association.) I was drawn into the crisis in August 1956 when accompanying Robert Anderson, later secretary of the Treasury and a close friend of President Eisenhower, on a quick trip to Saudi Arabia in an abortive effort to enlist Saudi support for SCUA.[13] As a result of the mission, King Saud agreed to send an emissary to Egypt and to support Dulles's efforts to bring about a peaceful solution to the crisis. The effort became moot when the British and French attempted to seize the canal in October.

Saudi Arabia had become increasingly important to Washington not only for its resources but also as a friendly outpost in a turbulent area. In 1951, a five-year lease was signed, permitting the United States the use of an airfield at Dhahran. The base was primarily envisioned as a recovery base for bombers in the event of a conflict with the Soviet Union, but it also implied a U.S. presence in a country with a growing population of American citizens involved in oil production. Saudi Arabia at the time was not yet the rich country it is today, and the financial assistance provided in the agreement was welcomed. In 1956, President Eisenhower corresponded several times with King Saud bin Abdul Aziz, eldest son of King Abdul Aziz bin Abdul Rahman Al Saud (Ibn Saud), founder of the kingdom who had died in 1953. I drafted some of the letters that assured the king of "the continuing interest of the United States in the territorial integrity, prosperous development and independence of Saudi Arabia."[14] This language was deemed as close to a firm security commitment as could be made without Senate approval.

At the time, the American ambassador in Jiddah was a veteran Middle East expert, George Wadsworth. (The Saudis had not yet permitted diplomatic missions in the royal capital, Riyadh.) Wadsworth had served in Jerusalem and Baghdad. A distinct personality, he had established a golf course in the Dead Sea area when he was consul general in Jerusalem; the tournament trophy was a statue of Lot's wife carved out of salt. When he came to Jiddah, he created a five-hole course out of the desert within the Embassy compound. He once had an aerial photo made of the course and came back to Washington to present it to the Foreign Buildings Office to insure that no future building would disrupt the course. He worked mainly from his residence and freely shared classified information with his Saudi assistant, Mohammad Massoud, who brought him the morning telegrams. Massoud subsequently became a Saudi vice foreign minister.

Wadsworth also had a passion for late nights, croquet, and bridge. Evening dinners with staff would often be followed by command performances on the croquet court. In a land in which alcohol was prohibited, the ambassador still managed to supply himself and his guests. Only after Wadsworth had left Jiddah did a Saudi friend tell me of the crisis during the ambassador's tenure when a box marked "stationery" was dropped on the Jiddah dock and a substance leaked that smelled a lot like gin. Wadsworth's standing with the Saudis was such that the matter was not pursued.

When Wadsworth came back on consultation for the first time after I had taken over the desk, the office director, Fraser Wilkins, told me, "Ambassador Wadsworth is coming back for consultation. He can sometimes get very excited. When he does, just walk away and he will calm down."

Wadsworth wished to impress on Washington that he was serving a king. At least one of his telegrams began, "As the king and I sat watching the sun go down over the Red Sea . . ." He was conscious of how one corresponded with a king. One of the ambassador's objectives on consultation (other than protecting the golf course) was to obtain a letter from President Eisenhower to pave the way for renewed negotiations on the Dhahran airfield. So we set the bureaucratic procedures in play. When the letter arrived from the White House in a normal-size, green envelope, I laid it before the ambassador.

"No. No," he shouted. "That's not the kind of letter you give to a king. It must be in a big envelope with lots of seals and ribbons."

So, taking Fraser Wilkins's advice, I just walked away. I came back in a few minutes and said, "Mr. Ambassador, if you will give me back the letter, I will have it prepared as you wish."

"No," he said, calmly. "I have been thinking. I will give this to the king and tell him, 'Your Majesty, this is not the ordinary type of diplomatic letter with ribbons and seals. This is on the president's personal stationery. This is a very personal message from our president." And that is what he did.

The wooing of King Saud culminated in an invitation for a state visit to Washington. The visit was preceded by negotiations, an essential preface to any official visit to the United States. We informed Ambassador Wadsworth that the United States normally paid for a party of twelve for three days in Washington and visits to other cities as agreed. Wadsworth complained that we could not dictate to a king how many he could bring with him. The royal party was coming by sea and it was ultimately agreed that the United States would receive a party of forty but would cover the expenses of only twelve. We had not counted on the ship's stopping in Cannes. Forty-two more boarded the ship at Cannes. Eighty-two disembarked when the ship reached New York.

Then there was the question of gifts. I was in Baghdad when Saud, as crown prince, had visited and, upon the completion of the visit, had presented automobiles to the Iraqi officials, ranging from Cadillacs to Chevrolets, depending on the rank of the recipient. I cautioned my contact in the Saudi Embassy in Washington, Faisal Hejelan, that U.S. regulations limited the value of gifts that American officials could accept and such presents would be an embarrassment. Secretary of State Dulles also addressed the issue in a January 25, 1957, memorandum to the president:

> In discussions with King Saud of his forthcoming visit, we have stressed that traditionally it is not customary for you to exchange elaborate gifts with foreign rulers. We have suggested that funds for such a gift might be used instead for the purpose of educational exchanges. Nevertheless we anticipate that King Saud will bring gifts for you and that you may wish to reciprocate.
>
> I suggest you give the King a leather desk set with a letter opener appropriately inscribed, symbolic of your correspondence with him. If you approve, I will make the necessary arrangements.
>
> I am suggesting to the Vice President that he present King Saud with a Steuben glass bowl suitably engraved. I plan to give the King a tape recorder in a fine wood cabinet.[15]

No automobiles were presented during the visit. However, when Chief of Protocol Victor Purse accompanied the royal party back to Riyadh, Mrs. Purse was given an Oldsmobile.

The visit broke precedents in many ways. The Saudis made clear that the visit would not be a success unless the president personally met the king at the airport—which Eisenhower did on a cold morning on January 30, 1957.

At the request of the Saudis, we had arranged for the treatment of one of the king's sons, Prince Mashur, at the Bethesda Naval Hospital. On the way in from the airport, the afflicted son was riding with the king and the president. King Saud apparently mentioned that he was grateful for the offer of treatment at the Navy hospital. Army General Dwight Eisenhower said, "Why Bethesda?" and we were required hurriedly to transfer the case to the Walter Reed Army hospital.

The king was accompanied by several tall bodyguards, sporting conspicuous scimitars, whom he wanted nearby. In what must have been a first, tents were pitched for them in the garden behind Blair House, the official U.S. guest house.

More adjustments were made inside Blair House. When I returned to the house an hour or so after the king's arrival, all the furniture had been pushed back against the wall, forming an Arab-style majlis, and a coffee server, a *ghawaji*, was clinking his small cups, and making the rounds. And instead of the normal three days, the king and his party stayed nine.

King Saud was entertained at a formal dinner at the White House on January 30. The king gave a return dinner for the president on February 1, an elaborate affair at the Mayflower Hotel. Financed in large part by ARAMCO , it featured a model electric train that carried the condiments around the table.

The presence of the king and his party provided an opportunity to negotiate an extension of the agreement on the Dhahran airfield facilities. Under Secretary of State Robert Murphy was assigned the task but was not enthusiastic about spending hours in such a negotiation. He appointed a negotiating committee and named me the chair. The experience was a graduate education in negotiating for the U.S. government.

The first negotiations were within the U.S. government. My committee consisted of lawyers from the Defense Department and the Air Force and military representatives from each service, in addition to representatives from interested parts of the State Department. As I recall, there must have been at least eight participants. My first task was to get their agreement on our negotiating position. They would then flank me at the table when we sat down with the Saudis and signal me if they thought I was departing from instructions.

Our task was not made easier by the discussions Ambassador Wadsworth had had with the king prior to the visit. Without instructions (this never bothered George Wadsworth), he suggested to the king that the facilities were valuable to the United States and that we might pay as much as $5 million annually and build a new terminal at the base as "frosting on the cake."

The second part of the experience was negotiating with the Saudis. The principal Saudi negotiator was Sheikh Yusuf Yasin, a Syrian, and one of four counselors to the king. The negotiations were conducted through an interpreter, although each side had some understanding of the other's language. Sheikh Yusuf had two memorable tactics. He would repeat back what he understood our side had said, but often with a slight twist in the Saudi favor.

As late night sessions drew to a close, he would suggest that one "minor" point might be cleared up in order to provide a fresh start in the morning. The "minor" point might be something major that he hoped the fatigued Americans would not notice.

At one point he raised something we could not accept, and I said, "We will take that under advisement."

He replied, "I do not know much English, but I know that when you say you will 'take it under advisement,' that means you are not going to do anything about it." He was right.

The king had other counselors as well. At times they would appear in Sheikh Yusuf's place and open the proceedings as if nothing had occurred before. All these tactics required vigilance and patience on our side.

We did reach agreement on a five-year extension at something below Ambassador Wadsworth's suggested price, but including the new terminal. The United States Air Force withdrew from the facility in 1961 when the five-year extension ended. The United States continued to assist in the management of the airfield through a private contractor.

The hot, sandy Dhahran facility was not a popular assignment in the Air Force. Shortly after the king's visit and the conclusion of the agreement, I visited Dhahran. Riding in from the airfield to the Bachelor Officer's Quarters (BOQ) with an Air Force officer, I said, with some pride, that I had just helped secure an agreement permitting us to remain for another five years. The officer replied with an expletive, "Don't tell anyone here or they will run you out of town."

The American presence at a Saudi airfield presented problems throughout the life of the agreement. It was not a base and U.S. activities were limited by Saudi concerns. Nevertheless, to many in the Pentagon it was a flag on the map, and I was thus constantly explaining that we could not assign additional personnel, stage troops through Dhahran, or preposition equipment without Saudi agreement. Saudi sensitivity about U.S. military activities, manifested in the late 1950s, reappeared to haunt us in the Gulf War of 1990.

One particularly vexing problem that was raised with the king and that was a constant issue in the Congress was the Saudi exclusion of persons of the Jewish faith—including military personnel. The Saudis did admit some Jews who were openly anti-Zionist such as Alfred Lillienthal, but they insisted that they had to assume that other Jews favored Israel, with which they were technically at war. The matter was highlighted during the king's visit when Mayor Robert Wagner of New York refused to receive him.

The king's 1957 visit ended on a sour note. The Saudis and Egyptians claimed that the water within the Gulf of Aqaba was territorial water, giving control of passage to the two nations and precluding Israeli passage through its outlet at the Strait of Tiran. The gulf runs between Saudi and Egyptian territory and the strait is the passage to the Jordanian port of Aqaba and the Israeli port of Eilat. While the king was in Washington, Herman Phleger, the State Department legal adviser, issued a finding that because the gulf was wider than the American view of territorial waters, the waters within the gulf were international waters. This meant that Israel had the right of access through the Strait of Tiran, an interpretation to which the Saudis strongly objected.

King Saud was a large, rather bulky man, with thick glasses that corrected his nearsightedness. Though Saud was the natural heir to the throne, he was not a person of great competence. He became increasingly unpopular within the Saud family and was deposed in 1964, to be replaced as king by his more capable half-brother, Crown Prince Faisal. I last saw Saud in the ARAMCO Hospital in Dhahran after his deposition. Sitting by this large, slightly stooped, and clearly stricken individual, I could think only of Shakespeare's King Lear.

During the king's visit and in subsequent communications, the Eisenhower doctrine was launched. President Eisenhower had explained the rationale on January 4, 1957, in a message to the king in advance of the visit:

> As you know, the United States in support of the right of nations to independence has encouraged the principle of collective security. For this reason it has supported the members of the Baghdad pact in their cooperative efforts designed to meet the communist threat. A further means which might have been employed by the United States to implement its policy of assisting countries of the area to develop their defense might have been American adherence to the Baghdad pact. I have however been disinclined to recommend this course, my primary reason being your Majesty's own attitude toward the Pact. . . .
>
> The program which I have decided to recommend to the Congress involves a joint congressional resolution which would state clearly and firmly our belief that the imposition by international communism of totalitarian regimes upon the free nations in the general area of the Middle East, by direct or indirect aggression, would undermine the foundations of international peace and hence the security of the United States.[16]

The Middle East Resolution as envisioned by the president was passed as a joint resolution on March 9, 1957. In addition to the language on security, the resolution authorized $200 million for economic and military assistance to the nations of the region in support of the doctrine. A retired congressman, James P. Richards, was appointed to visit the area and encourage nations publicly to support the doctrine.

I was in the meetings in the office of Near Eastern affairs when the original concept was discussed and the resolution framed. It was seen not only as a reinstatement of our concerns over Soviet ambitions in the region but also as a means to give the administration greater flexibility in providing aid. I joined others in questioning whether an initiative that required rulers in this area to "stand up and be counted" as supporters of the United States would effectively advance our interests. As with the Baghdad Pact, the results were mixed, and in many countries the doctrine became the basis for further anti-American attacks. When the Richards mission completed its visit to the region, only Iraq, Israel, and Lebanon had formally endorsed the doctrine. Jordan accepted the principles but gave no formal endorsement. Saudi Arabia also publicly endorsed the underlying principles but did not endorse the doctrine. The doctrine was rejected by Syria, Egypt, Yemen, and Sudan.

The Richards visit to Yemen illustrated the problem of dispensing the $200 million authorization. Accompanied by Ambassador John Jernegan, Richards met with the imam of Yemen in Taiz. They explained the purposes of the Eisenhower doctrine and their readiness to offer $2 million in economic assistance to Yemen. The imam passed on to other subjects but at the end of the meeting, "suddenly rose from his chair and said in excited tones, 'Only one percent of the $200 million has been offered to Yemen. How can I release anything to the press on this? It will be harmful to my prestige and I shall be shamed before the people of Yemen. It is much better therefore to leave everything in its place, as if nothing had been raised. Let us bury it and cover it with a stone.'" Jernigan, in his telegram reporting the meeting said, "Roundup on Yemen, playing in tougher league now—batting average hit slump."[17]

1958 was, for me, a memorable year. It began with my own visit to Yemen in May.

Yemen, at that time a kingdom, is a mountainous nation in the southwest corner of the Arabian Peninsula. Most Arab tribes trace their origins back to Yemen. Trade, primarily in coffee, between the United States and Yemen, goes back to the early nineteenth century. The United States was now interested in establishing a resident legation in the country.

One of the points of contention in negotiating the opening of a resident legation was whether we could fly the American flag over the building. The matter was resolved when we discovered in an early nineteenth century ship's log the sketch of an American trading post in Mocha, a Yemeni port, showing an American flag on the roof. The precedent satisfied the Yemenis.

Washington became concerned over developments in Yemen, both the increase in the influence of Nasser's Egypt and inroads by Communist China and Romania, a Soviet satellite. Both were seen as potential threats to Saudi Arabia. China had agreed to build a road from the port of Hodeida to the traditional capital of Sana'a.

Romanian firms were prospecting for oil. Diplomatic relations were conducted through Ambassador Wadsworth, who was accredited to the Yemen and made occasional visits from Jiddah.

One writer at the time described Yemen as "rushing headlong into the thirteenth century." Visiting the country was not easy. The ruler, Imam Ahmed, suspicious of the tribes surrounding the traditional capital of Sana'a, spent most of his time in the southern city of Taiz.

Although an airstrip did exist in Taiz for the imam's aircraft, required entry to Taiz was by road from the British colony of Aden to the south. Arrangements were made through the Yemeni legation in Washington for me to visit the vice foreign minister, Qadi al-Amri, in Taiz, and I was provided with the necessary visa. I was to be accompanied by another officer from the Office of Near Eastern Affairs, Michael Sterner, and his wife, Coco.

Our first stop was the British colony of Aden. Once a major port call en route to India, its importance had declined as the Empire contracted. It nevertheless remained important to the British as part of their presence in the Gulf and the Peninsula. As Fain notes, "Just as they had in the Persian Gulf, British officials worked diligently to convince the United States of Aden's value to Western, rather than merely British, interests in the Middle East. They believed they needed US cooperation in securing the colony and its military facilities from the depredations of the Imam of Yemen and especially the royal government of Saudi Arabia."[18]

The colony's governor, Sir William Luce, invited me to attend a meeting he was conducting with Horace Phillips of the Foreign Office. The differences of view between the two British officials were obvious. To the governor, representing the Colonial Office, Nasser was the enemy. Phillips took a more nuanced view; Britain would have to live with Nasser and work with him to the extent possible. I was also introduced to Colonial Office protocol.

Governor Luce gave a dinner in my honor at his residence. As I entered, his aide said to me, "The Guest of Honor leaves twenty minutes after the squash." Had I not known that squash was a British citrus drink I would have indeed been puzzled.

Upon arriving in Aden, we found that the official visa issued in Washington was invalid without a handwritten note from the imam's agent in Aden. The note was duly produced on a page torn from a spiral notebook. Thus armed, and accompanied by Mohammad, an Arab employee of the U.S. Consulate in Aden, and an American consular officer, we made the 110-mile journey over a rocky, winding mountain road to Taiz. It took us ten hours.

All visitors were required to stay in the official guesthouse. No one could arrive or leave without the imam's permission. When we arrived, we met a Pakistani diplomat who had been waiting four days for such permission. In addition to the Pakistani and a French diplomat, the other rooms in the guesthouse were occupied by Chinese and Russians.

The guesthouse was unique among all official accommodations I have experienced. Facilities were simple and centipedes hung from the rafters. Coco Sterner described the setting in a letter: "In spite of our mosquito netting and homemade paper-and-coat-hanger lamp shade, insects in droves are creeping in through pores in the wall. It still hasn't rained but grows humider, thicker, and smellier every night, with the garbage dump now very mature and jackals closing in on it, barking to each other, as soon as the guesthouse is dark." And, we were obliged to prepare our own food.

One room, furnished with Beirut brocade furnishings, was the VIP suite. During our visit, it was occupied by Roger Lescot, a French diplomat. Lescot had been in Yemen previously in 1947 to supervise a French economic assistance project. He pressed the Yemeni for permission to visit Sana'a in the north, where he had many friends. After some days, he was notified that the imam's plane (piloted by two Swedish pilots) was ready to take him to Sana'a. He spent a frustrating four days in Sana'a seeking permission to visit his friends only to be told that permission could not be granted until the governor returned. But, before the governor ever returned, Lescot was told that the plane was ready to take him back to Taiz. Returning to Taiz, he learned that he had been given permission to go to Sana'a only because the Yemenis needed the VIP room in the guesthouse for a diplomat from Peking.

In the sitting room of the guest house, I pursued the matter of a resident legation with the vice minister. In two sessions, I met polite evasion. Sensing there was something about the situation I did not understand, I asked Mohammed if there was a problem of which I was not aware.

"Yes," he replied, "It's the village."

"The village?" I asked.

Then Mohammed explained. "You know that as you sit in the sitting room of the guest house, you can see, out the window, a village on a hill. Well, when Ambassador Wadsworth was last here, he raised the question of a resident legation and, seeking to demonstrate the advantages to the Yemenis, he said the United States intended to build the finest legation in Taiz. He pointed out the window to the village on the hill and suggested that would be a fine site. But the Yemenis do not wish to move the village."

When next I met with the minister, I referred to the ambassador's visit and explained that he was merely illustrating our keen interest in building a fine legation. We had no particular site in mind—and certainly not the village on the hill. The minister was much relieved, and we were able to gain agreement on a diplomatic presence in Yemen.

I learned an important lesson in diplomacy: always try to find out what the real problem is. A permanent diplomatic mission was opened in 1959, but not on the village's hill.

The visit to Yemen in May 1958 was followed in July by another new experience: briefing Congress. In the summer of 1958, Lebanon was in turmoil. The government of Camille Chamoun, threatened by Arab nationalist elements, called on the United States for assistance. Any Washington reluctance to respond was quickly dispelled when, in July 1958, army elements in Baghdad overthrew the monarchy. Regimes friendly to the United States were seen as threatened throughout the region. U.S. Marines landed and took up positions in Beirut. They were followed by Ambassador Robert Murphy, then under secretary of state, who was sent as a special envoy to resolve the crisis. He successfully negotiated a political solution.

During this crisis, William Macomber, under secretary of state for management, and I were assigned to brief Congress on developments in both Lebanon and Iraq. Over several days in July and August 1958, we met daily with the House Foreign Affairs Committee in the morning and the Senate Foreign Relations Committee in the afternoon. The committee chairmen invited members of the Congress who were not on the committees to attend the sessions. Both were in closed executive sessions, permitting a full exchange with the members.

The differences in interests and attitudes between those in the House and those in the Senate were striking. House members, facing election every two years, were more concerned with how the American public viewed the Lebanese landings. Senators took a longer view and concentrated on the constitutional and foreign policy aspects.

The closed sessions permitted greater candor and openness from the members. To a degree probably impossible today, little leaked out from the candid and intelligent discussion of the issues. At one point Senator William Fulbright, a strong critic of Secretary of State Dulles, got up and walked out. In the corridor he said to the waiting press, "I will not be a part of Secretary Dulles's star chamber proceedings."

Throughout his time in Congress, Senator Fulbright was a critic of executive commitments that did not have full congressional approval. The following excerpt from the transcript of the hearings relating to Lebanon illustrates this approach:

> *Senator Fulbright:* What was the nature of the commitment that we honored?
>
> *Mr. Macomber*: I was speaking of a commitment in the sense that a friendly small country called on us for help and we gave them help.
>
> *Senator Fulbright:* Do we have that commitment with small countries all over the world? What is the nature of the commitment? Was there a written agreement, a treaty, or what was the kind of commitment you had?
>
> *Mr. Macomber:* In Lebanon we had a situation which we do not have in any other country at this time.
>
> *Senator Fulbright:* What was the special situation? Was there a written agreement?
>
> *Mr. Macomber:* No. there was not a written agreement.
>
> *Senator Fulbright*: What kind of agreement was there? What was the commitment that we fulfilled? You just said we fulfilled one, and now we have great credit among everybody for fulfilling our commitments.

Mr. Macomber: Maybe "commitment" was too strong, I will answer you as to what there was. I won't say we were committed. That is a little strong word.

Senator Fulbright: You used the word.

Mr. Macomber: I should not have used it, but we were under obligation—we were asked by a friendly small government to come to their aid when they thought that if we did not they would cease to be independent. Now that was the situation we were in. As far as any commitments are concerned, that is a different thing. There were words approaching a commitment but not a commitment.

Senator Fulbright: I think we are entitled to know about this. You skirt around this. What I would like to know is if we were responding to a commitment, what was the nature of it and what other commitments do we have of a similar nature?[19]

In a pattern that was to recur as other friendly regimes in the Middle East were overthrown in subsequent years, the senators in 1958 wanted to know why the Iraqi revolution came as a surprise:

Senator O'Mahoney: . . . When did you first know that the revolt was brewing in Iraq?

Mr. Macomber: This specific revolt, we knew that there was a shaky situation there and we knew all the time we were dealing with the Lebanon problem that Jordan and Iraq were probably the next on the timetable, but we did not know about the timing of this one.

Now as far as when we specifically knew, I understand that Mr. Allen Dulles knew in the early morning hours of Monday morning. What hour, I do not know. I found out at seven o'clock on the radio.

Senator O' Mahoney: By the radio?

Mr. Macomber: That is how I personally found out. I got up and turned on the radio.

Senator O'Mahoney: I was trying to follow Senator Humphrey's question about intelligence. It would appear then from your answer that from our own source of intelligence we had no advance information of the timing of the revolt.

Mr. Macomber: That is correct.[20]

Senator Lausche asked a pertinent question, "While I recognize that we ought to have knowledge as to what intrigues are being made concerning our country, what would we have done if we had known that the revolt was to take place at the minute that it did, and in a manner that it did? Can you answer that?"

Mr. Macomber answered, "Certainly one thing we would have done. If we had known, we would have warned our friends and one of the things that made this revolt so successful is that the people who would have fought it were dead, just like that, or rounded up. There was no opposition to it. It was very effective so I think if we had known ahead of time we could have at least done that."[21]

In 1959, my service as officer-in–charge, Arabian Peninsula Affairs, came to an end, and I was assigned to the National War College for a year of interacting with officers from the several military services.

11

UNFINISHED SENTENCES

For Middle East experts who had spent years involved with the complexities of the region, the most coveted Middle East assignment was in the embassy in London. Because of close interaction with the British in other regions of the world, the American diplomatic establishment in Britain's capital customarily included experts dealing with the Middle East, South Asia, East Asia, and Africa. Beginning in 1960 I had the good fortune to be for two years "the Middle East man in London." They were two of the most pleasant and interesting years of our Foreign Service life. Theaters, music, weekends in the country all remain vivid and pleasant memories. But there was work to be done, work that quite unexpectedly led to my spending the next ten years confronting the problems of U.S.-African relations.

In July 1960, my family and I sailed from New York on the SS *United States* for Southampton. I had just finished a year at the National War College at Fort McNair in Washington. Diplomats and soldiers often come at problems from quite different perspectives. The year together helps iron out misunderstandings and is valuable to all those who work with the military in the future. When I was later under secretary of state for political affairs, I could cut through a great deal of bureaucracy by fruitful conversations with my War College classmate General David Jones, then chairman of the Joint Chiefs of Staff.

The year at Fort McNair was also a year of both joy and pain for the family. Our third son, David, was born in January, and a few weeks later during a visit to Norfolk, our second son, Daniel, had his legs crushed when an automobile pinned him against a wall in a parking lot. Luckily, the emergency surgeon on duty in the local hospital had had extensive experience with crush injuries in World War II in the South Pacific. Dan's recovery was slow, but six months after the accident he was able to enjoy our new life in London. Soon, his budding piano talent qualified him as a junior exhibitioner at the Royal College of Music.

Unexpectedly, moving as we were to a country that we saw as much like our own, we had problems of housing and schooling—and even, on occasion, of language. Fifteen years after the end of the war, housing in London was still tight. We moved initially into an apartment and then stayed for two months in the home of an officer who was on leave. In September 1960 we moved into our own rented house, an 1820 mansion, one side of which was held up by wooden buttresses because "it had had a bit of a bomb in the war." When we asked the agent the usual American question about central heating, he replied that a new boiler was being installed. "The old one blew up but it didn't make much difference, because the owners only used it at Christmas time." In time, we learned how to operate a coal furnace.

The owner was Sir John Maud, British high commissioner in South Africa; we called the House "the Maudery." The house had been added onto over many years so that it had five different kinds of electrical connections. When we moved a lamp from one room to another we had to change the connection.

Lady Maud was a concert pianist and, much to Dan's delight, the house had back-to-back concert grand pianos. The rooms were furnished with genuine if somewhat tattered antiques. In the large garden at the rear of the house was a mulberry tree that dated back several centuries to the time when the property had been a priory. We were told it had been the setting for a ballad written by Sir Walter Scott.

We were somewhat saddened to leave the aging grandeur of the Maudery when, a year later, we were offered a modern embassy house. It was our fourth move in twelve months and the last for a year. Located within walking distance of Hyde Park and Marble Arch, it was a location convenient to my office in the new American Embassy in Grosvenor Square.

We had not anticipated the problem of schooling for our two sons, ten and twelve. The differences between the British and American systems for that age group meant that John and Dan would have been set back a year if they were admitted to a British school. After a year at the American School in Regent's Park, John returned to the United States to attend the Lawrenceville School in New Jersey. Dan continued for his second year at the American School. Our two little girls presented no problem. Fitted out in their prim uniforms they went happily to the nearby Connaught School. Young David, not yet a year old, was pampered by a series of English and Scottish babysitters.

In 1960, Britain was finally emerging from the grimness of the war years, although the sadness mixed with humor of those years still dominated the London stage. While still recalling the memories of the Blitz, the British were facing the reality of a fading empire. India, divided, was independent. During our two years in London, a parade of personalities, primarily from East Africa, came to negotiate independence: Jomo Kenyatta of Kenya, Julius Nyerere of Tanzania, Milton Obote of Uganda, and others.

Because of the major British interests involved, London was also watching the unfolding dramas in the former Belgian and French colonies, especially in the Congo. I once asked a Foreign Office friend what influence the British government had over the private mining interests heavily involved in the region. "No problem," he replied. "You see, the diplomats and the mining executives all went to the same schools. They speak to each other in unfinished sentences."

Encounters with history, theirs and ours, were inescapable in London. Here is a paragraph from a letter I wrote home shortly after our arrival:

> This is truly a great and fascinating city, probably more varied than any city on earth in its aspects. With almost every turn of every street, one meets some reflection of history, literature, or art. A building may have a small plaque indicating that some famous person lived in it. (There is a little house not far from where we are going to live temporarily where Anna Pavlova, the great ballerina, lived.) Or there may be another plaque indicating where some important

> event in English history took place. (There is a little hill not far from where we live now with a wonderful view of London; Lenin when in exile used to go there and survey the city, while pondering on the evils of capitalism.) Or literature: the orthodontist where Dan and John are going to go is on a little street between Harley Street (*Sherlock Holmes*) and Wimpole Street (*The Barretts of . . .*).

The rendezvous with history was particularly vivid when on November 1, 1961, we participated for the first time in the annual Buckingham Palace reception for the diplomatic corps. In our formal dress we gathered with diplomats from around the world. Those from Africa and Asia stood out in their more brilliant national dress.

Members of each embassy gathered in a group, and the queen and Prince Philip made the rounds, greeting those in the front rank of each group. Whether by design or serendipity, the American embassy diplomats were standing just under a portrait of George III.

Jean and I were standing behind Clinton Olson, our administrative counselor, when the queen stopped at our group. It was the year the embassy had just moved to the new chancery on Grosvenor Square. The queen asked Mr. Olson how things were going with the new embassy. He replied that some problems still existed with the heating. We were impressed when one year later at the next diplomatic reception the queen remembered Mr. Olson and asked him whether the heating had now been fixed.

Much of my work was in the British Foreign Office, a great dark pile of Victorian origin in Westminster near the Houses of Parliament. The furniture and the décor suggested they had not been changed since Queen Victoria's time. Unlike American offices, there is not a single nameplate on any of the doors, and one is either led to the proper office by a frock-coated attendant or, after being accepted, is free to go where business takes him.

Visiting the Foreign Office brought constant reminders of Britain's imperial reach. The walls of the India room and the Treaty room where modern meetings often took place could speak volumes about the building of an empire. If I took the passage that led from the Foreign Office to the Commonwealth Relations Office, I would pass by shelves of musty volumes of records of the India office. Britain ruled

India from a separate office that provided "advice" to the viceroy; this advice was inscribed in these files relating to water, land, relations with the princes, and a host of other administrative items. I frequently paused to examine a volume that carried me back into another era.

My relationship with individuals in the Foreign Office grew close, a counterpart to the friendships with officers of the British embassy in Washington. Ties were further strengthened by lunches together at the venerable Travelers Club, where I had an honorary membership. History dominated the atmosphere of the club. The extra rail on the stairs leading to the second floor was established to help Talleyrand. The library was filled with writings of British explorers who had created and maintained the empire. On an afternoon when I did not need to rush back to work, I often stepped over sleeping members to reach a tempting volume.

The work was chiefly a continuation of what I had been doing in Washington—maintaining communication with the British government on matters relating to the Middle East. The importance of a position such as the one in London depends greatly on where major exchanges and decisions are made. I was in London at the beginning of the Kennedy administration, and the close ties between the British ambassador in Washington and members of the Kennedy administration meant that Washington was where the action was. The embassy in London, however, could contribute insights into British attitudes and from time to time provide useful explanations to the British of circumstances in Washington. Sometimes it was necessary to educate my own colleagues. I once took a message about British views on the Arabian Peninsula to the political counselor, who had never served outside of Europe. He asked me as he looked at the paper, "Does anyone really give a damn about Saudi Arabia?"

Because of the numerous conferences that took place in London, the embassy was one of the principal sources for Washington on the details of decolonization. Broad worldwide cooperation in intelligence gathering meant that we had few secrets from each other. Often, however, the interpretations were different. Differences over policy existed within the British government; an understanding of those differences was useful in analyzing possible future British actions.

Inescapable divergences existed between the Colonial Office and the Foreign Office. Colonial Office officials were generally hired as administrators and looked at the situation in a given territory from the standpoint of keeping order. They saw emerging nationalist leaders as law and order problems, not as possible collaborators in a march toward independence. As noted in the previous chapter, some regarded Arab nationalism as a greater threat than communism. Foreign Office officials, on the contrary, tended to be closer to the United States in their views, recognizing that genuine nationalism required a degree of recognition, not suppression.

The time in London also introduced me to the parliamentary system. In this system cabinet members come from the Parliament. Unlike officials in Washington, who face congressional committees, often in an adversarial spirit, British officials did not have to testify at budget hearings or work under serious legislative restrictions in the administration of foreign aid. Life was simpler. The difference in systems perhaps explains why U.S. aid missions overseas number as many as eighty people in contrast to a British mission of four or five.

In response to invitations for an embassy representative, one of my tasks was to speak to British audiences in London and throughout the country. This was generally a pleasant experience, but the feelings lingering from the Suez crisis of 1956 remained strong in some places. On one memorable evening at the Chelsea Conservative Club, after explaining U.S. policy in the Middle East, I endured a tongue-lashing from a wing commander in the Royal Air Force who felt personally let down by the failure of America to come to Britain's assistance in the Suez invasion.

Visitors were common—officials coming on business or transiting the British capital en route to somewhere else, or personal friends. We made many forty-five minute trips to Heathrow and Gatwick airports.

Meeting visitors often involved not only the normal formalities but, in several cases, dealing with pets. Britain had very strict quarantine requirements, and those like myself meeting new arrivals were often required on very short notice to separate pets from their owners and arrange for a temporary kennel in Uxbridge. The owners and their pets did not always participate graciously in this operation.

Two of the most spectacular visits in which I was involved were the unofficial overnight visit by President Kennedy on June 4 and 5, 1961, to meet with Queen Elizabeth and Prime Minister Harold Macmillan and the April 1962 visit of Secretary of State Dean Rusk to attend a ministerial conference of the Central Treaty Organization (CENTO), the successor to the Baghdad pact.

Presidents of the United States do not just "drop in" to say hello to friends. They are preceded by occasionally arrogant advance people who seek to rearrange the landscape as they think the president would wish. They arrive not only with a substantial staff but also with a press corps that can at times number in the hundreds.

Embassy officers were mobilized and assigned tasks. Mine was to be available at the townhouse where Mrs. Kennedy was staying with her sister, Princess Lee Radziwill. The house was in a mews, a cul-de-sac with one entrance on a main street. The British police had stationed officers to control entry into the cul-de-sac.

I looked out and saw only two police at the entrance to the cul-de-sac. I asked the British police officer who was with me in the house whether that represented sufficient security. He replied, "We have thirty more waiting in a theater around the corner. We do not believe in overdoing security."

Screening members of the press for entry represented another task. For the Kennedy visit I was working with a young man from the Foreign Office. When I asked him whether we should admit a photographer from the French newspaper *Paris Match*, he replied, "Absolutely not. He will be under Jackie's skirts in five minutes."

A letter home on May 4, 1962, gives a picture of the visit of the secretary of state—a not atypical picture:

> This week involved, principally, the care and feeding of a large number of official visitors, headed by the Secretary of State. The movement of the Secretary in this day and age is no small undertaking. Arrangements must be made, not only for the business which brings him to the place he is visiting, but also for keeping him in touch

with developments throughout the world. Consequently, a considerable staff goes before him and with him. The advance man arrived, with one assistant, a week ago (three days before the Secretary.). He and I immediately began making arrangements for accommodations, transportation, security, office space, and other similar matters. Then we worked out with the British government the arrangements for the Secretary's arrival, for press handling, protocol, etc. By Sunday, we were ready and we headed, with a caravan of cars, printed information on the arrangements, and the senior officers of the embassy for the VIP lounge at London airport.

The Secretary's plane, a great, gleaming silver 707, touched down just on time on Sunday afternoon at 2:45. The sun came out, after a cloudy morning, to greet him. He and Mrs. Rusk came down the ramp to meet a crowd of cameramen, a representative of Prime Minister Macmillan, and our embassy delegation. Mr. Rusk then went for a brief meeting with the press. We loaded the rest of the party (23 in all) into the cars and sent them off to London. The Secretary arrived at 2:45 and by 5:00 p.m. he was in the Embassy meeting visitors and holding a working session with the members of the delegation. That night he dined with Lord Home, the British Foreign Secretary. We had a buffet supper for the rest of the party at our Minister's house.

Monday morning was the opening session of the CENTO conference he came to attend. We had to see that the delegation, including such notables as General Lemnitzer, Chairman of the Joint Chiefs of Staff, our ambassador here in London, and various assistant secretaries of state, were in their seats at Lancaster House by 8:55 a.m. Then transportation had to be arranged so that the Secretary arrived at precisely 9:25 a.m. to review an honor guard and to meet Lord Home before proceeding to the opening session of the conference.

Lancaster House, where most of the official conferences are held in London, is part of the cluster of royal buildings behind St. James's Palace. It is an ornate Restoration structure full of gilt and cupids, built by Charles II for one of his mistresses. Charles would probably not have been surprised to come back and see these strange people from the New World sitting with his subjects. He might have been somewhat more surprised a few weeks before when the Kenya Constitutional Conference took place to see the delegates from Africa with their monkey-skin headdresses and their lion-skin capes sitting where his favorites once danced.

On Monday night, the Secretary and Mrs. Rusk went off to have dinner with the Queen at Windsor Castle. We were not invited to that. The next night, however, we were invited to the dinner given by the British Foreign Secretary at Hampton Court. About 175 of us assembled for dinner in a long room underneath the state apartments through which the normal visitor passes. We were just at a level with the gardens, which were specially lighted for the occasion. This was only the second or third official function held at Hampton Court since George II closed it up almost two hundred years ago. Consequently, the catering is still a little rough; I had two entrées and no fish course! That didn't really matter because, after the dinner we were told that the palace was open for us to wander through. Guides were present who took us places we had never been before, including the Royal Chapel, some of the Woolsey rooms and the Orangery. It was a clear night, although a bit cool, but we did wander in the lighted gardens; one sunken garden, larger than a football field, was a mass of tulips.

Entertaining private visitors in London could be equally arduous. With visitors from California we packed into three days the Ceremony of the Keys (when they lock up the Tower of London at night), the Crown Jewels, Westminster Abbey, changing of the guard at the Horse Guards Parade at Hampton Court, Ye Olde Cheshire Cheese pub, the satirical revue *Beyond the Fringe*, a stately home, dinner at Royal Festival Hall, *Romeo and Juliet* at the Old Vic, shopping at Harrod's, and the American Embassy cafeteria. We had a wonderful time, but I'll bet they felt as dished in afterwards as we did.

We benefited greatly in our London stay from friendships with British diplomats whom we had known at our other posts. A British Diplomatic Service officer, Robert Belgrave, and his wife Susan, were among our friends when we were in Baghdad. When we were posted to London, they frequently invited us to their home, West Lodge, in Piddlehinton, Dorset, introducing us to British country life and the long weekend. We continued over many years to enjoy visits to West Lodge and to contribute occasionally through minor chores to its upkeep. Sadly, Robert died in 1991, but we remain in touch with Susan and visit her when she is not off on one of her equestrian adventures in Central Asia.

Susan comes from a British military tradition, and her house is filled with records of expeditions in the Far East, India, and Ethiopia. Her father was with Kitchener on a gunboat on the Nile during the Battle of Omdurman. The West Lodge "loo" is decorated with pictures of that battle, published in the *London Illustrated News* of that time.

American as well as British history intruded during our West Lodge visits. One of the Belgrave ancestors was James Dacres, captain of the British frigate *Guerriere,* defeated by the U.S.S. *Constitution* during the war of 1812. Susan told us the story of the surrender. Dacres and Isaac Hull, captain of the *Constitution,* had been friends at a naval training college in Britain before the Revolutionary War. They had made a bet that if one were ever defeated by the other, the loser would offer his hat rather than his sword. When Dacres came aboard the *Constitution* and offered his sword to Hull, Hull reminded him, "No, James, your hat, not your sword."

A copy of Gilbert Stuart's portrait of George Washington, framed with oak that had come from Mount Vernon, hung on a West Lodge wall. A letter on the back of the portrait from E. F. Sanderson, dated May 8, 1840, explained how the wood was obtained:

> Being instructed by My Friend to procure a piece of Oak Wood grown in reality on the Estate of the late Gen. Washington at Mt. Vernon in Virginia I found, after fruitless trials to accomplish my wishes by means of friend or Agent, that the only way was to take the earliest opportunity of performing this duty myself—Accordingly on the first day

of November 1838 I visited Mount Vernon—I met with the Overseer of the Estate who, on explaining my views, very readily afforded every facility—It happened that a few months previous the body of General Washington had been removed from the old tomb to a new Mausoleum, erected a short distance from his original resting place—Being accompanied by the Overseer I noticed at the new Tomb some oak planks laying about, I was informed by him that these planks were used at the disinterment of Gen. Washington in removing his remains and that he (the Overseer) assisted in bearing them—Of course I thought a piece of one of these planks would afford additional satisfaction as an interesting relic. Therefore at my request the Overseer very willingly sawed off for me the piece of oak plank recd, observing the wood was grown on the Estate.

One day we were invited to have tea with Susan's neighbor, a retired British brigadier, Sir Henry Jackson. In the course of the conversation he asked me if I had ever heard of Tom Paine.

"Of course," I replied, "he was one of the heroes of our revolution."

"We regarded him as a renegade," he said, "but would you be interested in letters from him that I have in a drawer?"

I replied with an enthusiastic "yes." He then disappeared inside and returned with two letters written from Paris by Paine. I had not known that Paine was an engineer. The letters were from him to his ironmonger agents, the Walker brothers, in Sheffield in 1788, with instructions about the building of a wrought iron bridge to be erected in Paddington. Included in the letters were paragraphs on recent conversations with Jefferson. I suggested to Sir Henry that he send these to the Massachusetts Historical Society, but I was never able to determine whether that took place.[22]

One of my other duties in London was to serve as political adviser to an admiral. Rear Admiral H. Page Smith had a command that encompassed the Mediterranean and South Asia. Stationed in London, he was a pleasant but brusque man. When I reported for duty to him he said, "I don't like to take orders from civilians, but if you will explain to me what you think I should do and give me a good reason, we shall probably come to the same conclusion."

Representatives of the U.S. armed services often played a significant diplomatic as well as military role. In Middle Eastern and other countries in which local military officers held political power, regional American commanders and attachés could establish contacts that were more difficult for civilian diplomats. Frequently the Navy, in particular, represented the United States where no diplomatic missions were present. For many years, two small vessels of the Navy's Persian Gulf command kept in touch through frequent visits with the rulers of the region's sheikhdoms.

I accompanied Admiral Smith on a tour of his region. Two memories stand out. When we visited Pakistan, I was able to see our old house in Karachi where the tree shoots we had planted twenty years before had developed into impressive trees. We were entertained at the Pakistan army mess in Rawalpindi. The ceremony was so close to the British pattern that one could almost see ghosts of past officers of royal regiments.

We also visited the Ethiopian Navy at Massawa in Eritrea. A Norwegian naval mission was training the Ethiopians, giving me a chance to brush up my Norwegian.

During the visit we made one mistake. We left our quarters in the late afternoon with the windows open and the lights on. When we returned, the lights were obscured by a host of flying objects attracted by the lights. Admiral Smith had a mild phobia about insects, and we had to round up and destroy the intruders.

Our two years in London came to a close in 1962. As a result of the hijacking of a Portuguese liner off the coast of Brazil I was to spend the next eleven years dealing with African issues.

In January 1961 a Portuguese opposition group seized the passenger liner *Santa Maria* as it sailed down the coast of Brazil. My embassy colleague in London, Fred Hadsel, who had the African responsibilities, was at that time on a U.S. destroyer as an adviser to a U.S. Navy goodwill tour of West Africa. The destroyer to which he was assigned was suddenly ordered to cross the Atlantic at flank speed to intercept the *Santa Maria*.

At the same time as his absence from London for several weeks, an international crisis was developing in the Congo. The newly independent former Belgian colony was at the center of United Nations efforts to preserve the unity of the country against pressures from activists in the copper-rich Katanga province. I was asked to assume Hadsel's duties and became engulfed in the African issue of the moment. My work on behalf of the Africa Bureau apparently caught the attention of Assistant Secretary of State for Africa G. Mennen Williams and his deputy, J. Wayne Fredericks. Fredericks asked me if I would be interested in returning to Washington to work on North Africa. I thanked him for the suggestion, but declined, saying that I was looking forward at the end of my London tour to going to Cairo as the deputy chief of mission. That was not to be. In July 1962 I received a letter from the State Department stating that I would be pleased to learn that I was assigned to be the deputy director of the office of Northern African affairs and would be returning to Washington.

So, we tore ourselves away from our wonderful London life and boarded the S.S. *United States* for New York, but not before I had made a quick visit to North Africa, my new area of responsibility. At the end of my National War College year, the class divided into groups for tours to different continents. I had chosen the African tour thinking that it would be a rare chance to see that continent. How wrong I was.

12

FROM PIRACY TO PETROLEUM

When I joined the Office of Northern African Affairs (AFN) in September 1962, first as deputy director and then as director, a period of rapid change in the region was coming to an end. From 1962 to 1965, I was to view the early adjustments to that change—but not the final results. Being a diplomat and moving from place to place is somewhat like walking through a Cineplex, watching bits of each movie without seeing the end.

Egypt had experienced its revolution in 1952. Although AFN's jurisdiction did not extend to Egypt, what happened in Cairo affected the whole region. Libya was formed as an independent nation by the United Nations in 1952, replacing Britain's military administration. Sudan, Morocco, and Tunisia gained independence in 1956, and Somalia in 1960. Algeria's long war with France was winding down, and that country was on the verge of dramatic change. Only Ethiopia, under Emperor Haile Selassie, remained unchanged for the moment.

Even more dramatic change lay ahead as the sands of the Sahara began to disclose the riches of oil and gas. In AFN in the 1960s, we saw the beginning of that change.

This was a time also when envoys from the new countries were bringing change to Washington—changes in customs and in attitudes. They were warmly welcomed by those who had supported the independence struggles. But for some in the Department of State, accepting that France was no longer dominant in North Africa required adjustment. Further, during a period still dominated by the Cold War, the concept of nonalignment on the part of the newly independent countries was widely unwelcomed by Washington.

At about the midpoint of my time in AFN, one of the great American agents of change, John F. Kennedy, was tragically assassinated. My office and the rest of the Department of State were suddenly engulfed in welcoming the many dignitaries from around the world who came to pay homage to him.

No part of the world has been as tied to the early American republic as this northern African region. Morocco in 1787 was the first country to extend formal recognition to the new United States. Seated at my desk, I confronted, on the opposite wall, another formidable reminder of that history in the form of a gilt-framed, full-length portrait of Mohammad al-Sadik, Bey of Tunis. It had been presented by the Bey's special envoy to President Andrew Johnson on October 30, 1865, "as a souvenir of his friendship," together with letters of condolence for the assassination of President Lincoln and of congratulations for the termination of the Civil War.[23]

Our historical relationship with the region goes back even further to another president, Thomas Jefferson. It was Jefferson who, in 1801, somewhat reluctantly authorized the construction of U.S. Navy vessels designed to confront the corsairs of the Barbary principalities of Morocco, Algeria, Tunisia, and Tripolitania. By so doing the United States ended the annual tribute paid to the Barbary rulers to protect its merchant shipping and seamen.

In 1943, U.S. forces joined the British and Free French in liberating Morocco, Algeria, and Tunisia from the Axis. More than 3,000 American dead rest in a cemetery outside Tunis. Later, prominent Americans were sympathetic to the movement for freedom from French domination in each of these countries. American diplomat Hooker Doolittle, when consul in Tunis during World War II, helped spirit the Tunisian nationalist leader, Habib Bourguiba, out of Tunis in 1945 ahead of French efforts to arrest him. John F. Kennedy, when he was a senator, spoke in support of Algerian independence in the Senate in 1957—a speech that resounded throughout the region. Irving Brown, an AFL-CIO official based in Paris who was concerned about possible communist inroads in the region, gave support to Algerian nationalists. William Porter, then director of Northern African Affairs and later ambassador to Algeria, met in Washington with North African opponents of the French, much to the consternation of Paris.

When I joined AFN, several dramas were unfolding as the countries in the region adjusted to independence. In the case of North Africa, that meant adjustment to boundary disputes and ancient claims upon neighbors, as well as meeting obligations to those who had supported liberation movements. Rhetoric from Washington supporting independence because "we were once a colony ourselves" led to expectations that made the United States a focus of appeals by several countries for aid and diplomatic support.

Those with boundary disputes with their neighbors brought pressure for recognition of claims long buried under colonial systems. Morocco laid claim to much of Northwest Africa, including portions of Algeria, Mauritania, and Rio de Oro—Spanish Sahara. Morocco and Algeria fought a brief border war in 1963 until claims were settled through mediation by the emperor of Ethiopia. In the Horn of Africa the five-pointed star of newly independent Somalia signified Somalian claims to Ethiopia's Ogaden and portions of Kenya. Ethiopia's claims to Eritrea were only settled when Eritrea became independent in 1993. Such claims created tensions and conflicts that lasted into the twenty-first century.

In the mid-1960s our bureau spent many hours poring over ancient and more current maps of the region. We were less interested in becoming involved in the disputes than in trying to understand the issues.

The American objective at that time was to ensure that the United States would continue to have relations with and access to the significant countries of the region. In Morocco and Libya the United States retained rights to military facilities established during World War II; and a vital U.S. Army communications center had been established at Asmara in Eritrea, at that time still part of Ethiopia.

We implemented these policies against the backdrop of the Cold War and Washington's concerns about possible gains on the part of either the Soviet Union or China. Achieving these objectives was often complicated by the desire of countries to remain free of the superpower conflict. To many in Washington "remaining free" seemed too often to benefit our adversaries.

Assistance, both economic and military, became a touchstone of friendship. The region's strongest supporters of the United States argued that internal pressures often made pro-American policies difficult politically and urged Washington to provide concrete evidence of the importance of the relationship. How much assistance, either economic or military or both, came to be a central issue in almost every visit by a North African leader.

This was true in other areas of the world as well, but it became an especially active issue in countries where the United States had military facilities or felt some special debt to the country's leader. Unsurprisingly, the White House informed the State Department that aid would not be increased as a result of an official visit. The U.S. Agency for International Development (USAID) argued that aid should be provided only on the basis of carefully crafted country programs. But when a visit actually occurred, the pressures for some gesture to the visitor generally prevailed. Pressures could come from special interests in the Congress or the public, reinforced by particularly persuasive pleas by the visitor or, during the Cold War, by allusions to competition from the Soviet Union or China. Even some of our best friends were not averse to playing that card. And the United States was at some disadvantage in this competition because of its different approach to the pledge of aid. Any assistance pledge required congressional approval, and Congress generally wanted specifics on how the aid money was to be spent. Members of Congress were averse to open lines of credit with details to be later negotiated. The Soviet Union, on the other hand, often made grand gestures promising substantial lines of credit open to later negotiation. One such gesture was a $100 million pledge the Soviet Union made to Ethiopia in 1962.[24]

The importance of aid to the relationships diminished in the 1960s, as oil and gas were discovered in substantial quantities, primarily in Algeria and Libya. Daniel Yergin, in his seminal work on international oil, *The Prize*, writes that the most prominent professor of geology at the Sorbonne once stated that he was so sure there was no oil in the Sahara that he would be prepared to drink any drops of oil that happened to be found there.[25]

The first major discovery came in Algeria in 1956. Three years later, geologists with Standard Oil of New Jersey (Esso) found oil in the western region of Libya. A country that had once depended for its existence on foreign aid and the export of esparto grass (used in currency paper) was on the road to matching the wealth of the

Persian Gulf. Discoveries of lesser magnitude were later made in Sudan, Tunisia, and Morocco.

The preservation of American interests in the region at this time centered to a large extent on our relations with three personalities: King Hassan II of Morocco, President Habib Bourguiba of Tunisia, and Emperor Haile Selassie of Ethiopia.

Both King Hassan and President Bourguiba had demonstrated moderate tendencies in their approaches to the Israeli-Palestinian conflict and opposition to Soviet and Chinese efforts in the region—two prerequisites for American friendship. Morocco also provided military facilities to the United States and, in subsequent years, would make Moroccan troops available in troubled areas of Africa vulnerable to communist advances. For the period 1948 to 1971, Morocco received the largest share of U.S. assistance to Africa—$314 million. Because of his country's policies and a generally favorable climate for economic development, Bourguiba's Tunisia received the second largest share. The emperor of Ethiopia had provided troops to assist the United States in Korea and was increasingly seen as a leader in Africa's emerging independence. All three leaders were autocratic rulers, although both Morocco and Tunisia had the trappings of democracy.

In the center of North Africa were two of Africa's largest countries in area—Libya and Sudan. Libya had been largely supported by foreign assistance until the discovery of substantial oil reserves in 1959. American assistance had been justified as a quid pro quo for rights accorded to the United States at Wheelus Air Force Base near Tripoli. I will have more to say about Libya in the next chapter, which covers my service as ambassador there.

Within the vast expanse of Sudan lay an example of one of Africa's most difficult problems: the divide between Islam and other religions, including Christianity. Sudan's southern region had been evangelized by Christian missionaries in colonial times. The Arab-led government in Sudan has to this day only reluctantly recognized the different ethnic and religious character of the peoples of the South. Conflicts between the two have been intermittent since the 1960s. Though the United States provided assistance, the relationship was never an easy one. It became increasingly troubled in later years.

I recall one unusual conversation relating to Sudan during my time in AFN. One day my phone rang and a voice said, "I am calling from Warner Brothers. We have just bought 'Kartum[*sic*]' [a film script about the battles at Khartoum] and Gregory Peck to go with it. Can you tell us something about Sudan? Is it a friendly country? The film we propose deals with General Gordon. I understand he is something of a hero in Sudan."

"Well," I replied, "we have satisfactory relations with Sudan, but they are not strong supporters of American policy in the region. And they have just moved General Gordon's statue out of the Central Park in Khartoum."

There was a pause at the other end of the line. "Thank you," the voice said.

In fact Warner Brothers did proceed with the film; *Khartoum* was released in 1966. Given the sensitivities involved, the filmmaker moved intelligently. They sent a representative who met with the family of the Mahdi and revised the script to meet some of their concerns. But it was Charlton Heston, not Gregory Peck, who played Gordon.

Visits to the president of the United States are an important diplomatic tool. They usually symbolize a close relationship and provide an opportunity for dialogue. President Kennedy was particularly interested in inviting leaders from the newly independent countries.

In March 1963, when King Hassan of Morocco visited President Kennedy, I was very much involved in the arrangements. The king was not an easy guest. Always aware of his royal status, he had few qualms about departing from the scheduled program, which called for the king to visit the State Department and call on Secretary of State Dean Rusk. A few minutes before the appointed time, I received a telephone call saying that the king was unable to visit the department and wanted Secretary Rusk to come to Blair House. I went to the secretary's office and informed him of the call. Always a gentleman, Secretary Rusk rose from his desk and said, "All right, let's go. Whatever the young man wants, the young man gets."

This attitude of the king was not confined to his two visits to America. A Moroccan friend told me that on a visit to France when

King Hassan was reminded by an aide that he was going to be late for lunch with President De Gaulle, the king, without stirring, remarked, "That is a matter of no consequence. I am a king and he is only a president."

There were also some nonvisits by King Hassan. He was scheduled to make another visit, and I was meeting in the office of Chief of Protocol Emil Mosbacher Jr. with Moulay Hafiz, his Moroccan counterpart. The discussion centered on the responsibility for paying the costs of the members of the Moroccan party during their visit to New York. Only twelve members, including the king, were considered the official party; the actual party was much larger. Moulay Hafiz asked how one could separate out the expenses of the official party from the rest.

Mosbacher said, "That should be easy enough. We know how much a king can eat and drink." At that point, Hafiz, much offended by this remark, arose, picked up his papers and walked out. The visit did not take place.

Morocco nevertheless was important to the United States, according it the use of three air bases established during World War II. In 1962, these air bases were being phased out under an agreement reached earlier with President Eisenhower, although Washington would maintain some communications facilities in the country.

Coming into AFN in the middle of the phasing out of the air bases in Morocco, I discovered that leaving a military facility can be as complicated as retaining it. Under the agreement to vacate the bases, the United States had agreed to transform the principal base at Nouasseur near Casablanca into a working civilian airport. This meant asking a reluctant U.S. Air Force to leave behind equipment central to the operation of the airport.

The principal representative of the Air Force in this matter was the under secretary for logistics, Philip Hilbert, a wily civil servant. I was constantly pressing him to be generous to the Moroccans. In response, he took every opportunity to demonstrate that the Moroccans, rather than cooperating in the transformation of the base, were stealing everything they could.

He called me one day to report that Moroccans had stolen the pump from a pumping station outside the base. "Not only have they stolen the pump, but overnight they have dismantled the station brick by brick." As far as I know the base was eventually turned into a civilian airport, but not without protests from the Air Force and at least the pump replaced.

Habib Bourguiba was also a frequent visitor to Washington, beginning with a visit to President Eisenhower in 1958. He recalled his friend Hooker Doolittle during each visit. As he grew older and increasingly senile, he looked to the United States for medical treatment. That is a story for a later chapter.

Between Morocco and Tunisia lay Algeria. The process of decolonization in Algeria was prolonged and painful. France considered Algeria a part of metropolitan France, and several thousand French had settled in the northern fringe of the country. Resistance to the French presence, dating back to 1830, intensified with the rise of an Algerian nationalist movement and the beginning of a bloody conflict in 1954.

France fought a long and brutal war against Algerian nationalists. The United States was inevitably touched by the struggle. France at that time was a member of NATO, and Washington, though concerned about the strength of the Communist Party in France, wanted to avoid any confrontation with Paris. Algerian nationalists and neighboring Arab countries accused the United States of helping France and, in particular, of providing napalm to the French forces.

After a conference at Évian-les-Bains in France between the French and the National Liberation Front (FLN), a troubled independence was finally achieved in 1962. The question facing us as I returned to the department was, "What can we do to support the new nation?"

Because of the interest shown by the United States in the nationalist struggle, Algerian expectations of American assistance were high, but so was resistance in Congress to shows of support to this new, left-leaning nation. Algerian ambivalence toward the Communist bloc and American concerns over an uncertain political situation in France inhibited wider U.S. involvement.

Ahmed Ben Bella, the first president of independent Algeria, came to Washington on an official visit in October 1962. Following the visit, he did not help his country's relations with the United States when, in the midst of the Cuban missile crisis, he went to Cuba to visit Fidel Castro. The incident was an early manifestation of the problems both we and "nonaligned" countries faced in balancing their interest in American assistance with what they felt were their obligations to the bloc of newly independent countries. After the Havana visit, Washington canceled a second Algerian visit that was to have taken place for a discussion of economic assistance.

Official American help to the new nation was a modest $4 million, limited to a medical team in Algiers, food aid, and efforts to mediate a border dispute between Algeria and Morocco. American energy companies and the U.S. Export Import Bank ultimately became involved in developing Algerian oil and gas, but not without difficult negotiations. The Algerians were reluctant to accept a price for their gas established by the world market.

A respected international oil consultant went to Algeria soon after the discovery of oil and gas. He carefully walked the officials of Sonatrach, the Algerian national oil company, through the intricacies of the international oil and gas market. At the conclusion he reportedly said, "So you see you cannot set a price at which you sell your gas. You must be attentive to the world market." But "this is our gas," said the Algerians. Ultimately, in 1969, they accepted that reality and signed a major agreement for liquefied natural gas with an American company, El Paso Natural Gas.

Being a diplomat often involves learning about intricate and unfamiliar matters. I became involved in the negotiations over the natural gas contract because the financing of the nine tankers necessary to carry the gas was to come from the U.S. Export Import Bank. Such financing raised political questions, given Algeria's nonalignment, and questions of technical feasibility, given the new technology involved in the transportation of liquefied natural gas.

I visited Algiers in late August 1962, just a few weeks after independence had been declared on July 3. The contest for power between those who had struggled against the French inside the country and those who had supported independence from outside continued. During my visit the color of the berets worn by the troops on the street frequently changed, indicating the temporary success of one group or the other. I flew to Algiers from Paris after observing the careful screening and searching of the other passengers. My letter home describes the visit:

We landed at Algiers in the late afternoon, arriving at the airport where, but a few weeks before, several thousand French residents of Algiers were encamped awaiting transportation back to France. John Root, our acting Consul General, met me, and we drove some five miles into the city of Algiers. There was a strange air of deceptive normality. The fields were well-kept; traffic and life seemed to move normally. Yet, at the airport gate there were several Algerian soldiers, their hands on the triggers of their machine guns. They did not smile as we went through. Along the road into town were several cars, some burned, abandoned in the ditch. Some had been bombed, others machine gunned. Some factories were closed. There were occasional bits of barbed wire where road blocks had been.

Algiers itself is a beautiful city, set on hills sloping down to a crescent bay. It is a city of trees, flowers, and lovely white Moorish houses. We drove into the city just as one of several demonstrations held that day was beginning, and shouting youths carrying placards ran by us toward the central square. We drove up to a vantage point and watched them for a few minutes, as they poured into the square and shouted on behalf of one or the other of the conflicting groups in Algeria. Suffice it to say, the political situation is complicated. I kept thinking of the old Abbott and Costello routine: "Who's on first?"

The first afternoon and evening I spent with the people of our consulate general, learning something of their past and future problems. They had had a most difficult time during the period when the extreme French settler group, the OAS (French acronym for Organization of the Secret Army) was making its last ditch effort to discourage independence by the indiscriminate murder of Muslims. The road in front of our consulate general winds down a hill. The large curve just before the gate to the Consulate was a favorite ambush point for the OAS. Eight Muslims were machine gunned during a two-month period as they came down this hill. They fell, mortally wounded, just at the Consulate gate. Fortunately, that aspect of the situation is over, although the political situation remains serious and there is still the prospect of other kinds of violence.

The next morning I had one of the most moving experiences of my life. The threats of the OAS and the uncertainty of the period after independence have forced most of the French out of Algeria. Doctors, lawyers, technicians, engineers, teachers, have left, virtually en masse.

Among the worst atrocities of the OAS was the bombing of the Beni Massous Hospital in the center of Algiers. The patients were moved out and placed in various other hospitals. One hundred twenty pediatric patients were moved to a large new hospital at about the time the staff of sixty French in the hospital left. The children were left entirely in the care of Algerian orderlies, without medical or nursing care. They were kept that way for over two weeks until an emergency medical and nursing team from the University of Chicago arrived. [The team was part of the U.S. assistance program under a nongovernmental organization, CARE MEDICO.] This group of three doctors (surgeon, physician, and pediatrician) and eight nurses went in and literally had to clean up the hospital before they could begin any treatment. Eighteen of the patients had died. None of the equipment worked. The staff had departed. The team got the hospital going again and were replaced a month later by a similar team from the University of Pennsylvania. This team had taken on the added responsibility of an adult surgery ward. John Root and I went through the hospital with the head of the Department of Surgery of the University of Pennsylvania, who was heading the team. We went from bed to bed. He described the problems (gunshot, napalm, fracture, cataracts, diarrhea, malaria, hernia, etc.), the conditions in which they had found the patient, and what they had been able to do. This was American aid at its finest.

That afternoon, we went with a pediatrician from the Pennsylvania group to visit a clinic in the Casbah, the old city of Algiers. Following the footsteps of Charles Boyer and Peter Lorre, we climbed its wandering steps and followed its narrow alleys for most of the afternoon. (Less than one

> week later, it was to be the scene of a battle.) As we walked down one narrow street, the Muslim owner of a coffeehouse saw the doctor in his white gown and rushed up to him to ask him if we would look at his brother. We turned and there, seated at one of the tables on the sidewalk, was a man with his leg in a cast. The doctor went over and we paused to help with the interpretation. The man in the cast had been shot in the leg by the OAS. A cast had been placed on it, but nothing else done. The man's brother had an x-ray, which he dug out from the dark recesses of the shop. In order to look at it, the doctor had to take it to the middle of the street where there was some light. There he held it up and examined it, while a crowd of small boys, men from other shops, soldiers, and, in the background, white veiled women gathered. The doctor was able to give him the name of a Syrian orthopedic surgeon who had just arrived in Algiers, and we went on.
>
> That evening we had dinner in the best hotel in Algiers, the St. George. Here, in an outdoor dining room, walled and roofed by an arbor of vines, we had a marvelous French dinner. In the unreal atmosphere of Algiers, we seemed far removed from the city below where gaping holes in buildings marked "le plastique," where shutters on more than half of the shops had been drawn by the departing owners, and where the principal traffic was the movement of large furniture vans taking the possessions of the French to the docks.

Unfortunately for our help to the Algerians, Congress decided that it could no longer fund ongoing medical programs, and after a few months the CARE MEDICO program in Algeria was ended in 1964.

Another country that was given considerable attention in the Kennedy years was Ethiopia. In 1963, an invitation to visit President Kennedy was extended to Haile Selassie, the emperor. This Byzantine autocrat, revered for his stand against the Italians in 1936 and as the longest-serving independent ruler in Africa, had received substantial help from the Soviet Union and was threatening to recognize Communist China. Ethiopia was also involved in an active border dispute with the newly independent country of Somalia. Later, Ethiopia's use of Cuban troops against Somalia in 1978 was to cause anguish in Washington.

I came to know the historic figure Haile Selassie, slight of stature, but rigidly royal in posture, when I accompanied Under Secretary of State Averell Harriman on a trip early in 1963 in efforts to discourage the emperor from recognizing Red China. The occasion was one of the few times in my career that I wore the morning coat and striped trousers that we had been advised to purchase upon entering the Foreign Service. Governor Harriman and I walked up the long steps to the palace, past a chained lion. The emperor, accompanied by two Chihuahuas, greeted us in the throne room.

That visit brought another lesson in negotiation. Ambassador (or Governor as he preferred to be called) Harriman and the emperor were approximately the same age—two veterans of their respective political systems. We knew that if the emperor did agree to hold off recognizing China, he would exact a price. We somehow had in mind a figure of $8 million.

The two men sparred for three hours, first across a conference table, then at lunch. Each time the emperor would raise the subject of aid, Harriman would change the subject to a wartime visit he had made to Asmara. The emperor was similarly evasive when the subject of China arose. The emperor's aides grew impatient and frequently passed him notes.

At the end of the session, I drafted a telegram for Harriman to send to the secretary of state reporting the conversation. I concluded with the sentence, "I (speaking for Harriman) believe we accomplished our mission, but, as I left the Emperor's office, the elaborate ivory gift from the People's Republic of China was still on display." Harriman read it over and called me in.

"Why did you put that in?"

"Well, sir, I was not sure we had a full agreement from the emperor."

"When I negotiate, I succeed," said Harriman and crossed out the offending sentence. He was right. We did provide additional aid and the emperor held off recognizing China for several more years.

Perhaps my least successful meeting with Emperor Haile Selassie took place when I sought, on a subsequent occasion, to sound him out regarding his succession. His cool relationship with and jealousy of his son, the crown prince, left this in doubt. But I found out, as I was later to discover with the king of Libya, that what will follow their death was not a popular subject with aging rulers. The emperor listened politely to my question and gave the standard response, that the crown prince would succeed. We later learned that the emperor had told one of his courtiers, "The American Mr. Newsom has been to see me to ask about the succession. I did not tell him that I really do not care what happens after I am gone."

As we prepared for a visit by the emperor later that year, we faced as always the question of a proper gift. The Ethiopians had sent Asrate Kassa, a cousin and counselor to the emperor, to assist in preparation for the visit. To entertain Kassa in Washington I took him to the Smithsonian Institution, where they displayed material relating to Ethiopia. One of the items was a Bible in a Coptic liturgical language, Ge'ez, containing a "tipped in" history of the monastery from which it had been taken.

Kassa turned to me and said, "This has been stolen from Ethiopia."

It occurred to me that a perfect gift might be this Bible. I called an official in the Smithsonian to see how I could arrange for the museum to release the item. He called back within a few days and explained that it was not a simple matter.

"This Bible had been taken by the British general Robert Napier when he led an expedition to rescue British hostages from the Emperor Theodore in 1868. General Napier in turn presented it to General Ulysses S. Grant in 1878 when Grant visited Gibraltar, where Napier was governor. The Bible became part of Grant's memorabilia, which were turned over to the William Henry Vanderbilt family to help Grant pay off debts. Vanderbilt subsequently donated the memorabilia to the U.S government so that they could be 'perpetually on display for the benefit of the American people.' If you want that Bible it will take an act of Congress." As I recall, time did not permit such a procedure, and the Bible may still be in the Smithsonian.

I was to see the emperor again when he returned for the funeral of John F. Kennedy. I wrote a long letter to the family on December 1, 1963, chronicling those events:

> It was just six weeks ago that I had the thrill of briefing President Kennedy on the Algerian-Moroccan crisis. I had shaken hands with him before, during state visits, and had taken notes at meetings between the President and visiting foreign dignitaries. This was the first time I had presented personally to him a situation and a policy, the first time I had the feeling of contributing so directly to the determination of U.S. policy at the highest level. President Kennedy liked to hear the facts and recommendations directly from those who are working daily and directly with them. Many other office directors and desk officers shared that experience during the three years he was in office. Most, I am sure, came away, as I did, impressed by this earnest man, keen to grasp details, impatient at nonessentials, quick to understand a problem, and dedicated to keeping America in tune with a dynamic world.
>
> My recollection of his passing is concerned more with the living than with the dead. As did everyone in the nation, I experienced that moment of disbelief and then shock when I first heard of the shooting. I was just coming back from lunch and joined others clustered around radios in the Department while we waited anxiously for news. Many around me who had known the President closely or traveled with him on trips wept unabashedly. All of us in the group, conscious as we were of America's image abroad, were doubly shocked as we thought of the impact this would have on that image. The sordid events in Dallas that followed only served to deepen that concern.
>
> We had little time for active mourning. Late that afternoon we gathered to consider what we would do if other nations chose to send delegations to the funeral—as they might be expected to do. It soon became apparent that they would. As word came in from every corner of the earth of chiefs of state, foreign ministers, and others who were

preparing to come, we set up a special 24-hour operations center to chart the arrival and arrangements for each delegation. Many, many questions needed answering. Where would they stay? Who would meet them? Would they be able to see President Johnson? Would Mrs. Kennedy receive them? Within the next 24 hours or so, most of these questions were answered.

General De Gaulle's decision to come made it inevitable that most of the European heads of state or, at least, prime ministers, would attend. By Sunday morning, most of them were on their way. From my area came the emperor of Ethiopia, the vice president of Tunisia, the speaker of the National Assembly of Algeria, and the brother of the king of Morocco.

I was awakened at 3 a.m. Sunday morning by the East Coast Army Relay Communications Station with a message that our ambassador in Ethiopia wanted to talk to me. We had to talk indirectly by teletype, but it transpired that the Emperor had just decided to go to Washington and was asking our ambassador to come along. What should he do? I told him to come on. Twenty-four hours later I was greeting him, with the Emperor, at Dulles Airport; they had come a third of the way around the world, via West Africa, in the Emperor's special Boeing jet.

Dulles Airport will probably not soon see a night such as that a week ago: Sunday, November 24. Jean and I went out, arriving about 9 p.m. A crowd had gathered by the incoming international gate. A plane was just landing bearing the Duke of Edinburgh and Sir Alec Douglas- Home. Shortly thereafter, a plane arrived bearing Crown Prince Harald of Norway. Then came the President of Ireland. Then came Pan-American flight 119 from Paris with four delegations!

Secretary of State Rusk and Under Secretary Ball were on hand to meet each delegation as they came in, together with the appropriate assistant secretary and office director. When Pan-American 119 came in, Secretary Rusk went out in the mobile lounge (for which Dulles Airport is famous) to meet the plane. He then escorted each delegation, in turn (while the others waited in the lounge) to the cars. First came the brother of the Shah of Iran with his delegation. Then came Prince Moulay Abdulla of Morocco with the Moroccan Foreign Minister and several other distinguished members. Then came the venerable Mr. Inönü, Foreign Minister of Turkey, and, finally, the Foreign Minister of Italy.

Meanwhile the aircraft bearing the Emperor of Ethiopia had been held in the pattern overhead. It landed a little before 11. I went out in the mobile lounge with the Secretary and Mr. Ball to greet this amazing little man. At 74 years of age he had, in the course of the past two months, paid a state visit to the United States, visited eight other countries, been instrumental in settling (temporarily at least) the Moroccan-Algerian crisis, and was now, on extremely short notice, returning to pay his respects to our President. He came off the plane very regally, but somberly. He expressed his deep condolences in French to the Secretary and rode silently with them into the airport. Here all the African ambassadors in Washington had gathered to do him homage.

The desk officers of the countries which sent delegations accompanied the guests to the funeral, to Arlington Cemetery, to the White House where Mrs. Kennedy received them, and then back to the Department for the supper which President Johnson gave. I was fully occupied preparing briefing material for the President on the guests he would meet that night, answering messages of condolence sent to President Johnson, arranging for meetings with the Secretary of State and others among our visitors, and keeping such other matters of foreign policy moving as seemed important at that moment. I caught only a glimpse out my window of the cortège as it passed Lincoln Memorial. From my window I could follow it across Memorial Bridge and could see the crowd on the hill below Lee Mansion where the President was to be buried.

The supper given by President Johnson for the delegations attending the funeral was an unforgettable occasion. Gathering on the eighth floor of the Department to meet the new President and do homage to the one gone were emperors, kings, princes, prime ministers, foreign ministers, and ambassadors from nearly every country in the world. I came somewhat late, escorting the Moroccan delegation. As I entered and they were being introduced to President Johnson, I looked across the room and saw a tableau of Queen Frederica of Greece, Britain's Prince Philip, and Mrs. Johnson. Not far away Paul-Henri Spaak of Belgium was speaking to Ludwig Erhardt of Germany. The princes of Norway and Sweden, resplendent in their uniforms, were nearby. A long buffet was set down the center of the main dining room. Tables were arranged on each side where the dignitaries and their escorts were seated. There was relatively little eating, however, as each guest made the most of the opportunity to meet people who might, on other occasions, be much more difficult to reach. Many sought out Anastas Mikoyan, the tough-looking little Soviet representative, undoubtedly with this thought in mind. It was our task to see that as many as possible met Secretary Rusk and others of importance in the Department.

Shortly after the majority of the guests arrived, President Johnson adjourned to a side room, where he received certain of the delegations for brief talks. He tried to pick those of particular rank whom he might not be seeing otherwise.

General De Gaulle arrived late. Tall, imposing, and gracious, he moved through the hall almost as if he were the host. Many clustered around to meet him and talk with him and he spoke to all. I did not speak with him, but I gather that I was caught on television backing out of his way at one point.

By Wednesday night, our delegations had all departed. To the credit of the Department, this great assemblage gathered and went its way without any serious incident. Fortunately, nearly all of the leaders who came recognized the special nature of the occasion and were prepared to accept departures in protocol and the lack of special attention which would be theirs were they to come at a normal time. President Johnson was most cooperative in meeting nearly all the principals who came and this, of course, helped greatly.

As President Kennedy and this past sad week pass into history, I cannot help but regret that those who, from afar, so often denounce the Presidency in their frustration and accuse administrations of failures in the face of problems that no man, really, can solve, did not have a closer look at the energy, dedication, courage, and wisdom of this dynamic young President and the men who, sharing his deep feeling toward America, worked with him.

In another year and a half my service in the Office of Northern African affairs would come to an end when I was appointed ambassador to Libya. As I prepared for that post, Jean and I met President and Mrs. Johnson in another setting.

We were invited to the White House, in June 1965, together with six other ambassadors-designate to meet and be photographed with the president. In my three posts as ambassador, Johnson was the only one to extend that courtesy. He received us first in the Oval Office and for a few moments complained to the photographer that his picture was not yet hanging in every executive office.

"Some of them still have Herbert Hoover hanging," he said.

After tea with President and Mrs. Johnson, the ambassadors-designate were ushered into the Rose Garden and lined up while the President gave us a little homily. I remember well his final words: "Now, if any of you find that you don't like the place where I am sending you, let me know. I don't want any of you messing me up out there." With that charge, Jean and I and four of our five children flew to Tripoli, Libya, in July 1965. It would be my first experience as a chief of mission.

13

SEEDS OF A COUP

Throughout my diplomatic career it was my fate to be involved, whether overseas or in the State Department, with countries on the brink of revolutions in which important American interests were at stake. Libya was a good example. As in Iraq and Ethiopia, and, later, the Philippines and Iran, our interests were tied to an unpopular, authoritarian regime that would do our bidding but was ruling over a population in which significant elements had a different perspective.

U.S. interests in Libya were defined as maintaining rights at Wheelus Air Force Base, protecting the substantial American investments in the exploration and production of Libyan oil and gas, and assuring the security of a community of more than six thousand Americans. Ostensibly to advance these interests, the United States had provided by the end of 1959 more than $100 million in aid, making Libya the single largest per capita recipient of American largesse in the world.[26]

The U.S. role in each of these objectives was surrounded by ambiguity. In past years many in Congress and the executive had objected to such "rent" for a military facility. During the Cold War, it was argued, countries such as Libya were on the "same side" and should provide facilities as part of the defense of the "Free World." It was often difficult to persuade opponents of such aid that foreign military facilities were politically unpopular, particularly in the Arab world, and that politicians needed to demonstrate tangible advantages from the arrangement. For several years after the 1967 war, in protest against U.S. policy, the Libyan government, to our embarrassment, declined to cash the annual payment for Wheelus, although it was dutifully deposited in Riggs Bank in Washington each year. I suggested to the Libyans that they might spend the money on equipment for their public security services, but for the Libyans the matter was too hot to handle.[27]

In justifying base rights, it was also argued—and I sometimes carefully implied—that the presence of a U.S. base provided security to a regime and to its country. In a personal message related to Wheelus, dated March 8, 1964, President Johnson wrote to King Idris, "The United States, since the days it fought beside the United Kingdom in furtherance of Libya's independence, has been keenly interested in the future and welfare of your Majesty's country." Referring specifically to Wheelus, the letter stated, "We believe the presence of this valuable installation helps to symbolize and demonstrate the substantial nature of our common efforts."[28]

Whatever the letter implied, it was highly unlikely that the United States would intervene to save the regime should it be threatened. A telegram from the State Department to our embassy in Tripoli during the June war crisis of 1967 spelled out what the United States was prepared to do: "We would contemplate intervening unilaterally with additional force only to protect American lives, and contemplate intervening with force to protect American interests (base and oil installations, or stake in survival of friendly government) only on express request by recognized Libyan governmental authorities."[29] Unlike the British we did not have a security treaty with Libya. I believe the king understood this. When the revolution occurred in September 1969, we had no requests for support from the king or any of his close supporters.

In Washington, in papers relating to Wheelus, it was common to cite the presence of American oil companies, implying that we would take action to protect such interests. Robert Komer of the National Security Council staff, in a memorandum to National Security Adviser McGeorge Bundy, dated March 17, 1964, relating to Wheelus, wrote: "We want to save this regime (the best we could have) and also protect our oil investment, now $670 million."[30]

I had serious doubts whether the Libyans would ever ask us for help in such cases and whether Washington—in the absence of a major external threat—would sanction the use of American forces in Libya. Whenever I raised a question about the relationship with the oil companies, Libyan officials wanted to know the basis on which I was raising an issue that they considered solely between them and the companies.

U.S. government responsibility for the protection of American citizens was clearer and was demonstrated in June 1967 with the outbreak of the Arab-Israeli war.

I arrived in Tripoli with Jean, Dan, Nancy, Katie, and David on September 4, 1965, and presented my credentials to King Idris on October 16. Given the history of U.S. struggles with the Tripolitanian pirates in the early nineteenth century, in my presentation to King Idris, I did not dwell excessively on past history. In 1965, we had close and friendly relations with the Libyan monarchy.

Outwardly at least, Libya was cordial to Americans. But the country had a long history of foreign invasions and brutal Italian colonialism. Under the surface lurked a strong xenophobia; even the Crusades were occasionally mentioned to emphasize past depredations from the West. In addition, the Arab population was heavily influenced by the Arab nationalist rhetoric of Gamal Abdel Nasser next door in Egypt. Libyans, too, felt what they saw as the humiliation of the Arabs in the creation of Israel and resented the U.S. role in that event. We were to find later in 1967 how deeply that affected Libyan attitudes.

A prewar Italian colony, Libya was created and brought to independence by the United Nations in 1952. Like Iraq, independent Libya was an amalgamation of three provinces with different histories: Tripoli, Cyrenaica to the East, and the Fezzan in the South. Following World War II, the first two had been under British military administration, the third under the French.

The independence arrangements created a constitutional monarchy with a king, Idris al Sanussi, the leader of a desert religious group. In 1965 when I arrived, King Idris was seventy-five years old. He was born in Cyrenaica but had lived for thirty years in Cairo. In another analogy to the Iraqi monarchy, he was seen by much of the population as a British implant. Except when stimulated by a crisis, he showed little interest in ruling the country. I once mentioned to the Libyan crown prince that I understood the king was going on vacation, to which he replied, "He is always on vacation."

Although the capital of the country was in Tripoli, the king and Queen Fatima spent much of their time while I was in Libya in Tobruk, 800 miles to the east. His entourage consisted primarily of Italians and Palestinians. He created an alternate capital at Baida, a small town in the Cyrenaican hills not far from the ruins of the ancient city of Cyrene. Our modest embassy office there had one officer and a communicator. I once asked the communicator, a retired Air Force sergeant, what he did for excitement in Baida. He replied, "I go outside and turn on the front porch light."

Because the American ambassador was frequently required to meet Libyan officials in Baida, one of my predecessors, Henry Villard, had leased the former residence of the Italian director of antiquities in the region from the local Islamic Foundation. The house stood on an escarpment adjacent to the ruins of ancient Cyrene, 2,500 feet above the Mediterranean. Ancient Greeks had tunneled tombs into the cliffs below; one of our servants lived in one of the tombs. I once asked the landlord to repair a sinking floor in the dining room. He advised us that to do so would require dismantling the room to excavate the site below because it had been built over a tomb.

On the shores of the Mediterranean below the escarpment were ruins of the ancient port city of Apollonia. Destroyed by an earthquake in ancient times, the ruins were still visible under the clear blue Mediterranean waters. A stone trough ran from Cyrene to Apollonia, curving down the escarpment. Constructed by the Romans to carry olive oil to the port, it was Libya's first oil pipeline.

To travel to Baida, we used some of the Wheelus base's old but still serviceable DC-3s and landed on a strip that had been built by German general Erwin Rommel during World War II. No tower or air control equipment existed. Someone from our embassy office in Baida would go out to the airstrip, chase the camels off the strip, and build a small brush fire. The smoke would give the pilot an indication of the wind.

During my four years in Libya I made frequent trips to Baida and Tobruk to meet with the king and other officials, usually accompanied by my indispensable Palestinian interpreter, Mohammad Salah. On some occasions, Roscoe Suddarth, an Arabist in our

Political Section would interpret. My Arabic had not reached the level of diplomatic conversation.

King Idris and Queen Fatima were always accessible and hospitable. Jean and members of my family often accompanied me. The royal hospitality at times presented us with more than we could consume. We learned never to completely clean the plate, because a clean plate was a signal to the queen to heap more food on it. After the meal, the queen prepared Libyan tea for our family. The small tea glasses were filled with crushed fresh mint or sliced green almonds. At one meal, as the king was carving a sheep, I asked him about the tradition of the sheep's eye being given to guests. He laughed and said, "It is our custom to show the guests an eye to prove that the lamb has been recently killed. One Englishman, handed an eye for that purpose, thought he was meant to eat it. Thus began the legend."

Many of my conversations with the king concerned the future of Wheelus Air Force Base. The base was established for bombers in World War II. By 1965 it had become a major training base for the 17th Air Force in Europe. Squadrons of F-100 aircraft would fly down to Wheelus to use a practice bombing range to the west of Tripoli. The base was also important to the American community for its school, hospital, and post exchange, the PX.

The presence of a foreign base and the noise of jet aircraft taking off over Tripoli were irritants, but both were manageable as long as the king agreed. The future of the base had become a major issue, stimulated in part by propaganda from Egypt and other parts of the Arab world. On February 22, 1964, Egypt's Nasser declared that no country could claim independence unless the military bases on its territory were liquidated.[31] This led to a Libyan declaration that the agreement on Wheelus, which expired in 1971, would not be renewed and to demands in the Libyan parliament to abrogate the agreement.

The situation was not helped by the decision on June 30, 1965, to close out the USAID program in Libya. The rising oil revenue in the country made it problematic to justify continued economic assistance. I was still director of Northern African Affairs at that time and very much involved in preparing instructions to my predecessor in Libya, Ambassador Allan Lightner. After a series of presidential letters, special envoys, and negotiations, the Libyan government agreed "on the principle of withdrawal" without setting a date.[32]

Although that settled the matter for the moment, the issue was still alive when I arrived in Tripoli. Clearly the king wanted us to stay, whether because it gave him a sense of security or because of services rendered by the base. I was never sure. We were constantly caught between the king and Libyan politicians, including many close to him, who were sensitive to both internal and broader Arab opinion. The king would never convey his own view to members of his government. By continuing to delay, he hoped to avoid definitive decisions. He would occasionally rein in individuals or change the government if statements got too far out of line. I had to deal with the foreign minister, Hussein Maaziq, who was a strong opponent of the base and occasionally made his views known. He had an interesting negotiating technique. When he did not wish to answer a question or address a problem, he would sit silently and wait for his interlocutor to change the subject.

The Wheelus issue remained relatively dormant until June 5, 1967. On that date Israel attacked Egypt and destroyed Egypt's Air Force. The Six-Day War had begun, and it profoundly affected the American community in Libya. Radio Cairo and the principal Cairo newspaper, *Al Ahram,* claimed that U.S. aircraft based at Wheelus had flown sorties against Egypt and that the United States had supplied satellite imagery to Israel—none of which was true. The impact of what was referred to as "the big lie" on Libya and on the American position in Libya was severe. It was also reported that King Idris had prevented Libyan army elements from going to the support of Egypt—which may have been true.

Angry demonstrations and attacks on American offices, including both diplomatic missions and oil company installations in Libya, occurred immediately following the outbreak of war.[33] The situation in the Cyrenaican branch embassy office in Benghazi was the most serious. Its personnel and that of our military advisory group were trapped in a vault by a mob and ultimately rescued by British troops stationed in Cyrenaica. John Kormann, the officer in charge, has given a dramatic account of the events in his memoir, *Echoes of a Distant Clarion.*[34]

On the basis of the developing situation I decided to implement our emergency evacuation plan for all dependents and nonessential personnel. Wheelus became the focal point for the movement of more than six thousand Americans to Rome and Athens by both U.S. Air Force and commercial aircraft. Although a few individuals resisted departure, the plan worked well. Only one factor had not been anticipated in the advance planning: what to do with pets. People showed up with their dogs and cats and other domestic animals. The personnel at Wheelus, in a remarkable achievement, quickly established kennels to hold the pets until, it was hoped, the owners could return.

Official Americans were shunned and all but routine contacts with the foreign office were cut off. One afternoon I was walking in downtown Tripoli and passed the governor of the National Bank, whom I knew well. I greeted him and said that I would like to visit him. He replied, "No. I will come to your house tomorrow evening and we can talk."

He came as promised, and we sat in our garden. He said to me, "I know in my head that the United States did not help Israel attack Egypt, but in my heart I must understand why a nation of two million people whom we consider second-class citizens can humiliate eighty million Arabs." It was one of the most candid statements on the Arab-Israeli issue I have ever heard.

Nasser's power in Libya was strong. A Libyan newspaper publisher told me later that when he took the news dispatch on June 9 saying that Nasser had accepted a cease-fire, his printers refused to believe it and would not set the type until he played a recording of the president's statement in his own voice.

With the concurrence of Washington and the Air Force, all flights in and out of Wheelus were suspended. The Air Force sent Major General Jack Lavelle, commander of the 17th Air Force, to work with me in the emergency.

On June 16 the new foreign minister, Ahmed Bishti, informed me that the king had decided to request our immediate withdrawal from Wheelus and had made a similar request to the British ambassador regarding the British bases. The Libyan government was concerned about what it might be able to say at a forthcoming meeting of Arab foreign ministers. With the department's agreement, I informed

Bishti that we were prepared to resume the 1964 discussions. I asked for time to prepare for discussions and suggested Libya might wish to form a committee for such talks.

On June 21 I had an audience with the king. My telegram to the department tells the story:

> 1. During audience with King on June 21 I said I wished [to] be certain he was aware [of] our reply to government on base issue. He asked what "agreement" we had with government. I explained we had discussed approach with PM [Prime Minister] and planned [to] have preliminary talk with GOL [Government of Libya] soon after which I might return for consultation. He commented, "The more delay the better."
>
> 2. In this context I stressed need get base operating again. I stressed also my disappointment at lack confidence in US on part RLAF [Royal Libyan Air Force]. He said he was shocked by conduct RLAF, including informing Egyptians regarding movements at Wheelus. He had not told government yet, but he intended move RLAF away from Wheelus to base which would be near neither Tripoli nor Benghazi. When I asked about further development RLAF, he said it would be slow.

I added a comment to my report, "Throughout audience, of which foregoing was part, King displayed relaxed relief that tough problems currently facing country were, under constitution, government's responsibility, not his."[35]

On the basis of my discussion with the king, I proposed to General Lavelle that we begin a slow return to operations at Wheelus, having two planes take off one day and testing the reaction. If the reaction is muted we will have four planes taking off for a couple of days, and if there are no incidents we will resume operations.

Sometime later General Lavelle told me that when I proposed this limited operation, he received a sharp message from Air Force headquarters about "letting the ambassador run the base." Lavelle told me that after the base was in operation, he responded, "You can't argue with success." Then later he wrote me a letter in which he said, "Because of the nature of the work and circumstances involved, working with you has not always been a pleasure. However, it has always been pleasant, easy and, without exception, has worked out well for the United States Air Force and the Seventeenth Air Force."

In the mid-1960s the development of Libya's oil resources was in full swing. Oil had been discovered in Zeltan near the western border in 1957. Libya departed from the common practice in the Persian Gulf region of awarding large concessions to a single major company. Instead, the Libyan oil law called for the granting of many concessions; by the mid-1960s there were more than a hundred separate concessions.

This meant the introduction into the North African oil scene of not only the major companies but a large number of smaller independents. The new Libyan policy provided ample opportunity for special deals and private arrangements that some labeled corruption. That situation was compounded by friends who surrounded the monarchy. The story is almost Shakespearean.

When Idris was young and destined to be the head of the Sanussi order, in accordance with Sanussi tradition a companion, Ibrahim al-Shalhi, was appointed to grow up with him. In October 1955, a cousin of King Idris assassinated al-Shalhi. Idris had only one child, a son who died at the age of 11. Ibrahim had several children whom Idris, in the absence of his own, came to regard as family. Whether by the king's encouragement or their own designs, Ibrahim's family became important agents in arranging oil concessions and other major business enterprises related to the growing petroleum industry. In so doing they enriched themselves and circumvented the normal processes of government. A young technocrat who was then minister of development once complained bitterly to me that he could accomplish very little because of constant interference by members of the Shalhi family.

I was very much concerned about the impact of the Shalhi family's excesses on the position of the monarchy and, by extension, on our own position in Libya. That concern deepened when, shortly before the king left for his vacation in 1969, he appointed a prominent member of the family, Omar Shalhi, as his special adviser. In messages that I wrote before my departure from Libya, I reported conversations with the crown prince, Queen Fatima, and a prominent member of the family, Abdul Aziz Shalhi, in which I expressed these concerns.[36] The crown prince discounted the power of the Shalhi family and stated that they would be obliged to leave Libya after the king's death. The queen nodded her head but was noncommittal. Shalhi assured me that he and his family remained loyal to the king.

Favors to the king were certainly a factor in the awarding of oil concessions. One effective entrepreneur was Armand Hammer of Occidental Petroleum. Through Libyan contacts he learned of the king's interest in Kufra, an oasis in the far southeastern corner of the country. Geologists had told Hammer that the water in the Kufra oasis was part of a major aquifer that flowed from the Nile. Hammer proposed to the king that Occidental bring engineers to drill for water. Their efforts brought in artesian water, and the desert bloomed around Kufra.

Hammer also introduced new seismic technology into the search for oil. His fame grew when his company located a substantial oil well just 300 yards from a dry hole abandoned by Mobil Oil.

Hammer has been described as a "deal maker." I can attest to that from my limited experience. He would fly into Tripoli with Mrs. Hammer in his converted A-26 bomber. As far as I know, he never went near the Occidental offices. He wanted to see the king and a few others. He was less interested in his current deal than in the next one.

I learned more about deals in the "oil patch" after I left Libya. In 1972 when I was assistant secretary of state for Africa, I was asked to appear before a subcommittee of the Senate Foreign Relations Committee, headed by Senator Charles Percy. An enterprising staff member had found a disgruntled accountant for one of the oil companies operating in Libya who gave a detailed account of the special payments made to various Libyans to secure a concession.

Senator Percy asked me, "When you were ambassador in Libya did you know about these activities?"

I replied, "These were matters between a private American company and private citizens and officials of another country. An American ambassador does not have authority to intervene in such matters. I confess that I was concerned about the rumors of corruption by American companies because of the impact of such rumors on our reputation and on the stability of the monarchy. I would occasionally raise the rumors with oil company executives, who would acknowledge that such activities went on but insist that they were not part of it."

The fact that an American ambassador had no jurisdiction in matters of this kind seemed to come as a surprise to the subcommittee. One member insisted that "something should be done about this." I believe that I thus played a minor role in the birth of the Foreign Corrupt Practices Act of 1977.[37]

In 1966 I became involved in another problem involving American companies. The Organization of Petroleum Exporting and Producing Countries (OPEC) had been formed in Baghdad in 1960 following a unilateral change in the posted price of oil by the major companies. The organization was becoming increasingly powerful and decided to seek a change in the profit split between companies and governments. Libya, following the lead of other OPEC countries, asked the oil companies to renegotiate their contracts to accept the new 75/25 split. Libya's unique concession arrangements involved both the major oil companies operating in the Persian Gulf region and independents with no interest in that region. The interests of the two groups were clearly at odds. The major companies felt obligated to follow the OPEC lead. The independents did not. They resisted the overture, and the Libyans threatened to change their contracts unilaterally. Until that time a unilateral change in an oil contract was rare. Washington believed it important to prevent the establishment of such a precedent, and I was instructed to approach the prime minister and argue strongly against such action.

The prime minister wanted to know on what basis the U.S. government was intervening in this way. I explained that most of the companies involved were American companies, that a large community of American citizens were in Libya to support the oil production, and that we, therefore, had a legitimate interest in doing what we could to prevent a major confrontation between the Libyan government and at least some of the companies. The independent companies supported our official intervention while the majors did not, thus creating a risk that the embassy would be seen to be taking sides in a dispute involving two groups of American companies. U.S.

antitrust laws that restricted discussions among companies further complicated the matter.

I decided to invite the lawyers from the respective groups to come to my residence to see whether a solution could be found. I was able to do so successfully only after the Department of Justice granted the Department of State a waiver under the antitrust act for such a meeting to be held.

Oil was not the only area of business in which I became involved. Libya with its newfound wealth was organizing a national airline and was in the market for jet aircraft. The competition for the sale was between an American company, Boeing, and the British Aircraft Corporation. The Boeing representative had called on me but had not asked for any assistance. He mentioned the name of his agent. When I made inquiries about the agent, I learned that he was associated with individuals that were out of favor with the Libyan government. I felt I owed it to the Boeing representative to pass on this information. He clearly did not appreciate my intervention, but he must have made inquiries on his own. He changed his agent, and Boeing was ultimately successful in getting the contract.

At one point, I raised with the king a misleading account in the Libyan press about the unreliability of Boeing aircraft. Unbeknownst to me, the agent reported to Boeing headquarters how helpful I had been, and a Boeing official wrote a letter to the Department of State expressing appreciation for my help. The next communication was from the department advising me that I had erred in assisting the Boeing representative. I should have notified Washington first and given the Department of Commerce the chance to inform all other American manufacturers of this opportunity. Had I done so I was quite sure that the Libyans would be flying British aircraft.

Libya presented a special problem for the U.S. government in the promotion of business. Other competing nations, including the principal European countries and Japan, offered experts to the Libyan government to help them with their procurement. In some cases—the national television was one example—advisors were provided without cost to the Libyans. These experts prepared the specifications for a proposal, specifications that were carefully tailored to favor the expert's country.

I brought this situation to Washington's attention and even contacted members of Congress that I knew. Libya had been a recipient of American economic assistance until the discovery of oil. Sending experts at U.S. government expense, even those related to commercial advantage, was seen by most people in Washington as a form of aid. The answer I got was, "Why should we pay for technical assistance to Libya when Libya itself can pay." The commercial advantages were never appreciated.

I tried to visit as much of every country in which I served as time and circumstances permitted. Libya was particularly tempting. Along the Mediterranean coast were some of the most impressive ruins of the Roman Empire anywhere in the Mediterranean. Many had been all or partially excavated by British, French, and Italian archaeologists. I have already mentioned Cyrene in the Cyrenaican hills.

Just west of Tripoli was an amphitheater, a remnant of the Roman port city of Sabratha. Through the columns of the stage one could see the backdrop of the blue Mediterranean. The Libyan cultural office occasionally arranged presentations of traditional dance and music in the theatre.

To the east along the coast, the road led to Leptis Magna, a city founded by the Phoenicians in 600 BC and built into its magnificence by Septimius Severus, the only Roman emperor born in Africa (146 AD). From Leptis, the French had taken columns to be used in Versailles in the mid–seventeenth century. Some barges sank under the weight of the marble columns and could still be seen under the water. Roofs and painted scenes in hunting lodges along the coast remained intact.

The Libyans were ambivalent about the Roman ruins. Many told me they did not relate to that period; they appreciated more the crumbling remnants of the Islamic civilization. At that time, at least, few were interested in tourism possibilities.

Dr. Froelich Rainey, director of the University of Pennsylvania Museum and a famed archaeologist, arranged for a $250,000 grant to reconstruct a basilica in Leptis Magna. Ahmad Jabril, the director of antiquities, insisted that $40,000 of this should be set aside for the purchase of a crane to lift various bits of the ancient fresco into place. Dr. Rainey pointed out that it would be possible to rent a crane from one of the oil companies for $100 a day. In so doing, money would be saved for the project itself. Jabril was insistent upon the crane and the project never got off the ground.

About 100 kilometers south of the Mediterranean coast stood a line of fortified farms that the Romans built as a southern defense. Although now in ruins, one could still see catchment cisterns that in Roman times irrigated substantial areas of the desert. Throughout my time in the Mediterranean region I never ceased to marvel at the wonders of the Roman Empire.

Below that line of farms lay the Sahara with its subterranean cities such as Ghadames, its natural wonders of rocks and sand, and relics of World War II. The remains of a bomber, the *Lady Be Good,* can still be seen.

I came to love the vastness and silence of the desert. I was reminded frequently of a phrase from the French writer, Antoine de Saint-Exupery, "In the desert you can hear the silence." I made several desert trips in our Land Rover. The longest was in January 1969 along the Chad-Libyan border. From Sebha to Kufra, there were no maps. In our convoy of five Land Rovers and two Bedford trucks, we followed old trails made by the Italians in the 1930s and made our way through the Rubiana Sand Sea with the help of photographs from the Gemini satellite. We also had with us a book by the German explorer Heinrich Barth, who had made the same trip in the nineteenth century. His accurate drawings of rock formations and other sites helped us identify where we were.

We passed camel caravans and occasionally stopped at the tents of the blue men of the desert, the Tuaregs, so named because of the indigo cloth that they wore to shield their faces from the wind and sand.

On one occasion we were dining under the stars with an elderly sheikh. We pointed out to him one of our early Eros satellites that streaked across the sky.

He asked, "How does it stay up in the sky?"

We explained that it went around the earth like the moon. More in curiosity than in disbelief, he asked, "The moon goes around the earth?"

So we sat there under the clear night sky drawing the solar system in the sand and explaining it to this man who had spent his life guiding caravans by the stars.

I was accompanied on the trip by officers of the embassy; Dr. Kenneth Dod, an amateur but enthusiastic geologist and an old friend from university days; Dr. Mohammad Ayoub, a Sudanese who was director of antiquities for the Fezzan, and two of his students; an Italian botanist and friend, Bruno Finnochiaro; the group navigator and geologist Dr. Angelo Pesce; and Dr. Rainey.

We learned much about the desert:

> Never go out with less than two vehicles. We had a friend who perished when his single vehicle broke down.
>
> If you break down, stay with the vehicle. It is much easier to spot a vehicle from the air than a person.
>
> In January the desert can be cold at night. Bring warm jackets.
>
> When driving on sand, break new trails. Once the crust is broken the chances of being bogged down become greater. Never stop on the way up the side of a dune.
>
> Dunes move as constant wind blows the sand. In the Sahara, when they move they are very likely to disclose ancient campsites and tools. We found a number of troves of prehistoric hand axes and other artifacts. On the basis of comparable findings in Europe, Dr. Rainey estimated their age at 250,000 years.
>
> Wind and flies are constant. Just open a can of rations and they appear from nowhere.

The desert is remarkably colorful, with its shades of brown, red, green, black, and blue. The archaeologists in the party were looking for and found ancient mines believed to be the only source in North Africa of a green feldspar stone that was used by the ancient Egyptians for jewelry. From a distance, the area of green stone looked like a cultivated field.

At one point, I waxed philosophical in my trip report: "There is something magnificent about standing on a deserted rocky peak just at sunset, watching for the minute bit of light that marks a distant vehicle. There is a feeling of loneliness, of vastness, and of smallness. One cannot help but ponder on the desolation of those who in the past crossed this hostile terrain, less prepared, less secure than we."

My trip report also records two other events:

> We are on top of the dune waiting for the trucks to get out when we make our regular midday radio contact with Tripoli. Unable to reach Tripoli, we talked with Baida and were informed that I have been promoted to Career Minister. [The second highest permanent rank in the Foreign Service.]
>
> I thought little more about it until about four o'clock, when Rocky [Roscoe Suddarth, one of the embassy's officers] asks that we stop the convoy to refuel. We had done so not long before and I felt this was unnecessary. However, the truth soon came out. From behind the various vehicles, as they pulled up, came members of the party, some with spears to cross over my head, another with a decoration, "The Order of the Tibesti," made out of Bob Wells's Army scarf and the top of a crackers tin, and Bruno Finnochiaro with a bouquet of "flowers" made of an onion he had found in the desert, wire, and toilet paper. Others turned cameras on the scene and I am officially invested with the honors of my new office. Just at that moment, a truck goes by on its way to Kufra. The driver takes one startled look and keeps going. I cannot imagine what he must have thought of this strange rite being performed in the midst of the desert.

Later, upon ending our journey at the Standard Oil port town of Marsa Brega, we encountered some suspicion. Security around the town was tight because of a successful attempt to sabotage it in 1965. I was driving the lead Land Rover and was dressed in Tuareg trousers. When I announced that I was the American ambassador and that word should have been left to this effect at the gate, the Libyan guard professed total ignorance. Rather coolly, he directed me to a phone on the fence and said I could call the security office. I guess that, in my rough clothes and somewhat disheveled condition, I did not look like an ambassador, since Rocky overheard the policeman say to his fellow guard, "If that's the American ambassador, then I'm King Idris." It was one of my proudest moments.

In May 1969 I received word that I had been nominated by the new Nixon administration to be assistant secretary of state for Africa. It was clearly time to take stock of the four years I had been in Libya and, if possible, to look ahead.

The embassy had heard reports of possible plotting against the government. The name of Abdul Aziz Shalhi was mentioned, but we had little information. Neither we nor the British were aware that at that time a captain in the Libyan Army Signal Corps, Muammar Qaddhafi, had been appointed by the government as liaison with a group of army officers in jail. He took advantage of that position to arrange for a coup. We later learned that when the young officers involved in the coup that took place in September went to arrest Col. Shalhi, he thought they were part of his own plot and said to them, "Not yet. Not yet."

Qaddhafi was born into a prominent tribe and was always conscious of his Bedouin roots. A British report on his experience at a military school in Britain said he isolated himself and had a picture of his Bedouin tent over his bunk. He returned to Libya resentful of the British and American presence and of discrimination he had encountered in both Britain and Libya. He claimed to have been turned away at one point by an American guard at the entrance to Wheelus even though he was in uniform.

The revolution of September 1969 and the reversal of American fortunes were, perhaps, inevitable. The presence of Wheelus and the sound of our fighter jets taking off and passing over Tripoli en route to the bombing range had become more and more unpopular. Our unpopularity increased after the 1967 Israeli-Arab war. Though Libya was not an active participant, it felt the defeat of Egypt's Nasser keenly, especially in light of the rumors that blamed Americans for supporting Israel in its attack on Egypt.

The widespread corruption ascribed to the royal establishment had undermined the credibility of the government. King Idris sought to strengthen the government in 1967 by appointing a young prime minister, Abdul Hamid Bakkoush, but replaced him in September 1968 when Bakkoush announced his intention to visit the United States, apparently without informing the king. Idris appointed another young Libyan, Wanis Qaddhafi, an oil engineer (no close relationship with Muammar). The king left June 9 for a four-month vacation, leaving behind political uncertainty. I departed Libya sensing malaise in the country and a feeling that we should not be surprised if the unexpected happened.

Under the circumstances, it was not difficult for a group of 140 young, disaffected Libyan army officers led by Muammar Qaddhafi to take armored cars and roll into Tripoli on September 1, 1969, in a relatively bloodless coup. Not even in Cyrenaica did anyone rise to support the king.

James Blake, my deputy, who became chargé d'affaires upon my departure, wrote to me on September 25 about the early actions of the new rulers. Their actions demonstrated the feelings of this young group that the Arab character of Libya had been violated in many ways by the royal regime, and they began by eliminating the vestiges of English:

> With the restoration of some normality in the community, including the return of regular Security Force personnel in front of the Embassy (unarmed, however), there are also some changes. Perhaps the most interesting has been the quick disappearance of English-language signs on business shops and other premises during the past week; . . . even traffic signs have had the English obliterated. . . . At Tripoli airport last Monday morning, I noticed that even the "Arabic" numerals marking the queues had been painted over leaving only the *authentic* Arabic numeral to mark the line in which the hapless traveler should stand. The English-language news broadcasts on the Libyan radio have also been dropped.

In my new position in Washington I had to deal with another manifestation of the revolution—the demand that all passports of travelers coming to Libya be printed in Arabic. As was expected, the Libyans also demanded the closure of Wheelus and the British base at El Adam. Wheelus was closed on June 11, 1970.

It was, perhaps, not unexpected that in an area fond of conspiracy theories some Libyans and some of the press in the Arab world attributed the coup to the Americans. In January 1981, I received a letter from P. Edward Haley, a professor at Claremont College in California, setting forth various interpretations of recent Libyan-American relations and suggesting that the United States saw the monarchy as increasingly unsupportive of American interests and arranged the coup. In 1998 I received a letter from a friend who had been an oil company official, enclosing an issue of *Al-Inqad,* a publication of the National Front for the Salvation of Libya, with a 150-page essay "devoted to the alleged role of Americans in the overthrow of the King Idris government and the establishment of the Qaddafi regime."[38] None of the assertions had any basis in fact but illustrated once more the difficulty that Libyans had acknowledging their responsibility for their actions.

If a revolution was pending in Libya, substantial change was taking place in our own country. The 1960s were a turbulent time, with protests against the Vietnam War, the civil rights movement, and rejection of established social customs. Some of the changes were hard for socially conservative parents to accept. The long hair and casual dress on all occasions were ultimately tolerated. New attitudes toward sex, drugs, and authority were more difficult to understand and condone.

In part we witnessed these changes from afar, but we also saw them through the eyes and experiences of our two oldest sons, John and Dan, who were then at the University of California in Berkeley. Through correspondence and occasional visits we maintained contact. John's letter of May 23, 1969, gives some of the flavor of Berkeley at that time:

> As you probably know by now, all hell has broken loose in Berkeley over the "People's Park" [an area near the university taken over by the homeless and protesters]. We are living under virtual martial law and military occupation. Tuesday I was arrested while I was standing on a street corner talking to a friend. There was no charge other than standing in the street, and luckily I have a witness, all of the charges will probably be dropped. Anyhow Karla [a friend] gave a bail

> bondsman $50 to bail me out, as my bail was set at $500 for the misdemeanor. A total of 85 were arrested that day, totally at random, and today over 250 were busted, herded together like cattle, and taken off to Santa Rita "concentration camp," where I spent five hours on Tuesday. All my professors have suspended their classes and consider the situation intolerable. Every foreigner I have talked to says it is just like home—Prague or Latin America. I talked to a Frenchman who was arrested along with me; he was deeply shocked and hoped that soon Americans would wake up and find out what has happened to their "democracy." I don't know what to think except that [Governor] Reagan and Alameda County Sheriff Frank Madigan are insane. But at the same time, so many professors and citizens have responded with outrage . . . that maybe there is hope yet for this country.

In 2007 John sent me a Father's Day card. The cover showed a man talking on the telephone with his wife at his side, saying, "Jail? Why no, officer, there must be some mistake, our son is at the library." Inside, the card read "Have we gotten to the 'look back and laugh' stage yet?" Then he wrote reminders of the past, including the time he and his girlfriend walked down Wisconsin Avenue in Washington wearing Roman togas and being briefly "interviewed" by a police officer. I assured him that we could look back and laugh. It was less easy to do so in 1969.

In July of that year, our children, Jean, and I left Tripoli with some sadness to head home to Senate confirmation for my new assignment and to become reacquainted with a changing United States. But my close involvement with North Africa was not yet over.

As a result of the Vietnam War, the end of the 1960s brought not only turmoil on the campuses but a reexamination in the Senate of worldwide American commitments. Senator Stuart Symington headed the Senate Subcommittee on U.S. Security Agreements and Commitments Abroad. Senator William Fulbright, then chairman of the Senate Foreign Relations Committee, was a prominent member of this special subcommittee. Because of my North Africa responsibilities, I was a principal witness in hearings relating to Ethiopia, Morocco, and Libya on June 1 and July 20, 1970.

The hearings sought to determine what commitments had been made to these governments, either through executive agreements, treaties, oral statements, or by the mere presence of military assistance groups. At issue was the question of what constituted a commitment and how widely knowledge of commitments had been reported to the Senate. At the heart of the matter, against the backdrop of American involvement in Cambodia and Laos, was the feeling in the committee that actions in these countries had been taken without any formal congressional approval and that future involvements should, wherever possible, be approved by a ratified treaty.

The hearings opened with an examination of our relations with Ethiopia. Some excerpts will give the flavor of the seven hours of testimony.

In response to a question from Senator Symington I said, "We have no security commitment to Ethiopia. We have, at various times, given assurances of our continued interest in the security and integrity of this country and our opposition to any activities threatening the territorial integrity of Ethiopia."

Senator Symington responded: "If you say you are interested in the security of Ethiopia, and are opposed to any activities threatening its integrity, don't you think the people have a right to know about these assurances? It is a commitment, isn't it?"

I sought to clarify what we meant: "In stating this, we had in mind our continuing grant military assistance and the clear intention in the event of any attack against Ethiopia, to use all our good offices in the United Nations and elsewhere to ensure the maintenance of Ethiopia's integrity. In so doing, we would act to recognize not only our own direct interest in the country, but the significance to us and to all of Africa of the continued integrity of this historic land."[39]

A representative of the Defense Department, George Bader, and I argued that the Senate had been informed of commitments through the annual appropriations and authorization process. Senator Fulbright did not accept this argument. A partial transcript of the hearing on Ethiopia follows:

Senator Fulbright: This whole series of hearings are for the purpose of trying to inform not only the Senate but the public about the extent of our involvement in these innumerable countries abroad. . . . How can you justify the public not knowing how their money is being spent?

Mr. Newsom: The public is aware . . .

Senator Fulbright: No. They are not.

Mr. Newsom: of the key points of this agreement.

Senator Fulbright: I don't think the public has the slightest idea how our money is being dissipated all around the world. They would have revolted long ago, as this committee would have. Senator Symington's inquiry—and this is the first time we have had one—not just about Ethiopia but in many places—has indicated that there has been a very artful, in-depth concealment of what we are doing.

You go to the Appropriations Committee, and in order to get the money, you tell them about these commitments, but the commitments themselves were never made public. In the Appropriations Committee all you have to do is convince a few people that this is necessary for the military, isn't that true?

Mr. Newsom: Well, Mr. Chairman, I would draw a distinction between making public precise documents which we exchange in confidence with foreign heads of state and through diplomatic channels. We feel there is certainly a great sensitivity among heads of state about our releasing private communications we give to them or that they give to us.

Senator Fulbright: But I am speaking here from the point of view of the American public. Whatever [a] foreign government thinks about these, that is determinative and whether we should know about it is up to the foreign government not the Congress or our own government, that is your attitude, isn't it?

Mr. Newsom: We have made public the fact that we have committed ourselves to support and supply equipment for the 40,000-man Ethiopian army, subject to the availability of funds through congressional action; that we were going to lend them a naval vessel, that we were going to help them with their university, that we were going to initiate a police program, all of these things which are the key points of this document.

Senator Fulbright: You told to the Appropriations Committee.

Mr. Newsom: We told to the Appropriations Committee and the Senate Foreign Relations Committee.

Senator Fulbright: I don't believe the latter part of that.[40]

Senator Fulbright was particularly critical of commitments made by "high-level visitors." He said to me at one point: "It is a very bad custom. I remember Vice President Humphrey was particularly prone to do this. He made a communiqué in Bangkok once, more or less promising to take the Great Society to all of Asia. Do you remember that case, Mr. Secretary? And when I answered "yes," the Senator said, "Can't you discourage this procedure, because it is a very dangerous one?"

I replied, "I can testify that we, at my level, have frequently done as much as we can to discourage this."[41]

Another exchange with Senator Fulbright focused on the powers of the president. (An echo is heard in the twenty-first century.) The question arose over the possible U.S. reaction in the event of a hypothetical conflict between Ethiopia and Djibouti.

Mr. Newsom: I think, speaking for the executive branch, our feeling is that this is an area in which we have very substantial interests, in which things, circumstances could change quickly and that we would feel the President should continue to have the flexibility, as Commander in Chief, to deal with the situation as it might arise. This is of course …

Senator Fulbright: Wait a minute, you have got this new theory. How does the Commander in Chief determine the policy that should be followed in Ethiopia? Have you extended this theory of the Commander in Chief's responsibility to the point where because we have 6,000 Americans there, among whom there are more than 2,000 military, that in order to protect those he can do whatever is necessary?

Mr. Newsom: We have an obligation, we feel, to our citizens abroad to assist them in getting out of a danger area, as something which has been done.[42]

[A bit later:]

Senator Fulbright: You do not really feel that the Senate has any role to play in determining where our interests lie?

Mr. Newsom: I did not mean to give that impression.

Senator Fulbright: Well, do you or don't you? What impression do you mean to give?

Mr. Newsom: Over the years the Senate has had a very definite interest and a recognized interest in events of this kind.

Senator Fulbright: What you say seems to mean that only the President should determine it.

Mr. Newsom: But there is, in a sense, what this is all about, the discussion that is now going on is a question of the division [of] responsibilities [between] the President and the role of the legislative branch, and I would not want to make a comment on where that line should be drawn in a situation of this kind.

Senator Fulbright: Well, it is interesting that you used the same phraseology that has been used justifying the entry into Cambodia that you use here.[43]

In another hearing that dealt with Morocco, Senator Fulbright made an issue of the classification of documents:

Senator Fulbright: You create a dilemma by classifying everything that has to do with the American commitments.

Mr. Newsom: Well, the fundamental dilemma, Mr. Chairman, is that so long as we conclude that these facilities are important to us, and it is our conclusion that they are important to us,{deleted}

Senator Fulbright: If they are all that important, why can they not be subject to the light of day and discussion in an authorization?

> The fundamental trouble that is afflicting all these arguments and these hearings is that the State Department, through neglect on the part of the Congress, is allowing you to do this type of classifying year after year, has become accustomed to it and you do not want to have to justify these programs publicly.
>
> Do you not still believe that our system of constitutional government has any validity?
>
> *Mr. Newsom:* I am a great believer in our system of constitutional government.
>
> *Senator Fulbright:* If you are, why do you not want to support it?
>
> *Mr. Newsom:* I believe, Mr. Chairman, that -- and here we may well part company -- we have operated satisfactorily over many years by sharing with the Congress arrangements of this kind.[44]

I have always enjoyed the give and take across a congressional hearing table. The Symington hearings, an exhilarating reentry into the Washington scene, were particularly stimulating. Over the years I became a good friend of Senator Fulbright, a dedicated public servant whose contribution to educational exchange has been without equal.

14

ONLY EIGHT PERCENT OF THE BLACK VOTE

For four and a half years, I threaded my way through the conflicting pressures that have traditionally influenced U.S. foreign policy in Africa. These included the politically oriented elements of the White House, relevant committees of Congress, lobbies, interested foreign governments, several American organizations concentrating on Africa, and the academic community.

I assumed the responsibilities of the Bureau of African Affairs in the State Department in 1969, at the height of the Cold War and in the immediate aftermath of the civil rights revolution, the turbulent sixties, and the march to independence of the black African nations. All of these elements increased pressures on our Africa policy.

President Kennedy, in particular, had reached out to the new African leaders. This was both his personal inclination and a reflection of his strong support in the African-American community. He had received several of the new African leaders in the Oval Office. His administration had played a significant role in United Nations efforts to maintain the unity of the Congo after it gained its independence from Belgium. Substantial commitments of development aid had been made to Nigeria and Ghana. Such actions had increased expectations of official U.S. help to black Africa, while increasing the risk of anti-American attitudes resulting from the disappointment of hopes unrealized.

I was never certain why I had been chosen to be assistant secretary for Africa. I had worked in the Africa bureau in a Democratic administration under a prominent Democratic appointee, G. Mennen Williams, and was recommended to the new Republican administration by Governor Williams's deputy, J. Wayne Fredericks.

Although my duties until then had involved only northern Africa, it was no secret that I shared many of the views of the outgoing administration.

In my initial assignment to the Africa bureau in 1962, I became aware for the first time of the domestic and foreign implications of the American civil rights revolution. I had grown up in California where, in my day, the question of race did not dominate politics. For the first time I met leaders of various American movements for racial equality. They were impressive and articulate.

The Republican administration of Richard Nixon entered office with a determination to correct what it viewed as the "black tilt" of previous Democratic administrations. The new Republican team was largely indifferent to Africa. When I suggested to one of the team that the president make a speech on African policy, his reply was, "Why should he? We only got 8 percent of the black vote."

Africa was seen less in terms of civil rights and more in terms of the Cold War. Soviet, Chinese, and Cuban assistance to African liberation movements, especially in southern Africa, were considered dangerous communist penetrations and threats to American interests. Restrictions that had been placed on relations with Portugal because of the continued Portuguese colonial occupation in Angola and Mozambique were considered serious constraints upon our use of important installations in the Azores and Portugal.

I was placed in a situation not uncommon in the federal career service. I would be asked to craft and support policies with which I was not totally in agreement. In areas of the world in conflict, long-term unresolved problems bred strong emotions both abroad and in the United States. Policy makers were inescapably caught between extreme positions and faced criticism if they did not follow one extreme or the other.

In the case of Africa, the division was between those who favored support for white-dominated regimes and assumed their long-term existence and those who felt the United States should actively work to change such regimes. Those favoring the status quo argued, in a Cold War context, that any changes risked favoring the communist world. Those representing the other point of view called for sanctions against the white-ruled regimes and support and encouragement to the liberation movements targeting such regimes. Throughout my career I have taken the position that civil servants should respect the democratic process and either carry out an administration's policies to the best of their ability or resign. Resignation, in my experience, sidelines opponents of policy without fundamentally changing its direction. During my tenure in the Africa bureau, I felt that as long as I could maintain reasonably effective communication with all the conflicting elements, both in the United States and in Africa, and could find opportunities within the limits of presidential policies to advance goals I believed in, I could maintain the position in good conscience. As a result, the next four years were, for me, an interesting test of how one can, in the complex machinery of the U.S. government, modify and shape policies. One cannot win all the battles, but with effort, one can maintain credibility and respect among most of the competing policy constituencies.

At the heart of the international and national debates on Africa in 1969 were three issues: challenges to white dominance, the possibility of Soviet and Chinese gains, and the most effective ways to promote economic development in the continent. In crises that foreshadowed events in later decades, we faced also the difficult tensions between the need for relief to populations caught in areas of conflict and the sensitivities of sovereign governments about foreign intervention. In addition, acts of terrorism and ethnic violence that were to plague the continent in future decades also appeared in the early 1970s. The tensions in the Horn of Africa that I had faced in my previous responsibilities for northern Africa continued, as a Soviet-armed Somalia stepped up its claims on Ethiopia's Ogaden Province.

Some of the issues I had dealt with in my North African responsibilities were still on the table when I assumed the assistant secretary position. Along with other Arab countries, Algeria had broken diplomatic relations with the United States after the 1967 war. Because of a growing interest by private American companies in Algeria's resources, Washington continued to hope that full diplomatic relations could be reestablished. In April 1972 I traveled to Algiers carrying a letter from President Nixon to President Houari Boumediene expressing "satisfaction with the favorable trend in relations between our two countries."[45] President Boumediene received me cordially and provided his private plane for a visit to Tamanrasset in southern Algeria. Foreign Minister (later president)

Abdelaziz Bouteflika saw us off at the airport. But it was clear that Algeria was not yet ready to move to full diplomatic relations.

As assistant secretary, I was caught in the middle of all these issues, conscious of my responsibility to an elected administration, but conscious also of the importance of preserving a meaningful position for the United States among black African nations. African-Americans saw parallels to their own oppression in the apartheid system in South Africa. Pressures to severely restrict all relations with Pretoria were strong from the Black Caucus in Congress and from several American organizations, both black and white, devoted to Africa. The demands for more forceful diplomatic action remained strong. Many would judge the administration's African policy solely on the degree to which it was prepared to confront the white-ruled regimes on the continent.

I came to the African position with a conviction that the United States could not ignore the considerable American constituency, both black and white, that supported such a policy, nor could any administration turn its back on the new nations.

As it turned out, the new administration discovered greater limitations to change than it had anticipated. Whatever their personal views on racial questions, President Nixon and Henry Kissinger, then the national security adviser, realized that the United States could not be seen to be supporting the racist policies of the white regimes. The American ship of state is never as maneuverable as incoming administrations would like.

In the United Nations, a positive approach to African issues was important not only as a reflection of the U.S. domestic constituency, but also because the African nations increasingly represented a significant bloc in international forums. Curbing Soviet and Chinese efforts in the continent required credible relations with the new nations of Africa. For many years, American success in maintaining the position of Taiwan in the United Nations rested primarily on the support of African nations. Similarly, in the early 1970s, when the United States sought to reduce its share of the United Nations budget to 25 percent, African nations helped our cause.

I worked closely in those years with our ambassador to the United Nations, George H. W. Bush. With a politician's touch, he reached out to representatives of some of the smaller nations of Africa, a policy that was deeply appreciated.

Each September I accompanied the secretary of state, William P. Rogers, to New York to meet with the leaders of African delegations to the United Nations General Assembly. Our task was not an easy one. Many Africans, with their rhetorical approach to problems, found unacceptable our complex and nuanced positions on such issues as colonialism, the Portuguese territories, and apartheid. Even the previous Democratic administration had, for example, opposed resolutions calling for sanctions against South Africa; that position did not change with the new administration.[46]

At the UN General Assembly in 1973 I first glimpsed Kissingerian diplomacy. Mobutu Sese Seko, the president of Zaire and an important friend of the United States, had just made a speech in the Assembly critical of Israel, just as we were pushing Congress to provide more assistance to Zaire. Once Secretary Kissinger heard of this, he asked me to make an appointment with Mobutu.

I accompanied him to the Zairian leader's hotel apartment. We entered, and after exchanges of greetings, Kissinger said to Mobutu "I have come to congratulate you." Mobutu looked pleased and a bit puzzled. Then Kissinger said, "You certainly know how to gain the attention of our Congress."

Mobutu knew exactly what the secretary was referring to and went into an explanation of how he, as an African leader, had to recognize the problems that Israel caused for the Palestinians. In a later meeting with President Nixon he went to considerable lengths to explain his position and to say, "I wish to give you the fullest assurance that you can always depend on Zaire's willingness and readiness to provide constructive and discreet assistance in solving any political or diplomatic problem involving any African nation or any other nonaligned nation—as in the recent case involving Cambodia."[47] Mobutu never again gave a speech critical of Israel, at least not in the United States.

A number of our problems with Africa resulted from the conflict between American domestic pressures for humanitarian intervention and the strong opposition to such intervention by the newly independent nations sensitive to their sovereignty.

Tensions among ethnic groups in Africa that had been encouraged or suppressed in the colonial period emerged as colonial controls were removed. One of the first appearances of this tragic reality was in the 1965 upheaval in Burundi, formerly a German colony in the heart of Africa and then a Belgian mandate. The Belgians had maintained the rule of a Tutsi minority. Foreshadowing the tragedy of Rwanda some years later, the majority Hutus rose against the Tutsi rulers and slaughtered several thousand. News of this human tragedy sparked demands for American intervention and an embargo on coffee exports from Burundi. Corporate and business interests may have played a role in the lack of forceful U.S. action, as some critics claimed,[48] but the principal inhibiting factor was the absence of international support for such measures.

Sanctions of any kind, to be effective, require congressional support in the United States and regional and international cooperation abroad. Although some of these elements might have been achievable, the most critical—African support—was not. As we were to find in similar future crises, strong negative African recollections of European humanitarian and missionary efforts and colonial interventions stood in the way of the kinds of actions being demanded in the United States.

I approached key African leaders to seek their cooperation in stemming the bloodshed in Burundi. One of those I approached was Okoi Arikpo, the foreign minister of Nigeria. I told him of the strong pressures existing in the United States for action on our part and said it seemed far preferable for Africans to step in.

He replied, "We do not want to intervene in our neighbors' problems. To do so would be to call attention to such events. That would reflect on Africa. People in your country and in Europe would say, 'See. That's the way Africans are.' When you talk about the troubles in Northern Ireland, you don't say, 'See, that's the way Europeans are.'"[49]

That same inhibition against interference applied especially to the actions of those who were seen as leaders in the liberation of Africa from colonial rule. The case of Robert Mugabe of Zimbabwe in 2007–8 is a prime example. As with the Ethiopian-Somali conflict discussed in the previous chapter and the Nigerian civil war later in this, Africans were also unwilling to involve themselves in disputes that challenged the colonial era boundaries.

The limitations on the U.S. ability to intervene in Africa—even when American interests were clearly at stake—was illustrated in a tragic way in Khartoum in March 1973. On the first day of that month, the Embassy of Saudi Arabia in Khartoum was hosting a diplomatic reception to say farewell to the American deputy chief of mission, George C. "Curt" Moore. The reception was invaded by eight members of the Black September movement, an offshoot of the Palestine Liberation Organization formed during a conflict with Jordan in 1970. The invaders took over the Embassy and released all of the guests except Moore, Cleo Noel—the incoming U.S. ambassador—the Saudi Arabian ambassador, and the chargés of Jordan and Belgium. They threatened to execute the hostages unless various Palestinian prisoners in Jordan, Israel, and West Germany and Sirhan Sirhan, the convicted assassin of Robert F. Kennedy, were released within twenty-four hours. These demands were subsequently reduced to include only the release of the prisoners held in Jordan.

The operations center of the State Department had facilities for worldwide communication, including a large wall screen on which words of a message could be flashed. (1973 was before the day of e-mail and computers.) The news of the capture of Noel and Moore in the Saudi Embassy reached Washington in the late morning of March 1. I was called into the operations center together with Joseph Sisco, the assistant secretary for Near East and South Asia. Although Khartoum was my area of responsibility, it was clear from the beginning that the kidnapping had a Middle East connection. William Macomber, under secretary for management, and Armin Meyer, coordinator for terrorism, soon took charge of the U.S. response.

The hours that followed were agonizing and frustrating. Washington clearly wanted to bring the perpetrators to justice, but attitudes toward American policy in the Middle East proved to be an insurmountable problem. No Arab leader involved, as embarrassed as he might be by the incident, was prepared to appear to be succumbing to U.S. pressure.

It was decided that Macomber would leave as soon as possible on a military plane for Khartoum—a flight that would take fifteen hours. My experience has been that the most vulnerable aspects of any crisis management are the communications—and this was no exception. While we were waiting for word of what was happening in Khartoum and of the Macomber mission, a sandstorm in the Nile area blocked out all communications from our embassy.

Other broadcast communications, however, were not blocked out, and the Sudanese and the hostage takers heard news of President Nixon's press conference on March 2, 1973, in which he said, "As far as the United States as a government giving in to blackmail demands, we cannot do so and we will not do so." I heard this news with a sinking heart. Not long afterward we received word that Noel and Moore had been killed. A subsequent RAND study of the incident confirmed that the Nixon statement had been heard by the hostage takers. Whether the presidential statement led to the decision to kill the hostages remains a matter of dispute.[50]

The days that followed were equally frustrating. The embassy was able to identify the seven members of the Black September squad. Macomber, who arrived in Khartoum after the killings, obtained a commitment from the Sudanese that the killers would be tried. More than a year later a Sudanese court pronounced life sentences, but "due to the hardships imposed by Israel on the Palestinians," President Jaafar al-Nimeiry of the Sudan commuted the sentences to seven years and announced that the squad would be turned over to the Palestine Liberation Organization in Cairo to serve the remainder of that sentence. On June 24, 1974, the squad was flown to Cairo and put in the hands of the Egyptian government. In the face of the general unpopularity of U.S. policy in the region and feelings of Arab solidarity, to hope that the killers would be severely punished was probably unrealistic.[51]

At the end of the 1960s, several situations brought the debates over African policy into sharp focus in the United States:

- In Washington, I was confronted with the draft of National Security Studies Memorandum (NSSM) number 39. The draft was intended, with the threat of the Soviet Union in mind, to open the way for greater cooperation with the governments in South Africa and Portugal in such matters as naval visits, the use of the Azores bases, and trade in items that had both civilian and military uses (so called dual-purpose).[52]

- In Nigeria, a civil war to reunite the breakaway eastern province of Biafra was seen by some in the United States and Africa as an effort to weaken a major black African country and by others as a matter of self-determination. This question was played out against the backdrop of a debate over relief.
- In Southern Rhodesia a white-dominated regime was holding out against strong African opposition through lobbying efforts in the United States and Europe.
- In a backlash against previous policies of generous economic assistance credits, Congress had voted to limit development assistance to ten countries in Africa.

This list includes at least some of the issues that confronted me in 1969 in the Bureau of African Affairs. Through bureaucratic efforts and by reaching out to our supporters, I sought to deal with each of them in a way that preserved our interests as I saw them. In Secretary of State William Rogers, who had his own problems with the White House, I had an important ally.

Critics of the administration nevertheless seized on what they had heard about NSSM 39 to make it a symbol of a shift toward white-ruled South Africa. On April 2, 1972, the *New York Times* published an article under the headline, "U.S. is quietly tightening its ties to white-ruled Southern Africa."[53] Words have a way of becoming pejorative symbols in the debate over African policy. In a speech in Chicago on September 17, 1970, I had spoken of the need for "communication" with all elements in Africa to initiate and encourage peaceful change. "Communication," it seems, became the target of condemnation, just as in later years my successor, Chester Crocker, faced the brickbats on "constructive engagement."

Although I do not recall ever receiving word that President Nixon had chosen a particular option under NSSM 39, it was generally understood that he had chosen Option Two, which read in part: "We would maintain public opposition to racial repression but relax political isolation and economic restrictions on the white states." Roger Morris, the NSC staff member who drafted the study, had this to say about it in his book, *Uncertain Greatness*. "Christened 'tar baby' by a State Department critic who foresaw early in the drafting that its only real result would be to mire the United States deeper on the side of the oppressors, this was ostensibly the option finally chosen by Nixon from the policy review. In retrospect, it was a disaster, naïve in concept, practically impossible for the government to execute, and thus a ready cover for pursuing the most reactionary and short-sighted US interests in the region."[54]

In fact, the changes under NSSM 39 were relatively few. The new administration, realizing the potential political damage of images of sailors being segregated in a South African naval base, did not seek further naval visits. Export-Import Bank credits on dual-purpose items were recommended, but few such items were purchased. And in official statements the condemnation of South Africa's policies of apartheid continued—but with the caveat that change should not be brought about by force. In his February 18, 1970, report to Congress on Africa, President Nixon stated, "Clearly there is no question of the United States condoning, or acquiescing in, the racial policies of the white-ruled regimes."[55]

The South African press showed great interest in my appointment and looked for signs that it represented a major change from that of the Kennedy-Johnson years. On August 28, 1969, *The Star* of Johannesburg published the following report from John Jordi, their Washington correspondent:

> When David Dunlop Newsom thinks about South Africa it is only natural that his memory should project a flashback picture of Cape Town in March 1960.
>
> For it is an eerie fact that the most recent visit that the new Assistant Secretary of State for African Affairs made to South Africa coincided with the Cape turbulence of the Sharpeville period. (He was there with a party from the United States National War College. His only other visit was as an itinerant student 20 years before.)
>
> With a rueful grimace, Newsom now recalls that 1960 experience simply as "a dour time." (He is a man of under-

statements, which is one change for the good). And since he doesn't make much of it, there is no point in others doing so. Still, that personal memory must reinforce in his case the lid-and-boiling-pot imagery which American officials must believe in, or at least insist they believe in, if they are to live comfortably with the orthodox State Department view of South Africa.

If that recollection does not influence Newsom, the best thing to hope for is that it does not become distorted by any subconscious need to justify policy decisions.

This has been the case, I suspect, with another senior official who likes to describe the "typical" white South Africans suburban home as "surrounded by a high wall topped with broken glass or barbed wire, with a spotlight playing on it and big dogs patrolling." He rounds off the picture with his recollection that "the first thing you see when you get in the door is a rack filled with rifles."

David Newsom seems too well-balanced a man to become prey to fearful fantasies. He has an excellent sense of humor (which is a second change for the good) and, better still, a sense of irony.

He has blue eyes in a crumpled kind of face and tends to look away while talking, and then directly at one as he makes his point. It is made quietly, without emotional show.

He is modest—about his knowledge of Africa, for instance—and likes his staff to call him simply "Mr. Newsom" rather than "Mr. Ambassador" (a title he can retain indefinitely following his Libyan envoyship) or "Mr. Secretary," which often replaces the conversationally cumbersome "Mr. Assistant Secretary." He likes to stress that he has been in the job only a few weeks.

One of the reasons that he got the job was said to be his lack of recorded identification with "positions" on Africa. But now, slowly, he must start to take "positions" publicly. There is nothing to suggest that these will be much different from the established State Department line, except perhaps in tone. But they will, also slowly, help outsiders to assess what power Mr. Newsom comes to wield vis-à-vis his counterparts among President Nixon's White House advisers.

Newsom's suite of offices is on the sixth floor at "State," with a view from his room to the wooded mall when the Venetian blinds are not down against the summer glare. There are the ubiquitous Stars and Stripes to the right of the desk, a pantry with a fridge to the left. Other doors lead off to secretaries, to the Deputy Assistant Secretary's office, and to the conference room where senior African Affairs Bureau officials meet at nine each weekday morning.

A bad colour photograph of President Nixon and a better one of the Secretary of State, Mr. Rogers, hang on the light-panelled wall, near the television set. Behind the big desk with diplomatic telegrams in the out-tray, the bookshelves, their backing painted a fierce red, are less than half-filled. There is a set of encyclopaedias. And a volume titled *Transition in Southern Africa.*

The furniture is all standard "G.S.A. issue" (General Services Administration, which is American for P.W.D.) of a grade appropriate to Mr. Newsom's rank. Brown leather armchairs and settee, gray-green wall-to-wall carpeting, brown glass ashtrays.

There are two wall maps of Africa plus a table-top globe, and sooner or later Mr. Newsom will begin to plot out the course of African tours which are likely to be just as ambitious as anything that predecessors like "Soapy" Williams undertook, though a lot less noisy.

He notes that he has visited "only 16" African states and he has a stack of invitations.

Obviously it is in South Africa's interest that he should go there if only to superimpose some less dramatic image on his memory than that of, say, the Langa march or troops protecting parliament. But such a visit is unlikely to come early on. This is partly because South Africa is not on Mr. Newsom's "still unseen" list of nations which will have priority. And it is partly because even if it were the only land still unseen, no prudent Assistant Secretary would launch his travels there, even if he did not want to make a speech.[56]

My predecessors had avoided making visits to apartheid South Africa. I decided to change that policy, but to do so in a way that would symbolize our support for change. In 1970, I visited South Africa myself, accompanied by one of my deputy assistant secretaries, Beverly Carter, a tall, impressive African-American. The following year, after some negotiation with the South Africans, I assigned the first African-American diplomat, James Baker, a Foreign Service officer, to the embassy in Pretoria with as much assurance as I could get that he would not face apartheid restrictions.

The 1970 visit to South Africa was one of the most fascinating experiences of my career. Beverly Carter had been editor of the *Pittsburgh Courier,* an African-American newspaper, and was one of the first American blacks to run for Congress.

Carter and I spent eight days in the Republic. We met with governmental leaders, educators, businessmen, journalists, students, and private citizens from every walk of life. We spoke with Africans, Coloreds, and Indians as well as with opposition political leaders in the white community.

On one occasion we had a taste of apartheid. We left the Republic for a brief visit to Lesotho. Returning by air to the Johannesburg airport, Bev and I went into the lounge and sat down. I ordered two bottles of Coca-Cola. I could sense some commotion at the bar. Soon one of the hosts came over and said to us, "I am terribly sorry but we can't serve you here. You'll have to go to the other bar" (meaning the bar for Africans).

I said to Bev, "I'm sorry about this."

He replied in a tone I have never forgotten, "That's all right. It's nothing new to me."

The South Africans did not quite know how to take Beverly Carter. At one of our official dinners, the wife of the Minister of Justice, looking across the table at Bev, said to me, "Mr. Carter is very impressive. Our blacks are not like that." I asked her what contacts she had with university-educated blacks. Her response made clear she had little contact with blacks beyond her own servants.

At Stellenbosch University, South Africa's principal Afrikaaner university, we met with a student group. One of the students asked, "Mr. Carter, why are you in the United States so critical of us when we are so good to our black people?"

Bev paused for a moment, then said, "I guess it's because you require people to go through separate doors because of the color of their skin." We both had the feeling that this was the first time the questioner and, probably the group, had ever thought about that.

Did our visit make a difference?

I was able to say at our final press conference in Pretoria that I was speaking with the full authority of the executive branch when I said, "The American official attitude toward the policy of racial discrimination in South Africa has been constant. We abhor racial policies which by law separate men and deny them rights solely on the basis of the color of their skin."[57] I believe this helped lay to rest any impressions based on other American sources that the Nixon administration or any other would accept the fundamentals of apartheid.

In our report to the House Subcommittee on Africa upon our return, we were able to note that the *Capetown Argus*, in an editorial shortly after our departure, coupled British Prime Minister Ted Heath's strong statement against apartheid with our own and pointed out that the South African government had been unable to convince either Britain or America of the rightness of apartheid. The paper asked whether the time had not come to reexamine this approach.[58]

It has always bothered me that the African community, with its strong feelings about apartheid, made almost no mention of what both Bev Carter and I considered a significant American visit. I recently read some of the academic work relating to the Nixon administration views on Africa, and there is scant reference either to me or to Beverly Carter or to our efforts to bring the anti-apartheid message to Pretoria.[59]

The emotions involved in the debate over the Nigerian Civil War came home dramatically when, before assuming my new office, I went home on leave to Berkeley, California. During my leave the *San Francisco Examiner* carried a full-page advertisement. In it was a picture of a child with a bloated belly suffering from kwashiorkor, a disease caused by malnutrition. The picture was frequently used in material promoting the cause of Biafra. This particular ad carried the message, "If you want to save this child, write to the new Assistant Secretary for African Affairs, David Newsom."

Upon reaching Washington I received a large stack of hate mail. It was symbolic of a bitter bureaucratic battle involving Congress, the staff of the National Security Council (NSC), and the Department of State.[60] I was again thrust into the middle of a debate relating to humanitarian relief.

The Nigerian Civil War had begun in 1968 when the Eastern Province of newly independent Nigeria broke away from the Federal Military Government (FMG) in Lagos and sought to establish an independent country, Biafra. The province was the home of the Ibo tribe, an active and enterprising people—mainly Catholic—who believed themselves persecuted and disadvantaged in newly independent Nigeria. They had been targets of riots in the northern region of the country just a few years before. The Nigerian government sought to suppress the secession both by military means and by a blockade.

The Biafran cause was supported in the United States by a group of educated Ibos, by Peace Corps volunteers from Massachusetts who had worked in the Eastern Province, and by a group of Holy Ghost fathers, also from Massachusetts. The Americans who worked in the province had convinced Senator Edward Kennedy of the rightness of their cause, thus stimulating congressional interest in the conflict. Internationally, Biafra had the support of the French and of a few Francophone African countries that gave formal recognition to the breakaway province.

A campaign was mounted in the United States and in Europe stressing the impact of the blockade on health, particularly of children, and, as the war continued, on the imminence of famine. Pressure grew in the United States for relief for Biafra. Supporters of Biafra airlifted relief supplies into the enclave. The Nigerian government insisted that unmonitored relief flights would be a violation of Nigerian sovereignty and would probably be carrying weapons. They insisted on the right to monitor and inspect such flights.

The State Department, conscious of the strong support for the unity of Nigeria both in Africa generally and within the African-American community at home, supported the policy of the government in Lagos. The African-American community generally saw the creation of Biafra as an effort to break up the largest black country on the continent and echoed the view of most African countries that colonial boundaries, however inexact, should not be changed by force.

The Nixon White House, sensitive to domestic political pressures, was generally favorable to Biafra and probably came close to recognizing the government of C. Odumegwu Ojukwo, Biafra's leader.[61] The NSC staff was unsympathetic to the position of the military government in Lagos and at one point sent two of its members to "bring the embassy in line with official policy." The State Department and, especially the Bureau of African Affairs, was accused of "clientitis" in its support of Nigeria.[62]

Support for Biafran relief was strong in Congress. Hearings were held by both Senate and House committees. I appeared before both committees with Clyde Ferguson, a Harvard Law School professor who had been appointed relief coordinator. The debate in Washington became sharply focused with the release in October 1969 of the report of a survey of the nutritional situation in Biafra by Dr. Karl Western of the Centers for Disease Control. The report painted a picture of severe starvation and suggested that many would die in the absence of a major relief effort.

The Nigerians were on the point of a final military push against Biafra and discounted the findings of the report. The NSC staff criticized the embassy in Lagos for not presenting the report to the Federal Military Government. The battle in Washington was joined.

Secretary of State Rogers was reluctant to see the United States involved politically in the conflict and opposed suggestions of mediation. The White House followed this position initially but changed when the domestic political pressure for some American action grew. Without informing the State Department, NSC staff members held secret talks with Biafran representatives and considered a mediation effort.

When I took over as assistant secretary in mid-1969, National Security Adviser Henry Kissinger was dealing primarily on this issue not with Secretary Rogers but with Under Secretary of State Elliot Richardson. Rogers, on this issue as well as on others, was increasingly isolated from the president. It was a challenge for me as an assistant secretary, dealing with an issue in which the secretary and the under secretary were on opposite sides, to maintain access and satisfactory relations with both.

Africa suffered then as it does today from the image of a troubled and corrupt continent. Murderous ethnic and tribal clashes plagued Africa then as they do today. The Biafran issue echoed the Burundi problem. It presaged issues to come such as Rwanda and Darfur, in which external efforts to respond to famine and genocide in an African country faced sensitivities over sovereignty and an inherent opposition to intervention.

In testimony before the Subcommittee on Africa of the House Foreign Affairs Committee on January 27, 1970, Clyde Ferguson explained the African attitude toward intervention:

> I think there are some historical reasons for this. One is, of course, the strong non-African face of the initial humanitarian relief efforts in Nigeria. They were principally from outside, did not come from other African sources; they came from Switzerland, Western Europe, and the United States. There is almost a psychological identification with humanitarians—which is a dirty word, for the most part, in Nigeria because it raises memories of missionaries who came with exactly the same sort of statements: "We are not interested in this, that, or the other; only the humanitarian concern," or "only an interest in saving your soul." They found what followed the missionaries wasn't just limited to that. Consequently the outside intervention which comes into Africa, given the history, is bound to raise these kinds of suspicions.
>
> There are also problems, I think, very personal and very human problems, of dealing with Africans. I sensed this. I sense in many cases very deep resentment about attitudes, about those interventionists who came almost with the assumption that Africans can't handle the problem. "If it is bigger than two people you can't handle it." That assumption, whether stated or not, gets through. There is resentment against it. I was surprised to find on my first visit, both to Biafra and Lagos, that exactly the same kinds of attitudes were expressed about one of the relief organizations, exactly

> the same. I think it is out of this feeling that you get, in the flush of victory, where they have shown they could do it, the feeling is that they had really had to do it themselves. The feeling was everybody else was grudgingly giving for their own purposes and not for the purposes of Nigeria.[63]

When the war ended with a Nigerian victory, I was sent to meet with President Yakubu Gowon of Nigeria to urge him to accept an international committee to oversee relief to the defeated province. Maurice Foley, British parliamentary undersecretary, and I were to approach him in separate meetings. Unfortunately, as we were having breakfast together that morning, we heard over BBC radio that American and British representatives were to meet President Gowon that day to urge him to accept an international commission. Whatever chance we had of success rapidly evaporated.

When I had presented my case to General Gowon, he turned around to the bookshelf behind him, dominated by Bruce Catton's volumes on the American Civil War. "Mr. Newsom," he said, "I have studied your Civil War and your reconstruction and I assure you we will treat Biafra better than you treated the South after your war." And, it turned out he was right.

Another issue, with similar domestic reflections, was that of Southern Rhodesia—the country that ultimately became Zimbabwe. A white minority that never rose above 5 percent ruled over a black majority. Pressures mounted in Africa and within the African constituency in the United States to encourage a move to majority rule. The whites resisted; and, under the leadership of Ian Smith, Rhodesia promulgated a Unilateral Declaration of Independence (UDI) in 1965.

As these steps were unfolding in Africa, a parallel debate was taking place in the United States, a debate every bit as virulent as that over South Africa. When Ian Smith likened the Rhodesian declaration to the struggle of the American colonies, he provided a rhetorical base for conservatives in the United States sympathetic with the white minority government and angry at Britain for its lukewarm support for American policy in Vietnam. Once more, as in the debate over South Africa, the white regime in Rhodesia was seen as the bulwark against communism in Africa. With strong support from conservative members of Congress, particularly Senator S. I. Hayakawa of California, and business interests in Rhodesia, the Smith regime mounted a major campaign in the United States, centered in the office of the Rhodesian Information Service in Washington.

Invariably, when I was speaking to audiences in American cities on African policy, questioners would rise and read from yellow slips provided by the Rhodesian Information Service: "How can we let down our true friends in Africa?" "Do you want to see the communists take over the vital minerals of Southern Africa?" "How is a struggle against the British in Rhodesia any different from our own struggle for independence?" The Nixon White House provided little support for a hard line against Rhodesia. Secretary of State Rogers, on the other hand, took a broader view and ultimately persuaded President Nixon that the United States should close the Consulate in Salisbury, the Rhodesian capital.

But not everyone agreed with the decision to close the Consulate. On October 24, 1970, shortly after the Consulate was closed, the president held a dinner in honor of the twenty-fifth anniversary of the United Nations at which the Emperor of Ethiopia, Haile Selassie, was the guest of honor. National Security Adviser Kissinger, possibly on orders from President Nixon, wanted to keep the program short and discourage speeches. I was asked to dissuade the emperor from speaking. I failed.

The emperor rose to speak after the dinner. After several minutes, Dr. Kissinger passed me his place card on which he had written, "Another five and the Consulate goes back to Salisbury." But, to my relief, the emperor sat down shortly after that and the Consulate remained closed.

We were less successful in maintaining sanctions. Britain had imposed a series of unilateral economic sanctions immediately after UDI. Nine days later, on November 20, 1965, the United Nations Security Council (UNSC) called on all states not to provide arms or oil. The Council followed up in December with bans on the export of copper, chrome, asbestos, and foodstuffs. Rhodesian funds were blocked in major capitals. One year later, when little progress had been made in reversing UDI, the Security Council declared the situation to "constitute a threat to international peace and security," thus making sanctions mandatory. Over the ensuing twelve years, until a settlement on independence was reached in 1980, sanctions were progressively tightened.

The United States supported the sanctions measures, but cast two vetoes in the Security Council: against proposals to cut off postal and telecommunications links and to tighten trade barriers among Rhodesia, South Africa, and Portuguese Mozambique. Both Britain and the United States also opposed Afro-Asian bloc efforts to promote the use of force—except to enforce the sea blockade preventing the supply of oil.

American support for sanctions was unpopular with the many conservative members of Congress who did not like the United Nations in 1970 any more than they did in the first decade of the twenty-first century. Many disagreed with the premises of the UN action and, as in the case of the Congo, contrasted Britain's punishment of anticommunist Rhodesia with its trade with communist Vietnam, China, and Cuba. In 1971, Congress found a way to circumvent U.S. observance of the sanctions in legislation that ultimately became known as the Byrd Amendment.

Originally introduced by Representative James Collins, Democrat of Texas, the law would prevent the United States from prohibiting the import of any strategic and critical material from a Free World country for so long as the importation of like material from a Communist country was not prohibited. What this meant was, if we were not blocking the import of vital materials from the Soviet Union, we could not do so from a Free World country such as Rhodesia. The act was directed primarily at chrome, available in Rhodesia, but also in the Soviet Union.

Through a series of legislative maneuvers in which the proposal was initially rejected by the foreign affairs committees, Senator Harry Byrd, Democrat of Virginia, attached the measure to the Defense Procurement Bill. The bill passed and was signed by President Nixon on November 17, 1971. In the Bureau of African Affairs, we sought to acquaint members of Congress with the implications for the United States in unilaterally ignoring a UNSC action, but we had little support from the Nixon administration.

African issues often became caught up in other legislative battles. The Nixon administration was not enthusiastic about blocking the Byrd Amendment when they needed conservative votes to defeat a measure by Senator Mike Mansfield, Democrat of Montana, to withdraw troops from Vietnam.

Joy greeted the passage of the Byrd Amendment (Section 503 of the Military Procurement Authorization Bill) in the offices of the Rhodesian Information Service, where "The 503 Club Marching Song," a parody to the tune of "O Tannenbaum," was sung. I figured in stanza 4:

> (To be sung with wistful melancholy)
> Oh, 503, oh, 503
> We faced a mighty enemy;
> Oh, 503, oh, 503
> We ran afoul of David Newsom,
> [Senator] Culver and [Congressman] Diggs —an awesome twosome;
> The U.N. fought you mightily
> And Harold Wilson [British Prime Minister] censured thee.
> The State Department thwarted thee.

With the establishment of the black majority government of Zimbabwe under Robert Mugabe on April 17, 1980, the sanctions issue and the Byrd Amendment became moot. Subsequent events in that country raise the question of whether we did the right thing, but in 1970 there were no realistic prospects for continuing white rule.

To further show the interest of the Nixon administration in Africa, Secretary Rogers became the first secretary of state to visit Black Africa, an official visit that was part of a ten-nation tour in 1970.[64] The itinerary included Morocco, Tunisia, Ethiopia, Kenya, Zambia, the Congo (Zaire), Cameroon, Nigeria, Ghana, and Liberia. Jean and I accompanied Secretary and Mrs. Rogers. As might be expected, the emphasis in the visits to North Africa was on the Arab-Israeli issue and in Black Africa on greater pressure on the white-ruled regimes in the South. Emperor Haile Selassie stressed the threats of Soviet influence in the Horn of Africa while President Mobutu in the Congo spoke of the menace of Chinese inroads. All of the African leaders emphasized the need for more economic assistance, "without strings."

In his discussions, the secretary seldom raised questions about internal policies, but the issue occasionally arose. One of the events in the visit to President Mobutu was a trip on his river yacht. Periodically as he sat with Secretary Rogers in the lounge he would get up and go to the railing to wave to passing canoes and other vessels. He explained to the secretary, "We have an election coming up and I am campaigning. But we have no Democrats—only Republicans," he said with a laugh.

The last stop was Monrovia, the capital of Liberia, a must stop for an American official at that time. Settled by former Americans slaves in the nineteenth century it was still ruled by descendents of those slaves. For an older generation of African-Americans it represented a special symbol of American interest in Africa. With its preservation of symbols and customs of a long-departed American South it was looked upon by a younger generation as an anachronism. As the Liberian chief of protocol announced their presence in stentorian tones, President and Mrs. William Tubman and Secretary and Mrs. Rogers entered the banquet room to the music of a slow march played by an orchestra on the balcony above. It was a scene that the secretary liked to recall to visitors when he was asked about his trip to Africa.

Just ten years after Secretary Rogers's visit to Monrovia, a military group composed of indigenous Africans overthrew the regime of the Amero-Africans, and Liberia descended into civil war.

Rogers's tour was generally successful except for incidents in Tunisia and Ethiopia. In Tunis Jean and other women from the party were in a car separated from the convoy when their car was surrounded and threatened by students armed with sticks angry about American policy in the Middle East. In Ethiopia, American Peace Corps volunteers in protest of the U.S. war in Vietnam refused to meet with Secretary Rogers.

In addition to the trip to South Africa and our trip with Bill and Adele Rogers, I made fourteen trips to Africa, visiting all but two of the fifty-two countries on the continent. I did not go to Equatorial

Guinea, where a murderous dictator made relations difficult, or Congo Brazzaville, where our USAID administrator had recently been expelled.

I also expanded our contacts with the eighteen countries of Francophone Africa. The African-American community and many Africanists saw the continent only in terms of English-speaking nations. Our contact with former French colonies had been restricted during the period of Charles de Gaulle, but after his retirement we expanded American activities, including the Peace Corps. We had no real problems except that the French objected when Peace Corps volunteers sought to replace French with the local vernacular as the language of education.

There was a common pattern to most visits: a press conference at the airport, a banquet, a cultural event with African dancing, meetings with officials, and visits to villages. In the villages we frequently had a session with the local administrator in front of a blackboard with statistics on local agricultural production and education.

I experienced a variety of aircraft from Russian helicopters to Piper cubs. One of the more memorable was a flying boxcar (C-124) assigned to the embassy in Kinshasa. Not only was it one of the noisiest that I ever rode, but the roof leaked when it rained. At the Wheelus Air Base in Libya, I traveled often in a C-54 that displayed a plaque showing that it had been the aircraft that in 1945 had taken General Douglas MacArthur to the Japanese surrender on the USS *Missouri*. My favorite aircraft was the reliable DC-3, in which I made several trips around Africa, landing on rough strips carved out of the jungle. In one such trip an elephant stood by as we rolled to a stop.

Whether meeting African leaders and their representatives in Washington or in their own countries, the question of aid invariably arose. In most cases, the emphasis was on aid for economic development. It was my intention to show by these visits the U.S. interest in all these nations; but unfortunately, many of my visits ended by pouring cold water on expectations for American help. Those expectations were high, and not only because of American rhetoric about our interest in the newly independent countries. Knowing something of the history of Europe, every leader had visions of a "Marshall plan for Africa." They were also aware of the more generous policies of the Kennedy administration, including large-scale, long-term commitments made to Ghana and Nigeria. The difficulty of reconciling African hopes with the realities of their governments and Washington's impatience never disappeared.

In the Cold War period, Congress was prepared to consider economic and military assistance to some African nations that provided military facilities, such as Ethiopia. To respond to most African needs, we were forced to rely primarily on international financial institutions, other donors, and modest "self-help" grants. The Peace Corps had a positive impact, but could never be considered part of our official response to African expectations.

The Nixon administration entered office at a time of growing U.S. disenchantment with Africa. As many of the new nations faced problems in implementing programs of economic aid, many in Congress became disillusioned. The early enthusiasm for Africa and assistance to Africa declined. Senator William Fulbright, for example, successfully introduced a measure in 1970 to limit development aid to no more than ten African countries.

In my stewardship of the Bureau of African Affairs, I was at a disadvantage. I was engaged in defending and explaining a complex body of legislation, the Foreign Assistance Act, which had grown voluminously with constant amendments over the years. Given the Congress's ten-country limit on African development assistance (meaning large-scale assistance), all I could discuss with African governments were modest self-help projects, Peace Corps programs, and technical assistance through private-sector organizations such as the International Executive Service Corps. I could also urge them to seek help from United Nations organizations and discuss with other donors the possibility of a group or regional program. I was required to pour buckets of cold water on expectations.

I was enthusiastic about the Peace Corps program in Africa. In 1970, 2,743 Peace Corps volunteers were working in Africa. In each of the countries that I visited I tried to meet with volunteers or visit their projects. While they may not all have been at the top of their skills or professions, they contributed one quality that Africa badly needed—motivation.

In Sierra Leone, for example, O. T. Long, a retired Chicago telephone lineman, discovered some abandoned truck chassis in a junkyard. He demonstrated how the truck chassis could be welded together to form bridges for small streams. In one isolated village that I visited this innovation enabled the village to build a six-kilometer road to link up with a main highway, making it far easier for them to ship their products to market. It seemed a simple thing to do, and I said to a villager, "Your village and the possibility of this road have been here for years. How is it that you have never built such a road before?"

"No one ever told us we could do it," the villager replied.

To make our assistance as effective as possible we had meetings with other aid donors in Africa, including the British, French, Japanese, and Germans. One of the more illuminating meetings was with a delegation from Romania.

I began the meeting by explaining our objectives for helping Africans. In a coffee break the Romanian ambassador to Washington took me aside and said, "My friend, you should understand that in Romania we are not so much interested in helping Africans as in helping Romanians. If a project will not make a profit we are not interested." I thought how ironic it was that this socialist country was more interested in profit than was capitalist America.

Each year Samuel Adams, the USAID assistant administrator for Africa, and I met with the subcommittee reviewing African aid for the House Foreign Affairs Committee. The subcommittee chairman was a Democratic representative from Louisiana, Otto Passman. I often wished that I could play for Africans a tape of a hearing before Congressman Passman to explain attitudes that we faced at home. To do so might have injected some reality into conversations about assistance, but the risk was always there that the hearers might not have believed what they were hearing, and the congressman's harsh comments might have done more harm than good.

Passman led the hearings with his legislative assistant at his side. The assistant handed him a sheaf of papers that contained questions to be posed to the witnesses and answers to be expected. If we did not answer as expected, we were then subject to harsh, if not insulting, comments. The congressman was a nervous man, constantly fidgeting in his chair. One of his staff once commented to me, "Congressman Passman is the only man I know who wears out his jackets from the inside."

The congressman posed quite effectively as an opponent of foreign aid generally. His tactics, however, were generally successful in getting a foreign assistance bill through a reluctant Congress. He would tell the House that he had squeezed every penny out of the spendthrift bureaucrats and that if there was going to be a foreign aid program this was the best he could do.

Transcripts of his hearings show various times at which he went "off the record." Such interruptions gave him a chance to vent his feelings in ways that he would prefer not to have publicly recorded. I can recall one such interruption in which he said, "Foreign aid is the worst disaster that has hit this republic since the war of 1812. Now you, Mr. Secretary, and you, Dr. Adams, don't accept this because both of you have your feet in the public trough." Then he would say, "Strike that from the record."

To give something of the flavor of a Passman hearing I went through the record of the appearances that Sam Adams and I made before Passman in April 1970.

In response to my statement that there is a great need for assistance in Africa, Passman spouted: "I am not asking you about need. I am asking you to answer my questions. There is need for everything. There is need for me to be younger, and a need for me to be healthier. I can point out a lot of needs. I am dealing with the fundamentals of what you ask for and what it is to be used for. I am of the opinion that you are on the minus side, not the plus side of this giveaway outfit. I don't mean to cut you off but I just want my questions answered because there are ten members on this committee and I have 4,000 questions and the others may have that many."

The demands for foreign assistance in the face of the curtailment of domestic projects brought special anger: "You throw away money as though it were chicken feed thrown out to a bunch of hungry chickens. All of these projects in America are being closed down because you can't get a penny for them. Contractors in my district were found to close down projects. Personnel were laid off. If you knew what I knew you would be wanting to shake my hand every 10 seconds [for] being able to operate in such a calm manner when I know what you people are doing to America."

Later, Passman elaborated further on this theme:

> That is a bit frightening when we take into account that in the last fiscal year, and for that matter this fiscal year, we had literally hundreds of projects close down in the United States for lack of funds—crippled children's hospitals, Hill-Burton Funds—we even bankrupted many small contractors in America because of the freeze order in the calendar year 1968.
>
> You remember the freeze order when we set aside literally hundreds of projects all over America but not one foreign aid program was affected by the freeze order. It looks like we have finally reached the point where you bureaucrats are so good with your voluminous information that you can sell the people in the Bureau of the Budget and the Director that foreign projects are more important than domestic projects. I kind of feel a bit ashamed that I have not been more successful in refuting some of the information that has been presented.

On foreign assistance in general, in commenting on a statement by Dr. Adams:

> We have gotten this world in a state of turmoil with this foreign aid program because everybody is trying to get their share. I think we established earlier that you were a church worker. Let me go back to Biblical days, and I could get you 40 or 50 quotes, but here is one in particular. In this day in which the Federal Government is talking of providing a guaranteed income for everyone regardless of whether or not he works, we wonder what the Apostle Paul of Christ's time on earth would have said on this subject. To find out what Paul thought in the day in which he did live we have only to read Second Thessalonians, chapter 3, verses 10 and 11, in which he said, "'For even when we were with you, this we commanded you, that if any would

> not work, neither should he eat, for we hear that there are some which walk among you disorderly, working not at all, but are busybodies." You have had these poor people from time immemorial in every civilization, even back before Christ's time. You are always going to have them. You can't remake and reform the world. What you people are doing is wrecking the economy of America, destroying our world markets, upsetting this intricate trade situation that means so much to our survival, under the pretense that we are straightening everybody's business out.

On another occasion Passman referred to the beginning of the aid program: "This may interest you, and I'm going to say it again for the record because it is good reading. When we first started the AID program it required the older members, well fortified with seniority, to walk down into the well of the House and address the Chair. They said, 'We are now embarking on a program that could conceivably take us into 17 foreign nations of the world, and it may require five years to complete this program, and it could cost as much as $15 billion.' You could have heard a pin drop. The very idea of embarking on a $15 billion, 5-year program just after the expense of that great war.

"Now contrast that, if you will, not to 5 years, but to 24 years and it is bigger than ever. Not 17 nations, but 123 nations of the world. Not $15 billion, but approaching $200 billion. We do not know where our friends are. The countries we have helped most are running us out the fastest."

He was not beyond taking a swipe at his congressional colleagues: "We have got a lot of smart men in the Congress. Some of them have so many diplomas they can't find a place on the wall to hang them but they don't know anything about business. They just haven't studied economics. That was not what they specialized in. We have gotten ourselves into an awful mess by giving away what we would normally sell."

The following exchange illustrates the congressman's attitude toward the World Bank:

> *Mr. Passman*: I note the World Bank leads the East African consultative group in arriving at the amount of assistance that your area needs, is that correct?
>
> *Mr. Adams:* That is correct.
>
> *Mr. Passman:* Who is President of the World Bank?
>
> *Mr. Adams:* Mr. McNamara.
>
> *Mr. Passman:* I think I have heard of that fellow before. He used to be at the Pentagon, did he not?
>
> *Mr. Newsom*: That is right, Mr. Chairman, yes.
>
> *Mr. Adams*: The World Bank itself, sir, contributes $135 million—
>
> *Mr. Passman:* The World Bank does not contribute a dime. The people through the taxpayers permit the World Bank to make the distribution for them. The World Bank does not have any money until it first gets it from the taxpayers. . . .

Passman was not sympathetic to emergencies. I told him a severe emergency existed in Nigeria (right after the Civil War).

His comment: "You will have another one this year somewhere. Don't let that excite you. You will always have emergencies. We had emergencies before we ever got into this mess."

Passman resented what he considered a diminished role of the Congress: "Let me say this, gentlemen. I do not know what you people are going to get by with. This Congress has abdicated to the executive. They run the show. It is a matter of formality to be in Congress. We do not have any more authority than your cook."

Passman showed his dislike of "temporary" agencies when Adams responded to a question about funds for a 1971 operation. When Adams replied, "This is only for the transitional period," Passman fumed, "That is all I want to know. Sometimes this transitional period lasts 10 years in some of these agencies. The most permanent thing in government is a temporary bureau or agency. You know that, don't you?"

Adams responded "I couldn't say, sir."

Passman's riposte: "We still have one outfit preserving saddles and bridles from the Civil War. That was concluded 105 years ago. It is a full-time job maintaining a warehouse containing saddles and bridles. They refuse to give it up. You understand that, don't you?"

In my four years as assistant secretary I appeared as a witness before congressional committees fifteen times. I always found them to be a stimulating experience and, at that time, relatively free of partisan rancor.

I was fortunate in the Senate that Hubert Humphrey chaired the subcommittee on Africa. I had known him from our meeting in Norway and frequently met with him to brief him on African issues. On one occasion there was a serious drought in the Sahel region in the southern part of the Sahara. I could not awaken much interest in the Nixon administration to this impending disaster. I mentioned the problem at one of my meetings with Senator Humphrey, and he asked whether I would like him to hold hearings. I said that this was a matter for him to decide. He did hold hearings and alerted the executive to the problem. The United States proceeded to organize a multilateral famine relief program. Jean participated in organizing a benefit ball for Sahelian relief, which President and Mrs. Nixon attended.

Four of my congressional appearances were before the House Subcommittee on Africa, headed by Representative Charles Diggs (Democrat of Michigan). Although he left Congress under something of a cloud I had great respect for Diggs. An African American, he demonstrated as much as any American an early interest in African affairs and became a genuine expert on the continent. When I left the position of assistant secretary, I was proud to receive a certificate of appreciation from the subcommittee, signed by Congressman Diggs. This certificate read in part (referring to me):

> It was his leadership that resulted in the following positive actions by the United States with respect to its African policies: The 1970 visit of Secretary of State Rogers to the African continent, the first time that a Secretary had visited Africa while in office; recognition of the urgency for relief and rehabilitation in the ravaged Sahelian African area; resumption of diplomatic relations with the Sudan and Mauritania, which had been severed during the 1967 Middle East War;

> the closing of the U.S. Consulate in Southern Rhodesia; the welcoming of much of the Lusaka Manifesto; publication of a Department of State document recommending fair "Employment Practices of United States Firms in South Africa"; the acceptance of the conclusions of the International Court of Justice's advisory opinion on the "Legal Consequences for States of the Continued Presence of South Africa and Namibia..." and Government action informing American firms it would not protect investments or rights against claims of any future lawful government in Namibia; the first assignment to the U.S. Embassy at Pretoria of a Black American Foreign Service Officer; program emphasis on the majority-ruled states of southern Africa: Botswana, Lesotho, Swaziland; and educating and encouraging the American business community to expand its interests and potential in Black Africa.

I was also a participant in the Anglo-American Parliamentary Conference on Africa, organized by the Carnegie Endowment for International Peace. It brought together legislators from the United States, Britain, and Canada at several annual conferences and was instrumental in awakening interest in the African continent in the legislatures of these countries. It was symptomatic of the approach at the time, however, that although African Americans were present, no Africans from the continent were invited.

Colonialism has probably left a greater mark on Africa than on any other part of the world.[65] Artificial boundaries created in European conferences laid seeds for future conflicts. In tribal societies, tribes favored under colonial rule bred resentments that overflowed when colonial restrictions were lifted.

Each of the colonial powers left its own distinct stamp. A Sudanese once said to me after attending his first all-African conference, "I felt at a disadvantage when in the presence of francophone representatives. The British trained us as administrators. The French educated their Africans as poets."

A Malagasy ambassador in Washington used to tell me about the brutality of the French in Madagascar, in particular about his brother's murder in a massacre by French troops. Referring to his experience with the French, I once asked him why it was that, whenever he had a few free days, he went to Paris.

His answer was, "I hate the French, but I love France." He then went on to explain that France had made it possible for any graduate of a lycée in Madagascar to apply to a university in France. "When I was in France," he said, "there were 5,000 African students in French universities. I went to visit a friend in Cambridge, England; there were 25 African students, all sons of chiefs."

The British, in choosing colonial officials, chose administrators who saw their task as maintaining law and order. They tended to create universities in Africa, rather than bringing Africans to British universities. French colonial officials saw their role as maintaining the influence of France, including the French language. When we introduced Peace Corps volunteers into francophone countries, we faced protests from Paris when they began to encourage African students to study in African languages.

Similar problems did not arise in Portuguese and Belgian territories, where little encouragement was given to the education of the African populations. Neither the Portuguese nor the Belgians contemplated giving up their African colonies.

When the Portuguese governor of Angola addressed the National War College group in 1960, he said, "We have been in Angola for 500 years and by God's grace we will be here another 500." That was just fourteen years before a military coup in Lisbon led to independence for Portugal's African territories.

In my time as assistant secretary, many Africans raised with me the question of the Portuguese colonies. There were pressures in the United States to recognize or speak with representatives of the liberation movements in these territories, as had been done in the Kennedy administration. Political pressures were muted, however, because of the vital role that the Azores bases played in permitting the United States to resupply Israel in the 1973 Arab-Israeli War. It was only later in the 1970s, when Cuban troops supported factions in Angola after the revolution in Lisbon, that the United States became actively involved in the affairs of Angola.[65]

In my determination to demonstrate American interest in all the African countries, I met most of their leaders. They were a varied group that included poets, visionaries, dictators, and tyrants. Too often, as in the case of Ahmed Sekou Touré of Guinea, charismatic leaders of independence movements developed into megalomaniacs, intoxicated with power and paranoid in their fear of opposition.

Sekou Touré had become prominent for defying Charles de Gaulle's plan for a French community in Africa. The French in retaliation pulled all their experts out of Guinea and stripped the infrastructure. Touré held an iron grip on Guinea. For some reason, in his paranoid fear of opposition, his suspicions focused on those he sent as ambassadors to the United States. None of those who returned to Conakry from Washington in my time was ever heard from again. I still have in my files a heartrending letter from the French wife of Fadhialla Keita, Guinean ambassador to Washington in the early 1970s, asking whether I could learn about the fate of her husband.

I made one visit to Guinea in which Sekou Touré took me, together with a German Socialist leader, on a trip from Conakry to his compound in Labe in the mountains. As we rode through various villages, crowds lined the streets to cheer the president. The cheering was less impressive when we learned of the coercion behind the crowds.

On the way to Labe, Sekou Touré said to me, without mentioning a name, "You will be having dinner with a fellow countryman tonight." The fellow countryman was Stokely Carmichael, a radical civil rights leader who had come to live in Guinea. Also at that evening's function was Miriam Makeba, prominent South African singer, who shared one of the rondola cabins with the president that night.

Another African leader with grandiose ambitions was Jean Bedelle Bokassa of the Central African Republic. He had been a sergeant in the French army in Vietnam and had taken power in a military coup in 1966. I visited the CAR capital, Bangui, in April 1971. Because of the somewhat unusual character of the visit I will quote from my notes:

> The president [Bokassa] had decided he would meet me up in his lodge at a national park in the northern part of the

country. I was to take off at 10 a.m. in a DC-4 for the hour and a half flight to Ndele.

1000: Arrived airport. Great uncertainty prevailed. No mechanic for aircraft. Waited one hour and a half. Frenchman raced up in Citroen—mechanic.

1130 Finally took off. Protocol man showed me to a settee with no seat belts; I persuaded him to let me sit in regular seat; . . . beer and champagne served alternately en route. Surprise expressed that we did not drink whiskey in morning.

1300: Arrived Ndele. Sat under thatched porch with local officials waiting for loading of Russian helicopter to take us to President's lodge. Dancers and drummers. Casualness about loading until I suggested the Ministers and President might be waiting for us and we [were] already late. Had feeling we could have sat all day.

1345: Take off in Russian helicopter; Russian pilots. Most comfortable helicopter I have ridden, including our President's. . . . Landed in bush. Bokassa met at camp which consisted of round concrete huts with thatched roof. Bokassa flanked by four women, one very attractive. I wondered what gave until they [were] introduced as his wife, sister, cousin, and wife of Minister. My hut had large bed with mosquito net; curtains with Bokassa's picture, large tub, water, icebox (kerosene) with Evian water, whiskey, Beaujolais, Lime juice. Bokassa hut had porch, no sign of any ventilation. Sat uncertainly for another hour, offered whiskey, took beer.

1500: Sat at table under thatched enclosure. Ate for two hours: hors d'oeuvres; fish, fish stew, manioc, wild pig, duck (with heads), small goat, chicken and rice, cheese, fruit.

1700: Nap time. Hotternhell in concrete hut. Slept an hour.

1900: Played card game with Ministers. Turned out to be crazy eights with variations. Wild game under stars. Will teach new rules to children on return.

2030: Supper: Fish soup, fish, steak, cheese, fruit, wine. Camp had generator for lights, but lights would not turn off.

Consequently flying ants and other insects attracted from as far away as Fort Lamy, forming curtain in and around huts. Largest insects were crickets (6 inches across, without exaggeration) in toilet hut. Somewhat disconcerting—if not constipating.

0530: Arose to accompany President on trip through game preserve. Saw lots of antelope, gazelle and birds. Elephant spoor but no elephant.

0830: Breakfast—in reverse. Waited until we finished coffee and toast before serving omelette, then fruit.

0900: Private "*entretien*" in my hut with President.

1000: Took off in Russian helicopter. Forced landing when bird flew into one engine. Arrived at Ndele, no plane to pick us up. Great uncertainty about what to do. No communications. No willingness to take initiative.

1300: Plane arrived. Delayed because at last minute President decided [to] buy two refrigerators and have them shipped in plane—not realizing difficulty of loading them. Refrigerators arrived. Dicey unloading. French pilots sat by drinking whiskey, preparing for return trip. Took off finally; arrived safely. *El Hamduilillah Salaama* [Thanks to God for your safe arrival].

0700: departure. Motorcyclists late. Departure delayed. Guard dancing girls.

That evening my aide, Tom Burke, and I were entertained at a dinner. Outside the dining room was a table laden with gifts. It looked something like the prize display at an Elks Club ball. In front of the display were seven square black cards—each with a circle of diamonds. It was explained that "one was for Mr. Burke, two were for me, and four were for President Nixon."

When we returned to Washington I notified the State Department protocol office of the diamond gift, which they valued at $7,500. I suggested that the diamonds be sold and a contribution made to an African scholarship fund, but the complicated rules of the U.S. Treasury made this impossible.

In a grandiose event, undoubtedly with a far greater display of diamonds, Bokassa in 1976 declared himself emperor and changed the name of the country to the Central African Empire. It remained that way until 1979, when Bokassa was deposed and went into exile and the name reverted to Central African Republic.

In a visit to Madagascar in 1970, representing the United States at the 10th anniversary of Malagasy independence, I had a glimpse of how the French held their empire together. Representing France at the ceremony was Jacques Foccart, de Gaulle's "Africa man." He kept the French colonies in line and arranged for the wealthier ones to funnel contributions into de Gaulle's political campaigns. I stood beside him in a receiving line at one of the receptions in Tannanarive. As each African official approached, Foccart knew his name and asked with knowledgeable detail about members of his family. He was either very well briefed or had a remarkable memory. If he displayed this personal attention to each one of the eighteen French colonies in Africa, he was one of the reasons for the loyalty of these colonies to France.

Paranoid tyrants were not unique to Francophone Africa. Idi Amin, whose towering figure dominated Uganda from 1971 to 1979 and fascinated Africans by his humiliation of Britons, wrote a series of letters to President Nixon critical of the American policy in Vietnam. On a trip to Africa that I made in April 1971, the White House asked me to see Amin and turn off the flow of letters. My meeting with him revealed a man somewhat detached from reality. I said that President Nixon appreciated his views but that he was a busy man and had asked me to convey to him any further thoughts that the general might have. Amin responded: "You tell President Nixon that he cannot send his bombers from Hanoi to bomb Kampala." I assured the President for Life of Uganda that President Nixon had no such intention.[66]

There were few true democrats in Africa, but there were men of vision and stature. I visited some of them. Jomo Kenyatta of Kenya and Kenneth Kaunda of Zambia were two. Julius Nyerere, despite criticism of his dreams of a socialist society, brought Tanzania peacefully to nationhood.

Leopold Senghor, a respected poet and intellectual, led Senegal to a peaceful change of power. A letter from Dakar on March 16, 1972, reports on my visit to President Senghor:

Today we spent accompanying President Senghor to celebrate the 100th anniversary of the city of St. Louis [Senegal] as a commune. St. Louis was founded originally by the French in 1650, changed hands several times over the next two centuries, and was the first French capital of Senegal. Most of it was built (on an island) in the late 17th century and it has something of the flavor of New Orleans. It was an active trading and slaving post in the 18th century. Some of the entourage of the French royal family escaped to St. Louis after the revolution.

We flew in the President's Caravelle to St. Louis. Then he had me ride with him, standing in his open Mercedes, through the crowds of St. Louis. It reminded me of my adventure in Guinea, although here the crowds were more spontaneous and less conspicuously organized. We then got down [from the car] at the old City Hall, where we were greeted by the mayor and I was given the Key to the City. After that, we visited a museum devoted to the development of the Senegal River Basin, and then adjourned to lunch at the old Governor's Palace. Following lunch, they gave us each a bedroom in the palace for a siesta! How about that for an addition to the program. I took advantage of it too.

The last event of the afternoon was a pirogue (canoe) race, a marvelously disorganized African event. The boats started off while the announcer was still welcoming the dignitaries. Each of the three boats was named for the wife, respectively, of the President, the Prime Minister and the President of the National Assembly. The boat named after Madame Senghor had the largest number of rowers in it and, of course, won. The race was given added excitement by dozens of boys in little pirogues (really only dug-out logs) who were paddling in and out across the course while the race was in progress.

After Senegal I visited the Gambia, the narrow, former British colony that lies along the banks of the Gambia River. In my visit to Prime Minister Sir Dawda Jawara, I was treated to a comment on progress in Africa. At the mouth of the Gambia River is one of the most beautiful beaches ever seen. A Swedish firm has built a hotel on this site and buxom Swedish tourists clad in very little could be observed. When I mentioned this observation to the prime minister he said, "Oh yes. But things have changed. The Europeans used to come down to stare at the naked Africans. Now the Africans come to stare at the naked Europeans."

I left the Africa bureau with a sense of accomplishment, although I did not achieve all that I would have liked to in terms of bringing change to the continent. We were able to maintain some balance in the Nixon administration, even though we made no major inroads in the apartheid system. Ironically, it remained for another Republican administration, that of Ronald Reagan, to adopt sanctions against South Africa, a move taken, like so many, for domestic political reasons. It remained for another of my successors, Chester Crocker, through a remarkable feat of diplomacy, to bring a measure of peace to southern Africa.[67]

In November 1973, I received a singular honor when I was invited to speak to the annual conference of the African Studies Association, a gathering of scholars traditionally critical of U.S. foreign policy in Africa. My speech was not as noteworthy as the introduction in the association's quarterly journal *Issue*:

> This is the first time in its sixteen-year history that the African Studies Association has been privileged to welcome an Assistant Secretary of State for African Affairs as a principal speaker at its Annual Meeting. Members of this association who follow African affairs in Washington ought to know why this welcome is made with particular enthusiasm and goodwill.
>
> Prior to his assumption of office as Assistant Secretary of State in 1969, David Newsom had specialized in North African and Middle Eastern affairs. It was widely and realistically thought that apart from the Middle Eastern problem, Africa would be consigned by the Republican administration to the region of low priority in official thinking. Some feared for the morale of dedicated Africanists in the Department of State; others doubted that African

> values would make any impression at all upon bureaucratic politics.
>
> These doubts and fears have long since been laid to rest by knowledgeable persons. Whatever may be said about the priority given to African questions in American foreign relations, there is no dispute about the competence and real distinction with which the Africa Bureau has been managed by Mr. Newsom. He has truly earned the admiration and respect of the Africanist community in this country and abroad for his forthright exposition of American policies and his advocacy, often but not always in vain, of proper regard for African values in American diplomatic thinking, [and for] his strong stand against the unfortunate Byrd Amendment. His papers and addresses will prove to be a valuable source of information for students of African-American relations during the Nixon era.[68]

Foreign Service officers serving in the State Department often have additional duties. During my time as assistant secretary I also served as president of the American Foreign Service Protective Association, the Foreign Service's health insurance organization. In addition, I was appointed to a task force to examine the role of spouses, male and female, in embassies overseas.

Traditionally, Foreign Service spouses were expected to assist the ambassador on social occasions and in other official activities. A spouse's activity was noted in the officer's performance report. With the cultural changes affecting the generation of the 1960s, this unpaid obligation was no longer acceptable to many in the Foreign Service. The task force appointed by Under Secretary William Macomber was asked to examine the issue and make recommendations.

We found that the demands some ambassadors were making on spouses of other officers were indeed unreasonable. In one case we had a letter from a young wife telling how the ambassador's wife at that post had demanded that she pack her (the ambassador's wife's) china and informed her that any broken china would be recorded on her husband's performance report.

We subsequently issued a report recommending that, in the future, Foreign Service spouses be treated as individuals in their own right and not be subject either to performance reports or orders from an ambassador. The recommendations were adopted as departmental policy.

I had the good fortune in November 1973 to accompany Henry Kissinger on his first trip abroad as secretary of state. He was visiting three countries in my former area of responsibility, North Africa. On the plane en route to Morocco, he asked me whether I wished to remain as assistant secretary for Africa or be assigned overseas. I replied that I had enjoyed the African assignment but was ready for a change.

He asked, "What about Indonesia?" I was intrigued—a new area, but, as a Muslim country with oil, not totally unrelated to my experience to date. So, Indonesia it was, and for the next five years I was involved in diplomacy in Asia.

21. During a visit to Jakarta, circa 1976, former governor and assistant secretary of state G. Mennen Williams meets with President Suharto of Indonesia and U.S. Ambassador to Indonesia Newsom.

22. David and Jean in the beautiful garden of the Embassy Residence in Jakarta. They enjoyed all their posts, but there was something special about Indonesia.

23. The ambassador attends the christening ceremony of the KRI *Martadinata,* with Indonesian naval officers and wives, May 1974.

24. The ambassador enjoys a ride in a pedicab in one of Indonesia's outer islands.

25. The new U.S. ambassador to the Republic of the Philippines, surrounded by family and friends, signs his credentials at a ceremony in the Benjamin Franklin Room on October 26, 1977. (From left) Katie Newsom, Aunt Agnes Walter, Jean, Mrs. Gregorio Abad (wife of the Philippine ambassador), and Under Secretary for Political Affairs Philip C. Habib.

26. Following the presentation of credentials at Malacañang Palace in Manila, David and Jean join President Marcos for a celebratory toast, November 11, 1977.

27. President Morarji Desai of India welcomes Under Secretary Newsom at a meeting in New Delhi, July 15, 1978.

28. President and Mrs. Anwar Sadat greet David at an Egyptian Embassy reception, circa 1978.

29. President Carter greets the under secretary at the White House, October 1977.

30. Secretary of State Edmund S. Muskie and former secretary Cyrus R. Vance, with their under secretary between them. Senator Muskie had just become secretary following Vance's resignation, May 1980.

31. The staff of the Under Secretary of State for Political Affairs (P) posing for a farewell photo. (Back row, from left) Anne Norris, Roscoe Suddarth, Mildred Patterson, Secretary Muskie, Geneil Maska, David Newsom, Helen Coleman; (front) Arvid Minott, Felix Vargas, Richard Baker, February 6, 1981. Not shown, Richard Jackson and Clara Galford.

32. Outgoing Secretary of State *ad interim* Newsom with President Ronald Reagan at the White House, January 1981.

33. Institute for the Study of Diplomacy Director Newsom with noted international economic consultant Robert R. Nathan, who spoke at ISD's 10th anniversary symposium, "As Others See Us: United States Diplomacy Viewed from Abroad," in November 1988.

34. Participants and guests at an ISD symposium on *The Modern Ambassador,* October 1983, Georgetown University. (From left, standing) Director Newsom, Judge Laurence J. Silberman; (seated) Amb. Charles S. Whitehouse, Dr. Elisabeth K. Herz, Professor Madeleine Albright, ISD Chairman Ellsworth Bunker; (behind Dr. Albright) Amb. Carol Laise and Amb. George C. McGhee.

35. Sharing a light moment with Senate Foreign Relations Committee Chairman Joseph R. Biden.

36. At Georgetown with Robert Gallucci (center), dean of the university's School of Foreign Service, and journalist Charles Bartlett, founding member of the Edward J. Weintal Awards committee.

37. At the March 26, 2003, meeting of former under secretaries of state for political affairs with Secretary of State Colin Powell. (L to r.) Marc Grossman, David Newsom, historian Stuart Kennedy, Joseph Sisco, Robert Kimmett, and Secretary Powell.

38. All seven Newsoms celebrate David's 90th birthday on January 9, 2008, in Charlottesville, Virginia. Standing behind David and Jean (from left) are John, Dan, Katie, Nancy, and David.

15

HALFWAY BETWEEN BEIRUT AND WELLINGTON

When I learned of our appointment to Indonesia, I said to Jean, "Not only is Indonesia a fascinating country, but we can hop down to Sydney, Australia for a weekend." Then I learned about distances in Southeast Asia. At that time, the flight from Jakarta to Sydney took seven hours by jet. Later, the New Zealand ambassador in Jakarta told me that Jakarta is halfway between Wellington, New Zealand, and Beirut.

With its 13,000 islands, Indonesia stretches for 3,000 miles across the South Pacific. It is a land of vast distances, variety, mysticism, and contradictions.

I arrived in Jakarta, the capital of Indonesia, in February 1973. Jean, who stayed behind to place our two girls in boarding school, arrived in April with our youngest son, David.

On February 24 I presented my credentials to President Suharto in the stately presidential palace on Merdeka (Freedom) Square in Jakarta. The scheduling of the ceremony was pushed forward so that I could be fully established before the arrival of our first official visitor, Deputy Secretary of State Kenneth Rush.

For four years I was to sit often with Suharto in that presidential suite, sometimes with only the interpreter between us, and frequently with visitors. On rare occasions, Suharto would receive me in his modest home in the center of the city. I found him a courteous but somewhat remote figure. Speaking always through an interpreter, he never seemed totally comfortable with foreign visitors. I encouraged visitors to state their business promptly to deter a forty-minute lecture on "national resilience," Suharto's favorite topic.

Indonesian friends described him as being in the long tradition of Javanese royalty— in effect, he saw himself as king.

I had looked forward very much to Jakarta as a post, recalling still my brief visit to the Netherlands East Indies in 1940. I benefited very much from the legacy of relationships with the embassy left behind by my predecessor and his wife, Frank and Martha Galbraith. Their advice was incorporated in a lengthy memorandum that reflected their own affection for the post and its people.

I did have to curb my curiosity about some of the places I had visited in 1940. When I asked one of our embassy officers to locate the hotel where I stayed in what was then Batavia, he said "Mr. Ambassador, no one in Jakarta today would understand what the American ambassador was doing in that hotel."

Indonesia, although different in many ways from the Arab world, had elements with which I was familiar: Islam and petroleum. Although 90 percent of Indonesia's population professed Islam, the society was in many ways different from the Arab world. Because the Indonesians had fought for their independence and had, under President Sukarno, made a sharp break with their Dutch past, the imperial experience was not as close to the surface. Unlike some postcolonial peoples, Indonesians were confident of their identity. They showed a remarkable capacity to face up to and resolve their own problems.

As Muslims, they resented the Israeli presence in Jerusalem, but rational discussions of the Israeli-Palestinian issue were possible. And the United States was not automatically blamed for all the nation's ills.

Official relations were on the whole good, although there had been difficult periods in the past. The United States had supported Indonesian independence in 1945, and a prominent American, Ellsworth Bunker, had helped mediate the last colonial dispute with the Dutch, involving West New Guinea (Irian Jaya). Washington, however, found it difficult to accept some of the policies of Sukarno, the first president. At one point in the 1950s, the United States considered supporting rebels in Sumatra against the Jakarta government.[69]

The presence of private Americans in Indonesia went far back in the history of both countries. This is well documented in James Gould's book *Americans in Sumatra*.[70] At the turn of the nineteenth century, Thomas Horsfield, an American medical doctor from Bethlehem, Pennsylvania, worked as a biologist with Sir Stamford Raffles, the British governor of Java, in the creation of Raffles's seminal work on the islands' flora and fauna. In 1834 two Methodist missionaries, Samuel Munson and Harry Lynn, who sought to work among the Bataks in Sumatra, became martyrs.[71]

Extensive trade in spices developed in the early nineteenth century. In 1883, while working for a Dutch company, American geologists from the newly developed oil fields of Pennsylvania discovered the first oil in Indonesia. In a strange footnote to history, in 1873 the Sultan of Aceh in northern Sumatra appealed to the United States for aid in repulsing the invading Dutch. The American consul in Singapore was reprimanded by the secretary of state for even receiving the request.

The United States in 1973 had a prominent role in the Dutch-led Intergovernmental Group on Indonesia (IGGI), which coordinated international development assistance. American-educated Indonesian economists were leaders in the nation's development.

American interests, both official and private, were substantial. Next to Japan, the United States was Indonesia's largest trading partner. U.S. investments in tin, palm oil, rubber, and minerals are extensive. Approximately 30 percent of Indonesia's oil production went to Southern California, and when I was in Jakarta plans were being made to bring liquefied natural gas to the Pacific coast.

Within the limits of its traditional nonalignment, Indonesia regarded the United States as the major benign nonregional power and wanted to see it remain as a balance to the influence of the Soviet Union. It nevertheless wanted to avoid formal security ties with Washington and was unlikely to grant any military facilities. It saw its security safeguarded by the Association of Southeast Asian Nations (ASEAN). As the fourth most populous country in the world, Indonesia's significance on the world scene was growing. In the 1960s, a group of developing countries led by Algeria had introduced the New International Economic Order, a series of demands on developed countries relating to trade, aid, and finance. Indonesia, as one of the more moderate voices in the group, became the principal negotiator with the developed countries in what came to be known as the North-South Dialogue.

Jakarta would turn out to be a busy post with a great variety of responsibilities. Here is a description of one of my early days in a letter I wrote to Jean in March 1974 before her own arrival in Jakarta: "On Thursday, a meeting at 8:15 with a group of executives from Pacific Lighting on their natural gas project and its problems. At 9, a two-hour meeting with the Minister of Planning on our revised aid program. At 11, a meeting with the officers and board of directors of the American Women's Club. At 12 a meeting with the executives of ITT on their satellite ground station project. At one, I gave a lunch for our regional treasury attaché down from Hong Kong. At three, presented the Legion of Merit to the last Indonesian military attaché in Washington. (A ceremony arranged by the military; white uniforms; formality; champagne—no kisses on cheeks.) At four, an hour reviewing the military assistance program. Home in time to get ready for *Kiss Me Kate,* the big show at the Joint Embassy School."

I had arrived in Jakarta as the United States was seeking a peace agreement and reducing its presence in Vietnam. The Indonesians were members of the four-party International Commission of Control and Supervision (ICCS) and maintained diplomatic relations with Hanoi. They did not consider themselves, as some did in Washington, one of the vulnerable "dominoes" in Southeast Asia. I recall one American businessman who came to see me during this period and asked how many months I thought he had to wind up his interests before Indonesia went communist.

In January 1975 shortly before the collapse of the U.S. and South Vietnamese forces, Graham Martin, the last American ambassador to Saigon, visited Jakarta and met with Indonesian officials. He assured them that things were going well for the Americans and that the Indonesians should not listen to "the little old ladies in Dubuque" who were demanding an American pullout. The Indonesians who had heard this took me aside afterward and commented, "What Ambassador Martin said was very interesting, but he must come from a different country than we were in." General George Brown, chairman of the Joint Chiefs of Staff, visited Jakarta shortly thereafter with a more realistic assessment.

Indonesians frequently complained that Washington did not pay sufficient attention to this significant Asian country. I was once in a group in Washington that included some Indonesian visitors and the Indonesian ambassador to the United States. The visiting Indonesians were complaining about the lack of attention being paid to their country. The ambassador, more familiar with congressional inquiries into the internal affairs of other countries, commented "You should be happy with that lack of attention."

When a diplomat goes to a new post, there is always a period of discovery. Reading books and reports and the advance briefings are valuable, but they can never convey the full picture of a new environment. It is as if one faces several curtains that must be pulled back one by one and, however long one stays, one always feels there are several more curtains to pull. Learning about a new country is a continuous process.

Particularly in a large post, an ambassador must make a special effort to reach out and get the insights of more junior personnel. Many of them, especially if they have a language facility, are in touch with elements of the country difficult for more senior officers to reach.

To try to resolve this problem in Jakarta, I held periodic seminars in which more junior officers from the various agencies made presentations. In addition to those from the Department of State, the embassy had representatives from five other U.S. government agencies, including the Library of Congress. I hoped to move away from the tendency of senior agency representatives to predetermine what their subordinates said. I was generally but not totally successful in this effort. Bureaucracies can at times closely resemble totalitarian states.

As part of my continuing efforts to understand the country, I tried to visit each one of the twenty-six provinces. Only one, East Timor, was out of bounds at that time for political reasons. Visits to provinces followed a certain pattern. I was usually accompanied by an Indonesian official who was following a program set down by the governor of the province. The escort clearly had little flexibility. If I suggested that instead of visiting one more factory, we visit a high school, the escort was clearly troubled. Any change required his going back to the governor and indicating that His Excellency, the Ambassador, was unhappy with the program as originally scheduled. We learned to follow the program as it was set forth and printed, even if at times we felt like a high-level political prisoner.

Even sightseeing opportunities were limited. We were taken by a motorboat up a river in Kalimantan, looking forward to a leisurely cruise that might give us a chance to see wildlife in the jungle. The driver of the motorboat, clearly wanting to show off his skill to visitors, drove at such a speed that every living thing was frightened away. But we were able to visit a center where a German anthropologist, Birute Galdikas, was rehabilitating orangutans whose mothers had been killed by poachers. As one walked through the jungle, it was not unusual to suddenly find one of the creatures in your arms, having just jumped down from the trees.

Provincial visits required calls on the two centers of power—the civilian governor and the military commander. At each visit we were presented plaques commemorating the event. We can now cover two walls with such plaques.

Visits involved meals—usually from a buffet table where the food, cooked early in the morning, was set out for the day. Breakfasts, with chocolate sprinkles and Cheez Whiz on the table, were one of the few reminders of the Dutch colonial presence. Other hospitality was not lacking. In one guesthouse, two bottles of scotch were side-by-side on the bedside table.

Visits by American officials provided further opportunities to learn about the country. The island of Bali was a favorite destination. This island, with its colorful Hindu culture, is without doubt worth a visit. In four years I made the 800-mile round trip to Bali's capital, Denpasar, eleven times. Many of these were for congressional visitors; we sometimes had the feeling that members or their staffs, doing the usual circuit from Japan to Australia, looked at the map and discovered Bali was on the way. "Why not drop down and see Bali?"

Some such visits were instructive. I accompanied Secretary of Agriculture Earl Butz on a visit to a rice farm in the hills of Bali. Balinese officials brought out records to show that rice had consistently been grown on the terraces of this farm since 900 AD.

Vice President Nelson Rockefeller came on what he hoped would be a private visit. He wanted to rent a minibus in Bali to take his new wife, Happy, to show where he had taken his first wife on their honeymoon. It took considerable diplomatic skill for my deputy chief of mission, Mike Rives, to persuade him that a sitting vice president of the United States could not come to a foreign country without meeting officials of that country. Foreign Minister Adam Malik graciously made a special trip from Jakarta to meet with Rockefeller.

Some visitors were entertaining. I quote from a letter written August 31, 1976:

> The next morning the Defense Attaché plane picked me up and took me to Bali to lunch with Mrs. [Clare Boothe] Luce. Although her eyesight is not good, she is still sharp and alert. This was her first visit to Indonesia and, poor lady, she spent the first week in Bali in bed with the flu. I briefed her briefly on Indonesia, but it was clear that she felt she had more fascinating things to say than I—and she did. Her conversation ranged over Carter ("no one-time governor of Georgia has the experience to be president"); Ford ("a really decent fellow who might just make it"); Kissinger ("I introduced him to Nixon; biggest mistake I ever made"); détente ("I was the one who suggested to the president that he stop using that word; no American really knows what it means"); Kennedy assassination ("there is strong evidence that it was a Castro plot").

Bali continued to be a popular tourist destination. Most Americans came and went without the attention of the American embassy. Two schoolteachers from a small town in the Middle West were exceptions. Kuta beach in Bali was popular with mostly Australian visitors, a number of whom swam in the nude. The governor of Bali tolerated this, believing such freedom was good for tourism. One day, however, the Minister of Religious Affairs from Jakarta visited Bali and observed the Australian practice. He ordered the federal police to raid the beach and a number of the offending bathers, including the two Americans, were jailed.

The embassy in Jakarta received a somewhat anguished call from the consular agent in Bali. The schoolteachers were pleading for our help in getting them released since they were due back in their classrooms very shortly. I raised the issue with the Indonesian Minister of Justice, Mochtar Kusumaatmadja. He said he hoped I would realize that this was a delicate issue since I was requesting him to override the authority of the governor of Bali. I said I appreciated that, but I felt that he, a graduate of both the Yale and Harvard Law schools, could find a way. He did, and two chastened and fully clad Middle West schoolteachers returned to their classrooms.

Another visitor—this time in Jakarta—demonstrated the sophistication of the street peddlers. Ancient Chinese tombs on the islands had revealed a treasure trove of antique Chinese porcelain, and many were being sold by itinerant merchants. When G. Mennen Williams, former governor of Michigan who had been my boss as assistant secretary for African affairs, visited Jakarta, he asked to see these peddlers' wares. We invited a few to lay out their inventory on the lawn of the residence. Governor Williams pointed to one piece and offered a modest price. The peddler, obviously offended, pulled a catalog from his bag and said, "Sir, Sotheby's is offering $600 for a similar piece."

I was told that Indonesians desired to avoid confrontation, but this puzzled me. The most popular cultural event, a shadow puppet play—the *wayang*—based on a Hindu epic, lasts from nine at night until five in the morning and ends with a great clash between good and evil. I asked an Indonesian friend whether the battle did not contradict their desire to avoid confrontation. He replied, "Oh, no. Remember, it takes us all night to get there."

I learned that in Indonesia, as in Norway, the supernatural was just below the surface. An Indonesian friend told me that the most significant *wayang* presentation occurs in Jogjakarta in Central Java and involves a puppet representing evil. At the conclusion of the play the puppet is carried to the beach and tossed into the surf. If it washes back onto the land, dire political consequences may lie ahead. Such an event, in the belief of many Indonesians, precedes political upheavals. As did many prominent Indonesians, President Suharto had a spiritual adviser, a *dukun*, with whom he would periodically communicate on a promontory in Central Java. A paper prepared for the embassy by an Indonesian sociologist explained, "People believe that it is for the best of the country and its population that power be entrusted to the king, because he has the inalienable ability to act as mediator between the people and the supernatural or cosmological forces which rule this earthly world."[72]

Javanese cultural objects such as the *kris*, a ceremonial dagger, had spiritual qualities. Ceremonies to appease the spirits were required before the kris could be moved.

One of the most prominent Indonesians, Soedjatmoko, an educator and philosopher who was Indonesia's first ambassador to the United States and later a member of the World Bank board, told me this story. When he was a young man during World War II, he participated in the resistance against the Japanese, who were searching for him. Staying with his father in the family home in central Java, he was trying to decide whether to stay or flee. His father told him to stay and explained that he had had a dream the night before that an army of ants had approached the house and then had suddenly turned away. "The Japanese will not come," he said.

Soedjatmoko told me that he faced a dilemma: "Do I trust my father's dream or do I leave the house? I decided to stay." A Japanese unit did start for the house, but as they approached, they were suddenly called away to meet an emergency. They never did reach Soedjatmoko's house.

The vestiges of World War II were still noticeable in attitudes toward the Japanese and in rusty remnants of combat in the outer islands. Just a few days before my arrival, anti-Japanese riots had erupted in Jakarta on the occasion of the visit of Japan's prime minister. Memories of the brutality of the World War II Japanese occupation were still fresh. At the same time, Indonesians credited the Japanese with encouraging the organization of the Indonesian army during the occupation. And President Suharto and other Indonesian military people kept in contact with Japanese officers who had trained them.

Indonesian attitudes toward Communist China were similarly ambivalent. In 1965, Indonesia had been the scene of a major confrontation between the military and what was then the largest communist party in Asia, a party supported by and identified with Beijing. Seven senior military officers had been murdered in what was seen as an abortive Communist coup. In retaliation, several hundred thousand suspected Communists (many of them local Chinese) had been killed or interned. General Suharto escaped the attack to emerge as the country's leader. Thereafter, at least until the democratic changes at the beginning of the twenty-first century, the army remained clearly in charge in both political and economic realms.

Throughout my time in Jakarta, the Indonesian army leadership was deeply suspicious of Beijing. The suspicion was enhanced each year when Adit, the exiled head of the Indonesian Communist Party, broadcast greetings from Beijing. Jakarta's negative reaction to the independence of East Timor is partly explained by the conviction that Communist China was supporting the independence movement. At the same time, through the local and overseas communities, the government maintained contact with mainland China, primarily through Hong Kong. Beijing China was officially recognized, but the diplomatic ties established in 1950 were suspended after 1965 and not restored until 1990. Indonesia refused to establish formal diplomatic ties with Taiwan, but did maintain trade representatives there.

Indonesia had a Chinese ethnic minority estimated at three million, many of whom still retained Chinese Nationalist citizenship. They had a strong position in local retail trade and were frequently the object of murderous riots in times of unrest. At the same time, many prominent Indonesians, including the president and foreign minister, had Chinese business associates.

Corruption was rife in many aspects of Indonesian economic life, from those at the lowest rung of the ladder, who had to bribe nurses to get service in a hospital, to those at the top, who benefited from the percentages they earned on contracts related to the expanding economy. Throughout my time in Indonesia it was accepted as a fact that the Suharto family benefited heavily from payments related to oil concessions and to the expanding trade and business opportunities in the country. A study prepared by the Center for Strategic and International Studies, a think tank in Jakarta, noted that "rather than being an aberration, corruption has been a core norm of Indonesia's political economy for decades. Corruption, of course, existed before the Suharto regime; but hierarchical, systemic corruption became one of the central features of the new order political economy."[73]

Concern about the impact of corruption on the stability of the country was not universal among the donor countries. Many businessmen from Europe and Asia established close and profitable ties with Indonesian middleman, many of them close to the regime. As was the case in Libya, I had no authority as the American ambassador to intervene in private business transactions even though the U.S. Corrupt Practices Act was in effect at the time.

Nevertheless, the regime created and encouraged one of the most impressive and honest development programs in Asia. A group of young, respected economists, most of them American-educated, led the program. Many held doctorates from my alma mater, the University of California at Berkeley. They were known as the "Berkeley Mafia." I encouraged American business representatives exploring investment opportunities to approach these honest technocrats first. Part of my argument centered on the experience of at least one businessman who met someone in a Hong Kong bar purporting to be a cousin of President Suharto, signed a deal, and paid a substantial amount for a property intended for a factory. Once he had arrived in Jakarta, he discovered that the property was in the middle of an active railroad yard. He came into my office in a state of agitation. My recollection is that we were able to help him through the intercession of a member of the Berkeley Mafia.

Although Indonesia is heavily influenced by Islam, I discovered that in the early days of the country's independence militant Islamic groups, many of them in the outer islands, were the young army's principal enemies. The idea of a country based on fundamentalist Islamic law was anathema to the army officers who ruled the country. When I paid my initial call on the interior minister, I remarked that I was pleased once again to be serving in a Muslim country. "Mr. Ambassador," he replied, "one of the first things you need to realize is that Indonesia is not an Islamic country."

American objectives at the time of my arrival were clear. We needed to find ways to recognize the importance of this major Asian country while respecting its independence and nonaligned status. I was pleased that, for once, I did not have to concentrate my time on the preservation of U.S. military facilities. We wanted to keep Indonesia free of commitments to the Soviet Union or China that would impede our own diplomatic and security access. Recognizing Indonesian reluctance to join any formal treaty arrangements, we wanted to maintain the freedom for American submarines to transit Indonesian straits and for our naval vessels to continue making port calls. Negotiations were proceeding on the International Law of the Sea Treaty, and Indonesia's role was crucial. We wanted direct discussions with them on some aspects.

When Suharto and the new order came into power in 1965, the United States joined with the Netherlands, Japan, and the United Kingdom in providing assistance through the Intergovernmental Group on Indonesia (IGGI). Assistance consisted of concessional loans for development, food aid, and technical training. For a number of years the American share exceeded $100 million a year. By the time I arrived in Jakarta, Washington and the international lending agencies were growing cool to the idea of concessional assistance to oil-producing countries. As a member of the Organization of the Petroleum Exporting Countries (OPEC), Indonesia was adversely affected by this. By pointing out that Indonesia had only 10 percent of OPEC's production and 80 percent of its population, we were able to sustain assistance through most of the four years that I was in Indonesia.

One of the most effective programs was one that trained individuals in both the United States and Indonesia. One cultural aspect that made the Indonesian program particularly successful, in contrast to those with other countries, was that Indonesians loved their country and wanted to return when their training was finished. Of the 6,000 participants in training programs in 1975, 5,500 had returned and approximately 85 percent of those were engaged in the occupation for which they had trained. In addition to official programs, two private American organizations, the Ford Foundation and the Asia Foundation, were active in the training field. It was a thrill for me when traveling in the outer provinces of the country to find Indonesians trained in the United States constructively working for their own country.

The United States also contributed substantially to the highly successful family planning program. With the cooperation of local Islamic leaders, a governor of East Java organized "mothers' clubs" for women participating in family planning. The approach created local social pressures and became a model not only in Indonesia but in many developing countries.

My personal role in the family planning program was incorrectly and sensationally highlighted in a column by Jack Anderson in the *Washington Post* on June 16, 1976. The column read in part: "While the public spotlight is focused on sex in Washington, the State Department is quietly promoting sex abroad. In faraway Indonesia, for example, U.S. Ambassador David Newsom has been notified that he will soon receive a shipment of over 50 million prophylactics as a foreign aid offering from American taxpayers."[74]

At that same time I was under treatment for a back problem, and the embassy doctor wrote in a note to Jean, "Here is a copy of the Anderson column. I must relate the news that I also protested shipping 51 million condoms to the ambassador. I thought they were for his personal use and protested that his back would never stand up to the stress!!"

In light of Indonesia's rapid development, we wanted to secure opportunities for the American private sector to participate. U.S. firms already had substantial investments in oil and gas, rubber, lumber, and minerals. The U.S. private sector contributed to the building of a modern banking system and other businesses by providing experts on a short-term basis through the International Executive Service Corps. As noted, American firms participated in the installation of Indonesia's first satellite communications system, Palapa. The footprint of the new system, covering all of Indonesia's islands, gave this far-flung nation new capacity in telephone and telegraph, telex and television.

I was present on February 15, 1975, when President Suharto inaugurated the domestic satellite project. The ceremony was not without its moment of humor. It had been arranged for the president to speak by telephone to the governors of the two most distant provinces, Aceh and Irian Jaya. The governor of Irian Jaya had obviously been waiting for a long time to unload his many troubles on the president; and as the crowd began to laugh, Suharto vainly tried to bring the conversation to a close. At least one governor had understood the power of the new system.

The most dramatic American investment in Indonesia was a copper and gold mine, 9,000 feet high in the mountains of Irian

Jaya. The Freeport Mining Company had constructed a town, a processing center, and a port out of the jungle. My youngest son David and I visited the project in 1975. A letter describes our approach: "We started off in the early morning since that is the best time for weather and drove up from the 6,000-foot town site to the mill site at 9,000. Then, as we rounded the road into the mill site, we looked up and there, 2,500 feet higher up a sheer cliff, was the mine."

Unlike Persian Gulf concession arrangements, foreign oil companies in Indonesia operated as contractors to the Indonesian national oil company, Pertamina. Only in very unusual circumstances was I, as the American ambassador, drawn into problems between Pertamina and the oil companies. One such problem occurred during my time.

Pertamina, an empire within a country, was run by Ibnu Sutowo, a military colleague of the president. During the petrodollar boom of the 1970s it borrowed heavily, much of the money coming from American banks flush with petrodollars. Pertamina was late in its payment of interest on a loan to one American bank, and this development sent shock waves through the banking community. I suddenly had a stream of American bank representatives visiting to inquire about Indonesians' creditworthiness. Many had assumed that because Indonesia was producing oil and gas, it was an "oil-rich" country. The lemming principle prevailed. One banker explained his firm's position, "Everyone is doing it. We cannot be left behind." I had to explain to them that Indonesia was not "oil-rich." They also discovered during their visits to Jakarta that the Indonesian government did not guarantee Pertamina's debts.

One day the bubble burst, and Pertamina faced the prospect of defaulting on several billion dollars of debt. It was at this point that the Indonesians displayed their capacity to resolve a serious problem. Despite his close ties with Ibnu Sutowo, Suharto, partly under diplomatic pressure, sanctioned a serious restructuring of the company and a curtailment of its power. He placed another respected army officer in charge of the restructuring.

In 1975, when the United Nations treaty governing the law of the sea was under negotiation. U.S. interest in ratification was high (although the United States has still not ratified the treaty as of 2008). Washington was then seeking to negotiate with other countries articles of the treaty that might make ratification in the United States difficult. One such article concerned the transit of international straits; freedom of such transit was vital to the interests of a major maritime and naval power. In this matter the United States and the Soviet Union were on the same side. Indonesia was seeking to establish an "archipelagic principle" that would make all waters within the boundaries of an island state territorial, thus requiring maritime powers to request permission for the transit of warships.

We did work out language that satisfied Washington, and Indonesian and other delegates went out on something of a limb to support us. It was not a happy day in relations with Indonesia and other similar powers when President Ronald Reagan, in 1983, declined to sign the treaty because of defects in the deep seabed mining provisions. This was one more instance of the vulnerability of American diplomats to political reversal of agreements negotiated in good faith with foreign governments.

All official relations with Indonesia were at risk because of concerns over human rights conditions. When I reached Jakarta in 1973, some 30,000 of the communist suspects rounded up after the abortive coup in 1965 were still detained on Buru, an island in central Indonesia. Many had been teenagers and younger in 1965, and many were only tangentially related to the communists.

U.S. legislation required that human rights be taken into account in American military assistance programs. It is not always recognized that the official impetus for including human rights in American foreign policy started in the Congress. In reaction to U.S. ties to military regimes in Latin America, Congress enacted eleven different requirements that mandated consideration of how governments treated their people in any implementation of U.S. assistance. Some key members of the House subcommittee staff involved in the enactment of this legislation moved into the White House in the Carter years and created further pressure for action in this area. In 1975, concerned members of Congress were focusing on the Indonesian case and threatening specific legislation that would sanction Indonesia.

Aware of this, I approached a well-placed Indonesian military officer. When I asked whether I should not find an occasion to mention the possibility of sanctions to President Suharto, he advised against it. "The President would only see that as a threat," he said. He asked for time to think about the matter.

Within a few days, he returned. "As I said," he told me, "the President would only see your mentioning this to him as a threat. But if *we* conclude this is a possibility and *we* mention it to him, he will take it seriously. We propose to send a delegation to Washington to speak to members of the Congress. If they tell us the same thing, we can then tell the President."

I was a bit skeptical, but recommended this course of action to Washington. The idea was accepted, and a delegation was sent, headed by General Ali Murtopo, a wily, politically savvy military officer closely tied to Suharto. The delegation was given a friendly hearing in October 1975, and General Murtopo's statement was inserted in the Congressional Record.[75] The delegation returned and reported the problem to President Suharto, and within a few weeks the decision was made to release the bulk of the detainees.

There was only one hitch at the end. Members of the diplomatic corps—ambassadors of Japan, Great Britain, the Netherlands, and the Holy See—who had interceded on behalf of the detainees were invited to witness the first releases at an army base in Sumatra. Army trucks pulled up to where the visitors were assembled, and several score of detainees filed into the hall. They took an oath of allegiance to the state and then all filed back onto the trucks and disappeared over the horizon.

I approached my military friend and told him, that this spectacle did not solve the problem. The detainees had to be seen to be released and reunited with their families. This was subsequently done, and all but 183 considered "hard core" communists were ultimately released.

By the time I reached Indonesia, the American community had grown to more than 4,000 individuals. Jean and I made a special point to reach out to this community. In 1976 we fostered a special commemoration of the 200th anniversary of the founding of the American Republic. In cooperation with Indonesians and members of the international community, we organized a community action council to provide both guidance and recreation. Young people in the expatriate community were as vulnerable to temptations of drugs and alcohol as those at home.

An important part of the American community consisted of Protestant missionaries. They even had their own air service, the Missionary Air Fellowship (MAF) that I occasionally used when visiting outlying areas. The Indonesians generally welcomed the missionaries, sometimes in surprising ways.

The Baptists had a hospital with an American staff in Bukkitingi in Sumatra. The governor of the province and some Muslims had been trying to close the hospital, claiming that the American medical staff were proselytizing patients. The hospital was saved by the military representative in the province, who looked upon the American presence as a balance to extremist Islamic elements.

Much of the American community life centered around the Joint Embassy School (JES), established originally for the children of embassy personnel and sponsored by the British, Canadian, U.S., and Yugoslav embassies. As the nondiplomatic expatriate community grew with Indonesia's development, so did the nondiplomatic student body.

One day I learned that a decree was in the works in the Ministry of Education that would have limited admission to diplomatic children. This would have had a serious effect on the American expatriate community requiring them to go through the complicated procedure of getting authority for a separate school.

As I have so often found in diplomacy, one needs to resolve the problem by finding out the reason for the government's decision. I was unable to do this until one night at a dinner where I sat next to a former Indonesian ambassador to Washington. I explained the problem to him and asked him if he knew the reason. He said, "Why, yes. It's the Chinese." He then went on to explain that, at that time, Indonesia was considering opening diplomatic relations with Beijing and did not want to establish a precedent under which nondiplomatic Chinese could attend a future Chinese embassy school.

Armed with this information I suggested to the Ministry of Education that all those nondiplomatic children currently in the school be "grandfathered," thus for the moment making the new decree unnecessary. My suggestion was accepted, and the school as it stood was saved.

A visit by President Gerald Ford in 1976 manifested the keen official U.S. interest in Indonesia. Ford came to Jakarta after a visit to Beijing, and for nineteen hours the embassy was inundated with presidential aides, communications, and press.

In the advance planning with the Indonesians, a question arose of where to assign various members of the party in the official guest quarters. These were in a four-story building with a presidential suite at the top. The third floor contained a special suite for a prime minister, posing the question of what to do about the prime minister's suite, since the United States did not have a prime minister. I told my Indonesian planner that this was no problem. Secretary of State Henry Kissinger was in many ways clearly comparable to a prime minister. I shuddered to think what the secretary would have said if he had been confined to a mere ministerial suite.

A more serious problem arose in the meeting between President Suharto and President Ford on December 6, 1975. I was present, along with Secretary Kissinger, Foreign Minister Adam Malik, and Minister of State Sudharmono. After a lengthy discussion of China, Indochina, and the situation in the ASEAN countries, Suharto turned to the question of Timor: "When it looked as if the Portuguese rule would end in Timor we sought to encourage the Portuguese to [begin] an orderly decolonization process," Suharto said. "We had an agreement with them on such a process, and we recognized the authority of Portugal in the carrying out of decolonization and in giving people the right to express their wishes. Indonesia has no territorial ambitions. We are concerned only about the security, tranquility, and peace of Asia and the Southern Hemisphere. In the latest Rome agreement, the Portuguese government wanted to invite all parties to negotiate. Similar efforts were made before, but Fretelin (the Timorese liberation group) did not attend. After the Fretelin forces occupied certain points and other forces were unable to consolidate, Fretelin has declared its independence unilaterally. In consequence, other parties declared their intention of integrating with Indonesia. Portugal reported the situation to the United Nations but did not extend recognition to Fretelin. Portugal, however, is unable to control the situation. If this continues it will prolong the suffering of the refugees and increase the instability in the area."

President Ford asked, "The four other parties have asked for integration?"

Suharto replied, "Yes, after UDI (unilateral declaration of independence), Indonesia found itself facing a fait accompli. It is now important to determine what we can do to establish peace and order for the present and the future in the interest of the security of the area and Indonesia. These are some of the considerations we are now contemplating. We want your understanding if we deem it necessary to take rapid or drastic action."

President Ford replied: "We will understand and will not press you on the issue. We understand the problem you have and the intentions you have."

Secretary Kissinger added, "You appreciate that the use of U.S-made arms could create problems."

A brief discussion followed on the legal constraints on the use of American arms. The session ended with a discussion of questions of trade and investment.[76]

The Indonesians invaded Timor the next day.

The failure of the United States to discourage the Indonesian takeover of East Timor has been the subject of much criticism. Although we had been following the issue, I do not recall that we alerted President Ford and Secretary Kissinger to the possibility that Suharto would raise the question and that the Indonesians would move so quickly. We were aware President Suharto held back the military after the Portuguese revolution in 1974. Both he and the Indonesian military were growing increasingly impatient. They had been seeking to negotiate with the Portuguese, but Lisbon was unable to produce a fully authorized interlocutor. Ever since independence the Indonesians had been unhappy that one half of one of the island remained under foreign control. Given the Chinese support for Fretelin, Indonesian action against the guerilla group was inevitable. It is only to be regretted that they handled the incorporation in an excessively brutal fashion. I doubt that objections on our part would have prevailed.

As my tour in Indonesia was coming to a close, I began to wonder whether I should not give up a life of wandering and seek employment in education or the private sector. I made some exploratory contacts, but the time was not ripe. Further challenges and adventures lay ahead.

At the end of four years in Jakarta, I was appointed U.S. ambassador to Manila. For a brief and exciting period, I was to continue my Asian education.

16

MY COUSIN NEEDS A VISA

At the end of four years in Jakarta, I was appointed U.S. ambassador to the Philippines. My tour in Manila, from November 1977 to March 1978, was the shortest of my career. Just as we were beginning to understand the complexities of another island nation, I was transferred back to Washington to replace Philip Habib as under secretary of state for political affairs. Habib, one of the nation's most skillful diplomats, had suffered a heart attack.

Those brief five months were active and stimulating:

> I had served in former colonies of other nations; this experience was my first in dealing with the residual responsibilities of our own colonial history.
>
> Once again I was faced with the task of preserving a military base presence in a third world country.
>
> As in Indonesia, I also encountered the special challenges of human rights issues under an authoritarian regime.
>
> In carrying out the objectives of my mission, I was to become acquainted with one of the developing world's most theatrical ruling couples.

I was not totally unfamiliar with the Philippines. My mother's oldest brother, John W. Dunlop (Uncle Jack), had gone to the islands as a Presbyterian missionary in 1917. He left to return to the United States in 1936, when he became chaplain at Folsom Prison in California. He never lost his love for the Philippines and its people and, after his wife died in 1960, he returned to Cebu to work and live out his life. In 1975, I visited him in Cebu from Jakarta, where we were then living.

Uncle Jack was an evangelical fundamentalist who believed strongly in "spreading the Word." He would drive around Cebu in an open jeep and when stopping at a traffic light would pass out religious tracts to the other waiting motorists. During my visit, I was using a car from the American Consulate. Jack was sitting in the front seat beside the driver. When we stopped at the first red light, he rolled down the window and out came the tracts. I had to remind him gently that being in an official car, we had to observe the separation of church and state.

When Jack died in March 1977, I flew from Jakarta to speak at his funeral in Cebu. More than four hundred devoted and tearful followers attended the service .

Meeting Uncle Jack's parishioners and touring the countryside around Cebu with him in 1975 gave me a glimpse of Philippine life that scarcely prepared me for the opulence of Manila that I was to encounter less than three years later. In many Asian countries there is a conspicuous gap between the rich and the poor. Nowhere was I more conscious of that gap than in the Philippines, perhaps because of our nation's own close association with the country.

Before taking up my position in Manila, I had to be confirmed by the Senate. This confirmation hearing before the Senate Foreign Relations Committee would be my fourth. Such a process is required for any presidential appointee. Previously I had been confirmed as ambassador to Libya (1965), assistant secretary for Africa (1969), and ambassador to Indonesia (1973). I had also observed other confirmation hearings.

These experiences ranged from the serious to the irrelevant. When I was officer-in-charge of Arabian Peninsula affairs in 1959, I accompanied an ambassador-designate to Saudi Arabia to his confirmation hearing. Another nominee that day was Earl W. Strom, who had been named ambassador to Bolivia. One of the members of the Senate Foreign Relations Committee at the time, William Langer of North Dakota, discovered that Strom's grandfather had been a member of the first North Dakota Legislature. The entire hearing was devoted to reminiscences of North Dakota's early history. As I remember, Bolivia was not once mentioned.

When I went before the committee for the African position, William Fulbright of Arkansas was chair. He conducted a serious exploration of the issues I was likely to face, but I learned one lesson. Never take steps of any kind that assume you will be confirmed. Fulbright was particularly sensitive on this point; he felt any such assumption challenged the legitimate role of the Senate.

My confirmation hearing for the Philippines assignment took place before the Senate Foreign Relations Committee on October 18, 1977. Senator John Sparkman of Alabama was in the chair that day. Two questions in the brief hearing dealt with human rights and the Philippine relationship with Indochina. (The Vietnam War had recently ended.) I was able to assure the senators of my experience and interest in human rights issues, and on the second question, to suggest that the Philippines wanted to maintain its freedom and identity. In Manila's view the question of Indochina could best be left to the states of the area.[77]

Once confirmed, I started the real preparation for the new post. The process included a trip to New York to call on Philippine first lady Imelda Marcos and Foreign Minister Carlos Romulo. Both were in New York for the United Nations General Assembly. Both greeted Jean and me warmly. Mrs. Marcos's Waldorf-Astoria suite was bedecked with at least a score of expensive bouquets. Romulo, a distinguished elder statesman of Asia, received me in simpler style. I was to see much of both of them in the months to come.

Jean and I arrived in Manila on November 4, 1977. I realized from the moment of my arrival that this would be a very different kind of diplomatic assignment. The American ambassador to the Philippines was clearly a significant public figure. The Manila press corps was out in force, and headlines the next day heralded my arrival—and my expected tasks: "US envoy arrives, is ready for talks"; and "Hard bargaining in store for new U.S. ambassador."

One press item, under the headline "Base Incidents Confront Newsom," was more specific: "American soldiers assigned at local bases have been committing indignities on people living near the bases. In one incident, military dogs were made to chase Filipino scavengers, and in another, Filipino women who were caught intruding into military or naval reservations were stripped naked."[78]

My priorities were clear: do something about the bases. At that time, as the result of the close cooperation in World War II, the United States had virtual sovereignty over seven military properties in the Philippines: Clark Air Force Base, Subic Bay Naval Base, San Miguel Naval Communications Station, one seismic station, an oil pipeline, a recreation facility at Baguio, and the American Cemetery. In addition, the United States had rights at two Voice of America sites. U.S. commitments to the Philippines were embodied in three agreements: the Military Bases Agreement (1947), the Economic Assistance Agreement (1947), and the Mutual Defense Treaty (1951). All would be subject to upcoming negotiations. Whatever other aspects were of interest to President Ferdinand Marcos, the amount the Philippines would receive in financial aid was of the greatest importance.

The bases were not the only symbols of the special position of the United States in the Philippines. The ambassador was still looked upon by many in the older generation as a symbol of real power. Because of the close wartime ties, the U.S. Embassy in Manila, the largest in the world at that time, included representatives of nineteen government agencies. In addition to the regular foreign affairs agencies and the Peace Corps, the list also included the Veterans Administration and the Social Security Administration, because of the large number of Philippine pensioners. Filipinos also continued to praise and benefit from the American-established educational system.

Diplomacy for the American ambassador in the Philippines had some of the aspects of a political campaign. Frequent visits to outlying provinces, attendance at public events, and speeches given upon request were designed to respond to expectations and to enhance the image and, one hoped, the influence of the United States. The visits included attendance at ceremonies involving our development assistance to the Philippines. For me, the most dramatic was held in La Union, a district near Manila, where, as a result of a U.S.-financed rural electrification program, I witnessed the turning on of electric lights for the first time in the history of the district. I learned how that simple project would enhance the educational and commercial opportunities of the district.

My visits also included stops at the major investments of American companies, including several oil companies, Goodyear's rubber plantations, and Del Monte pineapple groves. This was the only post

I held where I was asked for my autograph and urged to pose for photographs with local people.

The Philippines was still a poor country. Governed under both Spain and then the United States by an oligarchy of prominent families, the gap between rich and poor was startling. One Filipino told me that his people had an identity problem: "We were five hundred years in a monastery and fifty years in Hollywood." President Marcos sought to curb the economic power of the families—largely by garnering their wealth unto himself, making the gap even greater.

Having visited rural areas and slums, Jean and I were never totally comfortable living in a palatial Manila mansion inside a gated community, Forbes Park, when we knew what poverty lay not far beyond. One of my predecessors had acquired the official residence from a sugar baron. It was large and ostentatious and featured a small stream that wound through the first floor of the house. It was a mansion clearly designed for the Señora, not the Señor. I gave my reaction to it in a letter to my son Dan on December 5, 1977:

> If you think you've got problems, you should hear some of mine.
>
> So, you see, we move into this big house—and, I mean big. Orange County, Bel Air, Hollywood and all that. I'm told we're in the land of machismo, where the men are *it*.
>
> So, what do I find when we move in. There is a BIG bedroom. O.K. Then there is also a BIG FANCY TILE BATHROOM with sunken shower, etc., etc., but, I am informed by the maid, that it is only for Madame. Ambassador Sullivan, my predecessor used a smaller bathroom!! So I examine the other bathroom. No shelf. No medicine cabinet. No light over the mirror. So, I say NO. And so, I have sort of cohabited in the BIG bathroom with Missus, except that now, the Missus is getting up for her morning exercise class at about the same time I shave so where do I shave, of course, in the small bathroom.
>
> So, O.K., I don't rate a big bathroom, but how about the dressing room? Oh yes, there was a dressing room for the MASTER originally, but Mrs. Sullivan changed it into a kitchen. So, I have a dressing room in kind of a thorough-

fare with windows that are not shielded from the strolling guards. I feel like I am in Macy's window.

So, I've put up with that and draw the curtains for a little privacy, and then the maid enters with a stack of newly ironed clothing. My former dressing room not only has the dog's dishes and is a supplemental kitchen, but it is also the IRONING ROOM!!! (There are only FOURTEEN other rooms in the House where one could do ironing).

So, you see, this is a great house, and I love every inch of it when I can hide behind the curtain in order to get a little privacy and shave out of the fishpond just outside my window. It puts me in just the right mood to handle base negotiations, economic standoffs, irate visa applicants, dissatisfied veterans, and restless Washington.

Letters to my children provided an opportunity to express myself outside of official communications. I even used one of them in a speech. When I was asked to speak at the commemoration of the 33rd anniversary of the liberation of Manila by Filipino and American forces, instead of a speech I read the following letter I had written to my 18-year-old son, David.

On February 3, 1945, fifteen years before you were born, tired and dirty and gallant men entered this city. Men, women, and children in Santo Tomas University, who had been confined for three and a half long years, wept and cheered as friendly forces opened the gates.

Those days seem distant to you—as they are. Like every boy, you have been carried away by stories of that war. From the simplified accounts of history, you have formed opinions on who is good and who was bad. They were thrilling stories—but to you, not quite real.

You were curious when you and I saw the film *MacArthur* about events and names that were part of your father's life, but not yours. You wondered at—and perhaps did not fully share—your father's emotion as he stood at the monument at Corregidor or looked at the rows of crosses in the American Cemetery. You perhaps found little to identify with among the old men who marched with their medals on parade days or who sat about and recalled their adventures in a war which seemed to you so long ago.

Events have intervened since 1945 that, to some, have obscured the meaning of valor. The generation of your older brothers, the generation of the sixties, raised questions about one's obligation to one's country. The advent of the nuclear age has made the prospect of war more dreadful than ever before.

Everyone shares the hope that there will be no more wars—and none share this hope more than those who have fought. This should not, however, lead us to forget that there are times when men must sacrifice for a greater good.

To those who fought in 1945, the issues seemed clear. Nations were resisting the efforts of those who would conquer and dominate great regions of the world. Their efforts failed because of the courage and sacrifices of those years. People and nations today can determine their destiny; this would not have been possible if the tide had gone in the other direction. A new and beautiful Manila has risen from the devastated city liberated in 1945. The Philippines is a proud and truly independent republic.

Time has healed many of the scars of war. Those whom we fought are friends today. We respect the valor and the sacrifice of their soldiers, even though we opposed their cause. Peace and liberation are commemorated by friend and foe alike.

When the old soldier passes by with his medals and his memories, remember his sacrifice. It was no easier for him, at your age, to leave his home, his family, his loved ones, and face the fears and privations of war than it would be for you. There are those who watch him pass by who first saw him through the bars of Belsen or the gates of Santo Tomas. To them, he and his fellow soldiers were the liberators, and for them there will not only be respect, but eternal gratitude.

Every parent hopes that your generation will not face the awful challenge of war. Yet we feel a responsibility to

> help you to understand the true meaning of those days. In 1945, men fought and died against a desperate enemy to restore to men of other lands their right to be free. That is the true significance of liberation.

I came to the Philippines from a career spent largely in newly independent countries. From comments by some Filipinos I gained the impression that at least some of my predecessors acted as if the islands were still an American colony. I made every effort to dispel any notion that I felt the same way.

One part of the ritual of American ambassadors to the Philippines is, shortly after arrival, to speak to the Manila Rotary club, a sort of "state of diplomacy" speech. I took the occasion of that speech, on December 8, 1977, to suggest that the relationship was now on a different footing. A comment in a local newspaper suggested I at least partially succeeded:

> The heightening of the nationalist fervor the past few decades has forced the Filipino consciousness to adopt a more assertive stance in seeking to accelerate the multifaceted development of this emerging nation.
>
> Newly designated U.S. ambassador to the Philippines, David D. Newsom, in his first major policy speech the other day, displayed a firm grasp of this fact: "Like the citizens of other nations, newly independent in this century, you in the Philippines are asserting your nationhood, finding your roots, and your identity, reviewing and questioning culture and institutions brought from abroad"[79]

Because of the large Filipino community in America, pressures for visas were intense. The problem was brought home to me before I reached Manila. When I stopped at the headquarters of the Commander-in-Chief of the Pacific Fleet (CINCPAC) in Honolulu, one of his Filipino stewards approached me and said, "I have a cousin who needs a visa."

I was to discover that managing the long lines of visa applicants, and the many ingenious efforts by the Filipinos to provide the necessary documents, represented a major task of the embassy in Manila. So frequent were forgeries of passports, birth certificates, tax documents, and letters from sponsors that we had a special office to monitor visa fraud. As soon as our consular officers caught on to one dodge, however, the word went out through the grapevine, and our office was presented within a few days with some new type of forgery.

One former embassy employee, who was fired on suspicion of fraud, crossed the street in front of the Consulate and opened an office, Amity Travels, to advise people on how to get visas for the United States. His apparent advice was that the client should write to a congressman from a district where the client had friends.

I presented my credentials to President Marcos in a formal ceremony at Malacañang Palace on November 11, 1977. At the same time, I presented a letter from President Jimmy Carter agreeing to resume the discussions on the future of the military bases that had begun under my predecessor, William Sullivan.

We resumed formal negotiations on the base issue on November 25. Our objectives were to resolve the problem of base security and to respond to the Philippine request for greater symbols of sovereignty over the bases. Washington would have to deal with the question of compensation. In earlier negotiating sessions, the Filipinos had mentioned a figure of $1 billion for five years. We proposed a "good faith" clause that stated the United States would make every effort to provide $500 million over five years. In any U.S. negotiation, it is impossible to make a financial commitment without the approval of Congress.

We addressed, as a priority, the question of perimeter security, particularly at the two major bases. As indicated by the newspaper item quoted earlier, the inescapable contrast between the neat, wealthy, well-stocked U.S. installations and the shantytowns that existed just outside them led to constant efforts by Filipinos to break in and steal. Theft at the bases ran more than $1 million a year. The problem was ultimately resolved by passing to the Filipinos the responsibility for the outer security of the bases.

The United States also agreed to the appointment of a Filipino commander of the bases and to the flying of the Filipino flag. This formula, fully established under my successor, was incorporated into a new base agreement, on January 7, 1979. That agreement included the commitment to make the "best effort" to obtain $500 million in military and economic grants of aid to the Philippines over a five-year period. The new agreement generally reduced the pressures for complete closure until after the fall of the Marcos regime in 1986.

The Philippines during my time was, like Indonesia, under authoritarian rule. Ferdinand Marcos had seized power by declaring martial law in September 1972 after what many in the Philippines said was a period of violence and uncertainty. During my brief tenure, he was clearly the power. I found him intelligent, charismatic, and shrewd. David Joel Steinberg, in his book *The Philippines: A Singular and a Plural Place,* characterized him sardonically: "Ferdinand Marcos, brilliant, charismatic, wily, was a confidence man, a human being who believed his own falsehoods. Marcos lied audaciously to himself, his cronies, and his nation. He was able to dominate his people for two decades, first as a symbol of hope and progress, later as an omnipotent dictator, and finally as a worldwide symbol of corruption and decay."[80]

I met with President Marcos on an almost weekly basis, frequently alone, sometimes with visitors. On critical matters such as the base negotiations, he wanted to meet without advisers. We would go over the main points and he would agree or not agree. When he did agree, he passed that agreement on faithfully to the negotiators.

I do not disagree with Professor Steinberg's assessment, although I found Marcos generally straightforward in my dealings with him. He did duck issues, such as human rights, if he was not prepared to discuss them. On one occasion, however, he was candid with me. I had been instructed to raise with him reports of torture being carried out by his security services. He replied to this effect, "Well, you know, Mr. Ambassador, I have to depend on these men for my security. I can't always monitor closely what they are doing."

When he did discuss local political issues, he tended to be legalistic. And he gave standard responses, often referring to "our constitution based on yours." He was obviously very intelligent and probably the cleverest politician in the Philippines. Undoubtedly he could have been elected fairly for as long as he wanted. Instead, his ambition for power and wealth led to his excesses.

It is not possible to discuss the Marcos era without some words about the other half of what Professor Steinberg called the "conjugal dictatorship," Imelda Marcos, the "First Lady." Together they were a theatrical team. Mrs. Marcos gave the impression of making a special effort to co-opt the American ambassador and his wife and followed our movements closely.

Jean and I recall particularly the Marcos's reception for the Reverend Billy Graham and his party on Thanksgiving Day 1977. One of President Marcos political adversaries was the Catholic Cardinal of the Philippines, Jaime Sin. I was told that President Marcos invited Billy Graham to hold a crusade in the Philippines to show Cardinal Sin that the Philippines had a religious alternative. At the last minute, Jean and I were invited to a dinner at Malacañang Palace, a dinner given largely for Protestant clergy in the Philippines, with Billy Graham as the principal guest. Although we were entertaining guests at the Residence for the traditional holiday dinner, we were urged to bring them all with us to Malacañang.

It was the custom at the Palace for Mrs. Marcos to receive guests in the music room prior to dinner. We were ushered into the music room together with the Reverend Graham and his party. (Our dinner guests were to join the party in the banquet hall.) After a few minutes, Mrs. Marcos, who had been campaigning for her position as governor of Metro Manila, swept in wearing her campaign clothes.

She greeted Dr. Graham, "Oh, Dr.Graham, in my campaigning I have been telling the people of Manila that ours is the city of Man. Now I can tell them that it is the city of God."

Once we had all recovered from the introduction, we went in to dinner. The president joined us at that point. After dinner he rose to welcome the Grahams and gave a twenty-minute, apparently extemporaneous speech on how a country could not develop unless its soul was pure, and "You, Dr. Graham, have come to help us purify our souls."

I had the impression that this was not quite what Dr. Graham expected, and he paused for a minute or so before replying and thanking the Marcoses for their hospitality.

We were never sure how close the relationship was between the two Marcoses. Imelda would speak to Jean about how Ferdinand had written love songs for her—which on occasions she would sing. On only one occasion did President Marcos speak to me about his wife.

Mrs. Marcos generated many ideas. One of them was to hold the United Nations General Assembly in Manila. The idea was viewed with some alarm in Washington because of the elements of costs and precedent. I was instructed to see President Marcos and attempt to discourage the idea. He was remarkably candid in his response. "This is the first lady's idea. Perhaps you can find some way to discourage it in New York." With the help of James Leonard, the U.S. deputy representative in New York, a resolution was introduced thanking Mrs. Marcos for the idea without endorsing it. The concept was gently laid to rest.

Being the American ambassador in Manila, particularly during the Carter administration, was a balancing act. This balancing act is one of the most difficult of diplomatic tasks and especially difficult in a post where we had so many interests and so much history.

It was essential to have satisfactory relations with President Marcos. At the same time, the ambassador had two other tasks: to further the human rights agenda of President Carter and the Congress and to avoid such close identification with the Marcos regime that American interests would be harmed in the case of political change. In Iraq and Libya I had seen our interests severely damaged when regimes with which we were closely associated fell. I was to see it again later in the case of Iran.

Questions during my confirmation hearing emphasized congressional concern over human rights problems in the Philippines. The question of pursuing human rights issues in foreign policy was not confined to the Carter administration. The Reagan administration that followed came into office vowing to do away with the position of the Assistant Secretary of State for Humanitarian Affairs. They found out however, that this was a congressionally mandated position they could not touch. They had to turn around and embrace some of the same points of view as the Carter administration.

Upon the establishment of martial law by President Marcos in 1972, the democratic constitution was suspended, Congress was dismissed, the Philippine army was given greater powers, and political adversaries were imprisoned. In the Carter administration, with its emphasis on human rights, the violation of such rights in our former colony was especially troublesome. But, for the Filipino political elite, as with other authoritarian regimes, human rights questions touched the very core of sovereignty. Those who had thrown off the yoke of imperial rule did not welcome criticism from outsiders, especially from the former colonial power.

Without directly attacking local policies, an ambassador can raise the issue by emphasizing the circumstances in one's own country and the possible impact of foreign actions on attitudes in the United States.

Vice President Walter Mondale was to visit the Philippines in May 1977. In talking points drafted in the State Department for my discussions with Philippine officials as we prepared for the Mondale visit, I was instructed, with reference to President Marcos's declared intention to hold elections, to say the following:

> In our view, this visit [by the Vice President] presents a very special opportunity. Strong focus will naturally be on the countries which the vice president will visit and he will undoubtedly be accompanied by important representatives of the American press. The circumstances that exist, therefore, in regard to the aftermath of the elections and in regard to human rights when the vice president comes to Manila can have a profound effect on the future of U.S.-Philippine relations.... It is therefore essential that if the trip is to mark and to symbolize the new and improved relationship between our two nations that it take place in an atmosphere of visible movement towards greater democracy and individual and press freedom in the Philippines.[81]

In my Rotary Club address I had also touched on the problem. Speaking of the strong concerns expressed both in the Congress and in the executive on human rights, I said: "This consciousness in our foreign affairs is not wedded to particular institutions or to particular political labels. It is not seeking to intervene in the affairs of other nations. It does seek to make clear the strong preference of the United States for those societies in which there is respect for human dignity, due process of law and the people's right to express themselves and to participate in the process of government. In expressing this preference, the United States fully understands that these aspects are expressed differently in different societies and that the society of the United States has its problems, too." [82]

Foreign Minister Romulo addressed the question obliquely in remarks he made at the farewell dinner he gave for me on March 14, 1978:

> Having served a large portion of his career in Africa and Southeast Asia, Ambassador Newsom has a wide experience with the problems of developing countries. He has in consequence developed a wide knowledge of the diversity of the world in which we live today and acquired a deep understanding of the fact that in this diverse world there are many roads to freedom.
>
> No country, not even Rome, was able to impose its own values on other peoples. Today, three billion people in the developing countries live in conditions which do not meet even the minimum conditions for adequate food, shelter and literacy—the necessary matrix for the attainment of human dignity and freedom. Their basic priority therefore is freedom from starvation.
>
> But even in fairly advanced societies, the struggle to achieve faster growth and development is an essential human right. Indeed, it is a basic requirement for the achievement of all other rights.[83]

Much of the American interest in the issue centered on the case of Benigno Aquino, Jr. Marcos considered Aquino the most serious threat to his own political future. Aquino made history by becoming the youngest elected senator in the country's history at age 34. During his first year in the Senate, Aquino warned that Marcos was on the road to establishing "a garrison state." Aquino particularly angered Imelda Marcos when, in a speech in 1969, he criticized one of the First Lady's favorite, but extravagant, projects—a cultural center—calling it "a monument to shame."[84] When Marcos declared martial law on September 21, 1972, Aquino was one of the first to be arrested. He was imprisoned on what were generally seen as trumped-up charges of murder, illegal possession of firearms, and subversion. Shortly after my arrival, Aquino was sentenced to death by firing squad. The sentence was never carried out, but Aquino was in jail throughout my time in the Philippines.

His fate was a matter of special interest to Patt Derian, assistant secretary of state for humanitarian affairs, when she visited Manila on January 12, 1978. Derian had been prominent in the civil rights movement in the American South and joined the Carter administration to support the president's interest in human rights.

We arranged for her to see President Marcos, Secretary of Defense Juan Ponce Enrile, and other key Filipino officials. In my report of her visit I noted that I believed the visit "helpful" in that we conveyed directly to the president and Enrile "the strong feelings on human rights which reflect the views of an important segment of President Carter's coalition."

In her discussion with President Marcos, Derian sought to explain U.S. opposition to, or abstentions on, votes in international financial institutions on loans to countries that we considered violators of human rights. My report of the conversation notes: "She went on to say that she was concerned that if there were no human rights results as a consequence of our acts in these institutions, the amount of the American contribution would be lowered with consequence both for the banks and for the recipient countries. This sparked the strongest reaction from Marcos of any part of the discussion. He said 'You don't need to twist our arm. You don't need to employ dollar diplomacy.' He then went into a lengthy and emotional statement of the Filipino commitment to human rights, going back through their independence struggle and the war with Japan."

With the concurrence of Marcos, Derian met with Benigno Aquino in jail. My report notes that Patt "came back to the house euphoric, stating that there was a man who really understood what they were talking about and who could lead the Philippines back to true democracy. I cautioned that she needed to have some humility in making judgments on Philippine politicians in the course of a 24-hour visit, but she was not to be deterred from her strong feelings, that he represents our hope in this country."[85] My cautionary comment stemmed from my feeling, from reading and hearing about Aquino, that in background and attitudes he was not greatly different from Marcos. The main difference was that one was in, and the other was out.

When I returned to Washington as under secretary, I came to know and respect Patt Derian, but we always had a difference of opinion on how to approach human rights issues with authoritarian governments. She felt that we should emphasize the principles that we espouse and put less stress on how the U.S. Congress regarded such regimes. As my experience in Indonesia had demonstrated, foreign leaders were more receptive to the pressures from congressional action than from statements of principle by diplomats.

I must admit, however, that stressing to foreign leaders the strong feelings of members of the U.S. Congress on human rights has its risks. In January 1978 a large delegation from Congress visited Manila. I said to the members, "Now some of you have been very articulate in the House about the human rights violations in the Philippines. I hope that when you see President Marcos you will reiterate your concerns."

Their reply was, "Oh, that's your job. We are here as guests." They were surprisingly vulnerable to the charms of Mrs. Marcos, who led the visitors through the riches of the Marcos Foundation in houses next door to the palace. The visitors never seemed to realize how their silence undermined my efforts on this issue.

The Aquino story had a tragic end. In March 1980, Aquino suffered a heart attack. When Filipino doctors were reluctant to undertake surgery, he was permitted to leave for treatment and exile in the United States. In 1983, even though conscious of threats against his life, he and his wife, Corazon, returned to Manila. On his arrival at the airport on August 21, 1983, he was fatally shot in the head as he was being escorted off the airplane. The Philippine government claimed that a Communist hit man killed Aquino. The claim was never proven.

Satisfactory relations with President Marcos always had to be balanced with the need to avoid total identification with a dictatorial regime. I felt it important that while maintaining correct relations with the Marcos regime, the embassy do what it could to minimize identification with its excesses. I had observed revolutions in several countries in which we were so closely linked to a regime that, when it fell, our interests fell with it. In such cases, signals, often subtle signals, can be important to show a population that we are not totally wedded to an unpopular ruler. Even though different signals occasionally emanated from Washington, my predecessors and my successors believed we could take steps that protected our interests in the event of a regime change. This was easier to do in the Philippines, where we had many associations with the people and a strong reservoir of goodwill. U.S. Ambassador Michael Armacost recognized the importance of such symbols when immediately after Aquino's assassination he called on Aquino's mother to express condolences.

My wife Jean was an important partner in demonstrating independence from the regime. She assisted with arrangements for a benefit performance in the Embassy auditorium to raise funds for an orphanage for paraplegic children, organized by a Jesuit, Father James Reuter, a Marcos critic. The children presented a play, *The Dolls That Nobody Wanted,* and the performance was noted in the press. Its significance was not lost on either Mrs. Marcos or the Manila public.

Jean had lunch one day with Cory Aquino, the jailed Benigno Aquino's wife, who later became president when Marcos was forced out. Imelda Marcos, who had an excellent intelligence organization, knew of the planned lunch and invited both Jean and me to a luncheon on the presidential yacht on that same day. I accepted, but regretted for Jean. On the yacht, Mrs. Marcos conspicuously shunned me and spent her time talking with the Chinese and Russian ambassadors.

I set down some of my impressions of the Philippine tour in a letter to my former colleague James Blake (then ambassador to Iceland), dated February 14, 1978:

You would find this place fascinating. There is, first of all, the history. Everyone seems, at one time or another, to have come to the Philippines: the Chinese, the Dutch, the British, the Spanish and, of course, the Americans. A conversation of an evening can encompass tales of Chinese pirates landing at Lingayan Gulf or of outfitting a galleon for the long voyage to Mexico. Last week, I participated in a Navy Day celebration at which Mrs. Marcos dedicated a restored Spanish port, the first point in the Philippines captured by Admiral Dewey.

The American heritage is complex. There is much here that we can be proud of: the educational system, a significant middle class, one of the most substantial indigenous (non-Chinese) private sectors in Asia. The Philippine population shares our pride in our military heritage. Douglas MacArthur is a national hero. (I went to a luncheon in honor of MacArthur's birthday and found out I was the guest speaker; I intoned properly on the great heritage of the general.) A part of my duties consists of attending commemoration celebrations of all the major events in World War II: the fall of Bataan, the liberation of Manila, the landing in Leyte, et cetera. Another part entails entertaining officials of U.S. veterans' organizations and delegations, which come here in a constant procession.

We can be less proud of our political contribution. I had expected a somewhat wider appreciation of the responsibilities and tolerance of democracy. I have now come to realize that we ruled these islands through a series of significant oligarchies, much as the Spanish had done. These oligarchies then became centers around which political life evolved in the independent Philippines. By all accounts, the political life was borrowed more from Chicago and Jersey City than it was from Maine or Minnesota: tombstone voting, ballot stuffing, the private armies etc. . . . President Marcos and martial law have changed that, but there are many who regret this step.

It is gratifying for a diplomat to be remembered at the time of his departure. It is even more gratifying to be remembered favorably some years afterward. In an article in the *Manila Times Journal*, January 25, 1983, discussing the last four American ambassadors, Salvador P. Lopez wrote:

> Though David Newsom served here the most briefly of the four, he probably had the clearest and most balanced perception of the appropriate relationship that should subsist between the Philippines and United States during the difficult years of martial rule. In Washington in 1979, at a symposium on "ASEAN and the United States" [Newsom] set forth the official American policy at that time in these terms:
>
> "There are many in this country critical of the current situation in the Philippines. Filipino opposition figures in this country are free to speak their piece. On the official level, we have expressed our concern over the continuation of martial law.
>
> "Yet, this part of our dialogue should not obscure the deep reservoir of respect and affection for [the Philippines] which exists here. Neither should it obscure the genuine and valuable cooperation which continues to provide both our countries with valuable elements of security in an area of confrontation. After having served in the Philippines, I returned to this country feeling that, in some ways, that nation is among the least appreciated of our friends. That should not be so."

Lopez added, "I rather like that phrase 'the least appreciated of our friends.' Under Secretary of State David Newsom never got over the certain feeling he had for the Philippines and the Filipino people."[86]

17

HIS CONCERNS ARE GLOBAL

Jean and I were having breakfast on the terrace of the embassy residence in Manila in March 1978 when a telephone call from the State Department asked me to return to Washington to consider replacing Philip Habib as Under Secretary for Political Affairs. I fully understood that no one could replace Phil Habib, a legendary diplomat, but I took the job.

Shortly after I returned to Washington, a friend gave me a framed copy of a New Yorker cartoon. It showed a man at a reception sitting dejectedly in a corner with his head in his hands. The caption read "His concerns are global." Although I was more stimulated than dejected by my experience as under secretary, that caption correctly represented what I was to face in the next three years.

In the period between March 1978 when I returned to Washington and February 1981 when I retired, I was to witness and participate in intense diplomatic activity that accelerated significant changes in the world's political landscape, stimulated by decolonization and revolutions in Egypt, Iran, and Libya.

President Jimmy Carter was himself an instrument of change. He sought a resolution of the Arab-Israeli dispute by bringing together Egypt and Israel at the Camp David summit in September 1978. He pushed successfully for ratification of the Panama Canal treaties. He encouraged regime change in Nicaragua. He continued his emphasis on human rights. Although the confrontation with the Soviet Union continued, the seeds of decline behind the Iron Curtain were already apparent.

Change is not universally welcomed, even in the United States. The Camp David summit and the conclusion of the Canal treaties engendered criticism both external and internal. Efforts to promote human rights were continually complicated by the need for secure allies in the Cold War. And regime changes in Nicaragua, Afghanistan, and Iran proved beyond the capacity of Washington to control. The prolonged drama of the American Embassy hostages in Tehran finally doomed the political fortunes of the Carter administration even though all were eventually released. Each foreign policy success in Carter's administration had a political cost that ultimately undermined the administration.

Politics, diplomacy, protocol, and power come together dramatically on the seventh floor of the State Department. The position of Under Secretary for Political Affairs is the number three position in the department and frequently the highest post held by a career diplomat. It involves active interaction not only with the political structure of the White House but also with the Congress. Responsibility for major issues and crises can also devolve on the under secretary when the secretary and deputy secretary are away or preoccupied with high priority problems, as was the case in the Camp David negotiations on the Middle East in September 1978.

Each autumn the under secretary accompanied the secretary to the United Nations General Assembly in New York where, usually for a period of two weeks, the secretary met with foreign ministers from other member states. In one year, as I recall, we met with more than eighty foreign ministers.

Each secretary of state has used the position of under secretary in somewhat different ways. Secretary Cyrus Vance wanted me to serve as a chief of staff, coordinating many activities of the department and relieving him of direct responsibilities for some of the issues. Too numerous to mention were other ancillary duties—diplomatic receptions, greeting visitors at airports, and speaking engagements across the country.

Secretary Vance maintained the Soviet portfolio and the sometimes uneasy relationship on East-West issues with the president and Zbigniew Brzezinski, the national security adviser.[87] Vance was also heavily involved in the Camp David negotiations and in following the Iranian revolution in the hostage crisis.

Warren Christopher, as the deputy secretary, worked primarily with Congress and on issues with a strong domestic political component. He was action officer with Congress on the ratification of the Panama Canal treaty against a strong Republican opposition. He also played the primary role in untangling the bureaucratic controversies within the department over human rights issues. His final and significant contribution was the negotiation of the Algiers Accord, which ended the Iranian hostage crisis.

The Senate confirmed me as the new under secretary in April 1978. My confirmation hearing on April 11 provided senators with an opportunity to ask questions about my previous responsibilities, primarily in Africa and the Philippines. Few questions dealt with what were likely to be my future responsibilities.

Our day began at 7:30 a.m. with a meeting in Secretary Vance's office that included the secretary; Warren Christopher; Anthony Lake, head of policy planning; Peter Tarnoff, the executive secretary; Benjamin Read, undersecretary for management; Hodding Carter III, the spokesman; and me. The group discussed the major issues of the day and questions to be anticipated at the daily briefing of the press. On the basis of decisions made, it was my job to subsequently approve the guidance submitted by the various bureaus for that briefing.

As time went on my duties involved coordinating, mediating, and, as needed, overseeing the geographic bureaus, the Bureau of International Organizations, the Bureau of Intelligence and Research, and, on occasion, the bureaus of Humanitarian and Political Military affairs. Many were the evenings when I was about to depart that I received a frantic telephone call from C. William Maynes, the assistant secretary for international organization affairs, telling me that we had to make a decision within the next hour about a vote in the United Nations Security Council.

I was active in liaison with counterparts in the Central Intelligence Agency, Department of Defense, and National Security Council. Although there were tensions at the top in the Carter administration, I was able to work effectively with my counterparts on most issues.

The president's personal interest and an awareness of legislation on human rights made the concerns over how other governments treated their peoples a priority of the new leadership. But not everyone in the government was pleased with the human rights emphasis. Many were skeptical that such a policy could have beneficial results and believed that the emphasis could damage other foreign policy objectives. When I came into the department in March 1978, some fifty cases of disagreement simmered within and between bureaus over the implementation of legislation requiring attention to human rights. The cases involved not only legislative action against individual countries but also differences over how countries would be treated in the required annual report to Congress on human rights around the world. Deputy Secretary Christopher became the arbiter and ultimately resolved each one.

One administration focus involved Argentina, where a military junta was committing serious human rights violations in a "dirty war" against suspected communists. In 1977 an amendment to the Foreign Assistance Act, sponsored by two Democratic senators, Hubert Humphrey and Edward Kennedy, called for restricting military cooperation with Argentina unless that country, by October 1978, improved its human rights record.

Soon after my arrival in Washington, a Pentagon official concerned over the security of the South Atlantic approached me to see if the department would support the repeal of the Humphrey-Kennedy amendment. I asked him whether he really thought that the new Democratic administration, as one of its first acts, would seek repeal of a human rights amendment supported by two prominent Democrats. It was the last I heard of that proposal. But to respond to the Pentagon's concerns, I was sent to Buenos Aires in April 1978 to determine whether we could encourage any changes in Argentine policies. We hoped that, at the minimum, we could get the Argentine government to release political prisoners, agree to accept a review of their policies by the Inter-American Commission on Human Rights, and acknowledge the many disappearances of its citizens.

I met with Argentina's president and various other members of the ruling junta. Each seemed to be looking over his shoulder, wary of a knife in the back. Never have I seen such a balance of intrigue. They received me politely but insisted the United States should have a better understanding of the communist menace that they faced. I raised the question of the disappeared with Minister of Interior General Alveno Eduardo Harguindeguy. He waved his hand toward a set of file cabinets along the wall and said, "We know who the disappeared are. I have the files right there. But, if we acknowledge this, we will be deluged with legal claims, and we cannot countenance that." It was one of the more chilling experiences in my career and one of my less successful diplomatic interventions.[88]

In the years 1979 and 1980, the Cold War was still the central focus of U.S. policy. The Carter administration, and particularly the National Security Council staff, looked for and often assumed a Soviet hand in every development that seemed to threaten American interests, whether in Africa or Cuba or in the area that Dr. Brzezinski referred to as "the arc of crisis," the region stretching from India to the Mediterranean. The administration wanted to be certain that the Soviets "paid a price" for any aggression. At the same time, the administration wanted to avoid actions that would complicate efforts to gain Senate ratification for the second Strategic Arms Limitation Treaty (SALT II). Cold War dramas competed for attention with efforts to bring peace between Arabs and Israelis, decisions to prevent the spread of nuclear weapons, and growing threats to anticommunist friends.

Divisions that existed in the country over how to deal with the Soviet Union were reflected within the administration. Secretary of State Vance and his adviser on Soviet affairs, Marshall Shulman, generally sought to avoid confrontation. Zbigniew Brzezinski saw Soviet policy as an aggressive attempt to undermine American interests, both in the European field and in the Third World. President Carter sought, not always successfully, to bridge the differences.

Although other areas vied for attention, the central concern during much of the Carter administration was for the region embracing Pakistan, Afghanistan, and Iran. This came into sharp focus in April 1978 when a coup in Kabul brought a communist, Nur Mohammad Taraki, to power. The specter of a serious Soviet threat emerged in the region.

In July 1978 I was sent on a five-nation trip to explore the consequences of this development for U.S. policy. A press announcement on July 7 stated that I would visit Iran, Afghanistan, Pakistan, India, and Saudi Arabia "to hold discussions with leaders of the various countries on matters of mutual interest and concern."

My first stop was Tehran. The revolution in Kabul occurred at the same time as growing signs of instability and threats to the royal regime were appearing in Iran. On June 6, Ambassador to Iran William Sullivan had delivered to the shah a letter from President Carter responding to a May 6 letter he had received from the Iranian monarch that had expressed concern about developments in Kabul. Carter's letter informed the shah of my mission and stated that "domination of Afghanistan by the Soviet Union would be a development of great seriousness for the free world. It should, therefore, be a matter of high national policy for those of us who share this view to cooperate closely over the coming weeks and months."[89]

I met with the shah in his palace on the Caspian Sea on July 9. The audience, lasting an hour and forty-five minutes, ranged over Soviet ambitions in the region, internal problems in Pakistan and Turkey, the Arab-Israel conflict, and Rhodesia. Though my reporting telegram does not reflect this, my recollection is that when the shah turned to Iran, he seemed preoccupied with "turning over a democratic Iran to my son."[90] I came away with an impression of an indecisive, troubled man. None of us knew at the time that he was already suffering from cancer.

I followed the visit to Iran with one on July 11 to New Delhi, where I met with Prime Minister Morarji Desai and various ministers. Much of the attention in the discussions was on relations with Pakistan and the reluctance of India to make overtures to Islamabad in the absence of initiatives from Pakistan. India would reluctantly accept some U.S. military assistance to Pakistan in the light of developments in Afghanistan. The Indians, however, were reasonably relaxed about developments in Kabul and stated that "they want to treat Afghanistan as a nation still independent and welcome the fact we wish to do the same."[91]

In my visit to Kabul on July 13, I met with Taraki and his foreign minister, Hafizullah Amin. I found them friendly and desirous of maintaining relations with the United States. Each one had spent some time in America. A U.S. aid program had operated in the south of the country for many years. The Soviets had similarly been active in the north. In my recommendations to Washington after my visit,[92] I suggested that we not voluntarily withdraw our activities until the new regime raised the issue. As it turned out, our withdrawal would probably have made little difference in events as they unfolded. Conflict soon developed between the principal communist elements in Afghanistan. Both Taraki and Amin were later killed in the struggle for power. Keeping an American presence in the country did permit us to observe developments. The matter became moot when the Soviets invaded Afghanistan in December 1979.

From Kabul, I was driven on July 14 through the famous Khyber Pass to Peshawar in Pakistan. In 1978, the central issue in our relations with Pakistan was the clear evidence that Pakistan was seeking to develop nuclear weapons. They had signed an agreement with the French for a reprocessing plant, a development that threatened to trigger U.S. legislation that would prohibit assistance to countries breaking the nonproliferation barriers. Throughout my time in the department, this was to remain a serious obstacle to full relations with Islamabad.

My visit came at a troubled time in Pakistan. In 1977, the Pakistan army had overthrown and jailed the elected prime minister, Zulfikar Ali Bhutto, and established General Zia al-Haq as Martial Law Administrator. My report noted the Pakistani conviction that the Soviet Union was completely in control in Afghanistan and represented a major threat.[93] Suspicion of India remained high, and relations between Pakistan and the United States were troubled because of the threat to terminate aid and because of previous arms embargoes. Relations with Pakistan in the next two years were to be little better, with the hanging of Bhutto in 1979, Pakistan's continued pursuit of a nuclear weapon, and pressures created by the Soviet invasion of Afghanistan.

In my brief visit to Saudi Arabia on July 18, I encountered little interest in the problems of Afghanistan. The Saudis were, as might be expected, primarily concerned with nearby developments—in Yemen and Somalia. Words of the concluding paragraph of my reporting telegram could have been written in 2007: ". . . [T]here is no doubting the fact that this is a very important piece of real estate as far as we are concerned. We should continue to consult closely, bear patiently their litany and their contradictions, and find imaginative and acceptable ways to assure them of our constancy and support."[94]

My hurried trip gave us a view of a troubled area but resolved little. In the months after my return, even more dramatic changes were to occur.

A series of riots in various parts of Iran in the fall of 1978 weakened the shah's position, and he was ultimately overthrown and left the country in January 1979. Washington's hopes that a secular regime might emerge were dashed with the appearance and rise to power of the Ayatollah Ruhollah Khomeini.

I will never forget Valentine's Day 1979. The crises in Afghanistan and in Iran came together. I was called to the Operations Center in the department by word that, for the first time since the revolution, mobs had invaded the U.S. Embassy and were holding the ambassador and others hostage. On the same night, we received word that Adolph Dubs, our kidnapped ambassador to Afghanistan, had been killed in a botched rescue attempt in Kabul.

We were fortunate on that occasion to be able to find Iranian authorities to help restore the Embassy and free the hostages. Communications are vital in a crisis of this kind. The Swedish Embassy had an office on an upper floor in an adjoining building, and by peering into the American Embassy compound was able to inform us of what was happening. We were not so fortunate in November 1979, when the Embassy was seized again.

With Khomeini's seizure of power on February 1, 1980, it became clear that America's time in Iran was over. My office was subsequently heavily involved in ensuring the safe departure of 40,000 Americans and a fair termination of contract obligations. A number of Americans were working in the oilfields of Iran and did not see the need to leave the country. Their attitude changed when leaders of the emerging oilfield unions made life for them more difficult.

A particular problem arose with two employees of EDS, a Texas company run by Ross Perot. The revolutionary authorities had jailed the two men on grounds that EDS owed the government of Iran $24 million. Perot denied any such debt and insisted that this charge represented harassment by the new authorities. In a telephone call to me, he threatened to take action on his own to free his men. I urged him against it, arguing that any precipitate individual action would complicate efforts then underway to assure the safe removal of all

Americans. Perot later claimed that he had organized an operation that had freed the men by force. The alleged operation became the subject of a novel by Ken Follett, *On Wings of Eagles.* In the embassy in Tehran and in the department, we were skeptical of Perot's claim. The best information we had suggested that the men had walked out of prison when mobs stormed the prisons during the hectic days following the revolution.[95]

The shah, upon his departure, had been assured that he could, if he wished, come to the United States. Still hoping to return to Iran, or to be returned by us as he had been on previous occasions, the shah tarried in Egypt. As the revolution gained strength, however, admitting him to the United States became more and more of a risk to our people and interests in Tehran. Pressure for his admittance grew, led by David Rockefeller and Henry Kissinger. They appointed a former aide to the late Nelson Rockefeller, Robert Armeo, to lead the charge. I became the point man in the department for calls from Armeo and other friends of the shah.

Aides to high-level politicians develop a blunt and often arrogant persistence in pursuing the interests of their chiefs. As an advance man for Rockefeller when he was vice president, Armeo had developed these characteristics in full. His pressure increased when it was disclosed that the shah was suffering from lymphoma and related blockage of the bile duct. We had some heated exchanges as I sought to discourage efforts to bring the deposed Iranian ruler to the United States. Ultimately, after the shah had traveled from Egypt to Morocco, to the Bahamas, to Mexico, President Carter made the decision to admit him on compassionate grounds. He entered a hospital in New York on October 22, 1979. When it was suggested that the shah enter the hospital under an assumed name, Armeo, probably out of pique at my opposition, chose to admit him as David Newsom.[96]

Despite our best efforts to explain the circumstances to the Iranians and to assure them that we had no intention of returning the former ruler to Iran, the new regime remained deeply suspicious. Iranians had not forgotten the role played by the United States in removing their elected prime minister, Mohammad Mossadeq, and restoring the shah to power in 1952. Thirteen days later, on November 4, a mob took over the American Embassy, seizing 52 hostages. A 444-day drama ensued.

The administration immediately took steps to make contact with the new revolutionary officials to seek release of the hostages. President Carter suggested sending Ramsey Clark, a former U.S. attorney general, who had been acquainted with leaders of the Iranian National Front during Mossadeq's time. I was on the telephone to an officer in the Iranian foreign office to propose that we send Clark by U.S. military aircraft. The idea of a military plane immediately raised suspicions that we were seeking to reinstate the shah. Clark ultimately arrived by other means, but the mullahs who led the revolution had by then overtaken the influence of the National Front in Iran.

This first effort did not succeed, although within a few days the Iranians released six women and seven African-American men among the hostages, explaining "they are not spies."

In January 1980, just a few weeks after the hostages had been taken, I was visited by Sadiq al-Mahdi, a Sudanese lawyer. He had been involved in advising the Ayatollah Khomeini on the drafting of a new Iranian constitution. He told me that it was unlikely that Khomeini would agree to the release of the hostages until his constitution was in place, the new Majlis (parliament) had been elected, and responsibility for a release could be shifted to the parliament. As things turned out, that is exactly the pattern that took place. A new Majlis was elected, Khomeini presented what he considered the conditions for release, and a secret emissary agreed to meet Deputy Secretary Christopher in Europe.

But that process did not begin to unfold until August, and no U.S. president, given the pressures on him, could afford to do nothing until the strange new government in Tehran had spoken. This meant that for seven months the United States tried doubtful emissaries, arrangements with discredited Iranian politicians, and a failed military rescue mission. Secretary of State Vance strongly opposed the idea of a rescue mission and resented the fact that it took place, without consulting him, while he was away from Washington. He resigned on April 28, 1980, and Senator Edmund Muskie of Maine was appointed to take his place.

The major responsibility for managing the hostage crisis in the State Department had been with Secretary Vance and Harold Saunders, Assistant Secretary of State for Near East and South Asia. In addition to my involvement in overseeing the evacuation of 40,000

Americans, I joined Secretary Vance in periodic meetings with the families of the hostages and went to Frankfurt, Germany, to meet the first group released by the hostage takers.[97]

We could not have managed this crisis without the invaluable help of the Swiss, our protecting power in Tehran. Three paragraphs from an essay I wrote for a volume honoring Raymond Probst, Swiss ambassador in Washington at the time, describes their role:

> During the long days of 1980, when 52 of my diplomatic colleagues were held hostage in Iran, it was my custom to take an early morning walk. My route passed the Swiss Embassy, only a few blocks away. Each day as I passed, I could not help looking up at a window on the second floor—the office of the ambassador. Frequently a light would be burning at five or six in the morning. I knew that the ambassador was at work. I went to my own office with a special anticipation. That light suggested that our sensitive link with Iran, Ambassador Raymond Probst, had a new message, possibly of hope, possibly of disappointment.
>
> Throughout those days Ambassador Probst played a critical role as communicator, counselor, and friend to those of us struggling with the frustration and impenetrability of postrevolutionary Iran. He became to those of us involved in the issue a symbol of extraordinary help to a friendly nation facing a serious crisis abroad.
>
> Ambassador Probst, ably assisted by his minister, Frank Muheim, was our link to his colleague in the Swiss Ministry of Foreign Affairs, Ambassador Edouard Brunner, and to the end of the chain in Iran, Ambassador Erik Lang.[98]

The Swiss have had long experience as the protecting power in situations where diplomatic relations have been broken. They take the matter very seriously. But they draw a sharp distinction between protecting interests and representing a foreign government. Although the Swiss were helpful in sharing with us, through Ambassador Probst, Ambassador Lang's reporting from Tehran to Bern, they never agreed to our speaking to Ambassador Lang personally when he was in Switzerland on leave.

The seizure of the hostages in November 1979 was followed in December 1979 by the Soviet invasion of Afghanistan. In early December, as the civil conflict in Kabul worsened, we began to detect in satellite photos movements of Soviet troops toward the Afghan border. On Christmas day they moved into the country in force.

Opinions differed on the Soviet objectives in Afghanistan. Some saw the move as part of a grand plan to establish a Soviet presence in the Persian Gulf. Others related it to Moscow's concerns over the internal situation in Afghanistan and to Russian fears that the growing influence of Muslim fundamentalism might infect Islamic tribes in the Soviet region. Whatever the reason, the event was seen as a dangerous escalation in tensions with the Soviet Union, and policies were developed "to make Moscow pay a price." Sanctions were immediately imposed on the Soviet Union, and the decision was made to withdraw American participation in the Moscow Olympics of 1980.[99]

I was asked to inform Armand Hammer of Occidental Petroleum that he had to suspend a project to build a petrochemical plant in Russia. I was also involved in discussions with the Department of Agriculture about imposing a grain embargo, the most serious of the sanctions. I learned much about the complexities of the international grain trade.

The United States was able to maintain an embassy in Kabul during much of the Soviet occupation. It faced the complications of the occupation when, in September 1980, a Soviet soldier appeared at the door to the Embassy and requested asylum. The possibility of moving the soldier out of Afghanistan did not exist under the occupation. One option would have been to turn him over to the United Nations, but the UN representative in Kabul at that time was a Bulgarian. Naturally the Soviets wanted access to him, but our officials insisted that contact with him could only be made with a pledge of fair treatment. At one point the Soviet embassy brought the soldier's teacher from his village school, but referring to her as "an old bitch," the soldier refused to speak with her. Eventually his release was negotiated with an assurance that he would, as he wished, go to a technical school. One wag in the embassy commented, "Yes, Gulag Tech."

Few events in history have had as great an impact on the international scene as the Soviet invasion of Afghanistan. The encouragement of Islamic militancy as an instrument against the Soviets in tribes within Afghanistan and among the thousands of fighters who flowed in from other Muslim countries created a pattern of terrorism that has plagued the world since that time. Radical Islam found its strength and its voice. Al-Qaeda was born in the efforts to defeat the Russians in Afghanistan.

The invasion also dealt a mortal blow to arms control. Until the Soviet move into Afghanistan, the Carter administration had worked for the ratification of the second Strategic Arms Limitation Treaty (SALT II), despite strong congressional opposition. Throughout the period, decisions were weighed for their possible impact on SALT II. In the end, the invasion of Afghanistan, viewed as proof of Moscow's unreliability, doomed the treaty. Moreover, many feel that the Soviet decision to invade Afghanistan marked the beginning of the end of the Soviet Union.

The country most affected by the events in Afghanistan was Pakistan. Afghan refugees flowed into the western tribal territories. Given the tribal ties across the disputed border between Afghanistan and Pakistan, the government in Islamabad felt seriously threatened by the presence of formidable Soviet forces next door. President Zia ul-Haq turned to the United States for help.

The problems involved in responding to Zia's understandable call for help dramatically illustrated the complexities built into programs of American aid—even in the case of emergencies. In such cases not only is the credibility of the United States at stake, but so also is the credibility of governments that depend upon us in times of threat.

Congress has never agreed to a contingency fund that would give presidents the authority to commit resources in the face of unexpected developments. Immediate responses must be scraped together by reprogramming (with congressional consent) from existing resources. In the meantime, until it creates a more substantial response, Washington must resort to soliciting help from other countries, promising consultations on requirements, and making forceful public statements. This was the case with Pakistan after the Soviet invasion.

My memorandum to the secretary on May 3, 1980, described the situation:

> Following the Soviet invasion of Afghanistan, President Carter and others stated that an urgent effort to strengthen Pakistan would be a "central element" in the US response. As a first step we publicly reaffirmed the validity of our 1959 bilateral agreement with Pakistan.[100] Privately we put together a $400 million assistance package.... We also decided to seek congressional acquiescence in lifting the effects of the Symington amendment on Pakistan for this purpose.
>
> News of this package leaked to the press before we had time to present it to the Pakistanis. By the time Dr. Brzezinski and Mr. Christopher reached Islamabad on February 1, Pakistani leaders had already concluded that our offer was grossly insufficient, and Zia had publicly denigrated it as "Peanuts." The Pakistanis asked for a firmer security commitment to be embodied in treaty form, as well as for more resources. They argued that our offer would unnecessarily provoke the Soviets without contributing sufficiently to Pakistan's security to justify the risk. He adamantly refused to permit us to submit legislation to the Congress, despite our warning that the budget window was fast closing.
>
> By mid-March, the Pakistanis had calmed down sufficiently to clarify their position in a way that had not been obvious to us earlier—they would rather forgo military assistance altogether than accept the amounts we had offered, but remained interested in strictly economic aid. Regarding the latter, their first priority was debt rescheduling (which they have always considered as just another form of aid), followed by more traditional assistance.[101]

The memorandum highlighted three difficult problems for the administration: the nuclear issue, the request for a treaty, and debt rescheduling.

The reference to the Symington amendment signaled the nuclear issue. A paragraph from a review of nonproliferation issues explains the problem of providing military assistance:

> Notwithstanding the concern about Soviet adventurism in the Persian Gulf region, Section 669 of the 1961 Foreign Assistance Act prohibited such aid to Pakistan. This provision, added to the Act as the "Symington amendment" in 1976, stated that the United States could not give economic or military assistance to any nation that imported uranium enrichment technology, unless that nation agreed to full-scope IAEA [International Atomic Energy Agency] inspections. Pakistan, known to have imported such technology, had refused to permit the necessary safeguards. The amendment contained a proviso allowing the president to waive the ban on aid—but only if he certified to Congress that termination of assistance would have a serious adverse effect on vital U.S. interests and that he had received reliable assurances that the country in question would neither acquire or develop nuclear weapons nor assist other nations in doing so. The satisfaction of the first waiver condition was not difficult under the circumstances, but the administration was unable to certify that Pakistan had renounced nuclear weapons. Despite General Zia's insistence that his country's nuclear program was entirely peaceful, intelligence reports leaked to the press indicated that Pakistan was continuing its active efforts to develop nuclear explosives. Hence no aid could be provided without a change in the Symington amendment.[102]

A request for a treaty presents any administration with formidable obstacles. The Senate has historically been reluctant to commit the United States through treaties. Nearly every treaty agreed to by the United States has been the result of a serious legislative battle. At the time of the invasion of Afghanistan at least fifty treaties negotiated in good faith by American diplomats awaited ratification; at least one went back to the time of President James Madison.

Debt rescheduling not only presented budget problems but also risked establishing precedents that would cause other debtor countries to request similar privileges. Other problems inherent in any response to Pakistan included the sensitivity of India and the reluctance of a Pakistan government to have a high-profile American military presence in the country.

In recognition of the complexities of American assistance, Washington turned to other countries, particularly China and Saudi Arabia, urging them to consider financial and military equipment assistance to Pakistan.

It was not until the Reagan administration took office that the problems of aid to Pakistan were more fully worked out. Sanctions against the Soviet Union were accompanied by a major diplomatic effort to persuade other countries, and particularly allies, to help Pakistan and to press the Soviets in various ways to withdraw.

On January 24, 1980, I met with King Hussein of Jordan in London. In a career that included contacts with a variety of less than admirable world leaders, my conversation with the king of Jordan stands out as an exception. The man whom in my days in the Office of Near Eastern affairs we used to call "BYK"—the brave young king—was personable, honest, and skillful in keeping his kingdom intact in a dangerous world. Our conversation in London covered not only the common apprehensions regarding the area created by events in Afghanistan and Iran, but also Iraq, the Palestinian problem, and the implications of a possible union between North and South Yemen. Because of counter pressures from Palestinians, the king had not supported the Camp David agreement but nevertheless welcomed the chance to improve relations with the United States.

The meeting took place on the eve of an Islamic summit in which the case of hostages in Iran, the Soviet invasion of Afghanistan, and the Palestinian issue were likely to be raised. My reporting telegram infers from King Hussein's remarks that the Arabs would seek a resolution that would publicly condemn the Soviet invasion while linking the condemnation to a united Islamic appeal to the United States to press Israel to solve the Palestinian problem.[103]

Later that month, on January 28, I flew to Bucharest to deliver a letter from President Carter to President Nikolai Ceausescu, a quite dissimilar sort of leader. Nonetheless, as a communist who had refused to slavishly follow the Soviet Union, he was regarded differently from other Soviet satellite rulers.

Bucharest, at least in January, was one of the drabbest cities I have ever visited. The center of what must at one time have been a reasonably beautiful city was the site of a massive boulevard with Lenin-style block buildings on either side. The woman provided by the embassy to assist us said she was fearful every day that the bulldozers would show up at her house to begin demolishing another area.

In his letter to Ceausescu, Carter stated, "I am confident that I can count on your full support for efforts to find just and peaceful solutions to the grave crises that currently jeopardize our common desire for a more stable and secure world."[104]

My telegram (in telegraphese) summarizes the discussion: "Had lively two-hour session, during which President Ceausescu expressed continuing criticism of Soviet invasion of Afghanistan while indicating personal puzzlement over motives for their actions, other than presumed Soviet reaction to foreign backing of Afghan rebels. In lively give and take discussion Ceausescu: (1) was skeptical that the US counter actions to Soviets or sanctions on Iran would have desired effect; (2) expressed confidence in prospects for Yugoslav stability post-Tito; (3) felt US should do a lot more re Palestinian issue and, despite counter arguments, promoted idea during current Camp David negotiations of parallel initiative involving Soviets, and relating to Palestinian rights; (4) emphasized Romanian hopes for continuation of CSCE [Conference on Security and Cooperation in Europe], specifically stressing military disengagement and nuclear missiles issue; (5) cautioned US about promoting relations with China at expense of Soviets or other nations." [105] Nine years later, on Christmas day 1989, Ceausescu was overthrown and executed.

United States interest in Romania stemmed not only from Ceausescu's stand against the Soviets, but also from interest in the Jewish community. Under congressional pressure Washington had linked the granting of most-favored-nation trade status with the annual emigration of a certain number of Jews. I visited Rabbi Moses Rosen, the head of the Jewish community; his house and center were one of the few buildings spared from destruction.

In June 1980 I accompanied President Carter as he carried the diplomatic torch on a trip to Lisbon, Rome, Belgrade, Madrid, and

Vienna. In Vienna he attended an economic summit that produced a joint declaration condemning the Soviet invasion and calling for a complete troop withdrawal.[106]

We arrived in Yugoslavia just a month after Marshal Tito's death. Tito, even more than Ceausescu, had demonstrated his independence from the Soviet Union. He had been an important world leader, a founder of the nonaligned movement. He had also held together the restless republics that formed Yugoslavia. I had previously visited Belgrade in April 1979. At that time our ebullient ambassador, Lawrence Eagleburger, had warned me of the fragile nature of the Balkan state and, with considerable foresight, predicted that, upon the death of Tito, Kosovo would become a serious problem. I was not therefore surprised at the tension during the Carter visit when we met with the Council of Presidents of the various republics that made up Yugoslavia. The presidents clearly had little regard for each other and few spoke without looking for guidance from Stevan Doronjski, the secretary general of the Communist Party. I was not surprised when Yugoslavia broke up.

It had been a message from Marshal Tito that played a role in taking me back to my old haunt, Libya. In September 1978, a visit to Libya by Billy Carter, together with a delegation from the state of Georgia, attracted press attention. Without informing the State Department, President Carter called in Ali Hudairi, the head of the Libyan People's Bureau (Libya's post-revolutionary equivalent of an embassy) for a private talk. The president presumably wished to disassociate himself from any actions of his brother.

When we learned in the State Department that our head of state had received a Libyan representative, we believed this provided an opening for the United States to request that Muammar Qaddhafi, the Libyan ruler, receive a senior official. The idea was reinforced when a message was received from Marshal Tito stating that the Libyans wished to improve relations with the United States.

Accordingly, I visited Tripoli on June 17, 1979. My chances for progress and a meeting with Qaddhafi were seriously diminished when, on the initiative of Senator Jacob Javits of New York, Congress placed a ban on further aircraft sales to Libya. A Libyan role had been suspected in a Palestinian attack on an El Al airliner in Istanbul in

1976 in which an aide to Senator Javits had been killed. In addition, Libya had used two Boeing 727 airliners to transport troops to Uganda in support of Idi Amin and was an outspoken critic of the Egyptian-Israeli peace agreement negotiated at Camp David. In addition, Washington was refusing to release C-130 transport planes that Libya had purchased before the revolution.[107]

In my one-day visit to Libya I met separately with the secretary general of the foreign office, the minister of foreign affairs, and Major Abdul Salam Jallud, Qaddhafi's number two. The conversations ranged over Camp David, Libya's relations with Egypt, and Libya's relationship with the Palestinian movement. In each meeting, the Libyans returned to the ban on aircraft. It was clear that if a basis did exist for an improvement in bilateral relations, such improvement would not be possible without a solution to the aircraft problem. My request to see Qaddhafi was met with the statement that he was "250 miles away."[108]

Concerns were expressed in both Cairo and Tel Aviv over my visit to Tripoli. A telegram to our ambassador in Cairo explained the rationale: "We have had a dialogue with the Libyans reaching back over some time in an effort to find the basis for a reasonable if limited relationship given our interests there. The present situation results more from our own decision not to sell 747s to Libya than from Qaddhafi's statements, and we felt the need to put that in the least unpalatable perspective possible."[109]

In the Cold War era, troubling Soviet activities were also present in Latin America. Cuba, since Fidel Castro appeared on the scene, had become a treacherous issue for American politicians, made so by pressures from the Cuban exile community, particularly in Florida, and by Cuba's close relationship with the Soviet Union. This was certainly so during the Carter administration.

My participation in secret talks with Cuban representatives introduced me to the complexities of our relations with Castro's Cuba and also to the deep divisions within the administration. In early 1978 the administration had been approached by a Cuban exile businessman in Florida, Bernardo Benes, who had been in touch with officials in Havana. He suggested that the Cubans were prepared to open talks on the release of political prisoners, including a number of American citizens captured in the Bay of Pigs, the abortive 1961 invasion of Cuba.

President Carter decided to respond and authorized David Aaron, deputy national security adviser, to meet secretly with a Cuban representative, Jose Luis Padron, in New York on April 14, 1978. Aaron was to stress (and presumably did) that any normalization of relations with the United States would be contingent on Cuba's ending its military intervention in various parts of the world.

In a memorandum sent to Dr. Brzezinski on April 13, 1978, Aaron wrote that he would tell the Cubans "specifically, military intervention elsewhere in the world—in particular in Africa—is the principal obstacle to improvement in our relations. We have no objection to normal involvement in economic development, in medical and educational activities, but we cannot accept Cuban combat forces operating at will in Africa or elsewhere."[110]

I was subsequently authorized to meet with Padron, to discuss prisoner release, and, on the basis of my previous African experience, to explain U.S. policies in Africa. Together with an interpreter, Stephanie van Reigersberg, I met Padron and another Cuban, Antonio de la Guardia, in the St. Regis Hotel in New York for a six-hour conversation.

The Cuban interest in the prisoner question was clearly motivated by their concerns about attitudes in the Florida exile community, as reflected by Benes. They also wished to raise broader issues in U.S.-Cuban relations, including the U.S. embargo. My instructions from the White House were to avoid responding to any other issues raised by the Cubans. Those were to be discussed only in an exclusive NSC channel.

It was difficult in a daylong conversation to avoid other issues, and when I gained access to NSC documents in preparing this memoir, I discovered that I had been sharply criticized for exceeding my mandate. The following is from a memorandum from David Aaron to Zbigniew Brzezinski dated July 20, 1978:

> It is difficult to make this point but it is a fact that Newsom exceeded his mandate (which was to talk only about prisoners) and invited a discussion of other substantive matters as well as consideration of the procedure for following up on

> those other matters. Moreover, Newsom took [a] position on at least two issues which go beyond the administration's line. First, he suggested that their bill for damages and our bill for expropriations ought to be equal. [I do not find such a suggestion in the record of the conversations.] Second, he told the Cubans that he thought they were in Africa on their own and not as tools of the Soviets. At the same time he indicated that others in the administration had different views. This is bad for two reasons. First, my line, which you and the President approved, is that regardless of their motivation they are in effect serving as tools. Secondly, Newsom openly acknowledges past differences with the administration and put[s] himself on the side of being more pro-Cuban.

Aaron suggested that I not be included in further discussions with the Cubans.[111]

I presume that Secretary Vance did not agree, for I continued to lead three more sessions with the Cubans. Indicative of the close ties between Havana and the United States, both Cubans I met with had relatives in the United States and one, at least, was a New York Yankees fan. Meetings took place in the St. Regis Hotel in New York, a hotel in Atlanta, my own house in Cleveland Park in Washington, and in a motel in Cuernevaca, Mexico.

In the sessions, when we raised the question of Cuban activities in Africa, Padron placed the blame on us. The following is the Cuban's statement from the memorandum of my conversation with him on June 15, 1978:

> ...[O]ur links with Africa are historic and began with many of the countries before their independence. ... Plus, there are strong historical ties. In the liberation struggles of Guinea and Angola against the colonialist government of Salazar, many Cubans fought, and in one way or another, we have close relations with all existing liberation movements in Africa. This is a part of our foreign relations philosophy.
>
> The US attempted to isolate Cuba politically and diplomatically, to blockade us economically, and to harass us

> systematically. We felt that the proper alternative for us was to unify closely with the Third World, both for self-defense and for self-preservation.[112]

American administrations during the Cold War had a fixation about the Cuban role in Africa. Henry Kissinger accompanied President Gerald Ford to Indonesia in 1976, when I was ambassador in Jakarta. I could scarcely get Dr. Kissinger to focus on Indonesian affairs because of his clear preoccupation with the Cuban troops in Angola. On the basis of my African experience, while not denying that the Soviets could be exploiting the situation, I saw the Cuban presence as related, at least in part, to their ideological support for the African struggle for independence. I believed that Cuba had a role of its own in its relations with that continent, and I reflected that in my statement to Padron. Later research on recently opened Cuban archives demonstrates that the Cubans did make the decision to send troops to Angola without consulting Moscow.[113]

Although I believed that I was indeed following the instructions I was given, I also felt that we were unlikely to move the Cubans with blunt demands that they withdraw their troops without giving them some indication of what benefits to them might follow if they did. Perhaps I was naïve, but I could not help but wonder whether, if we had been ready to discuss substantive bilateral issues with the Cubans, leaving the African issues aside, we might have made some headway in resolving those issues. We could then have made clear to the Cubans that their presence in Africa was an impediment to moving forward with the resolution of those issues.

We did get an indication of the dire state of the Cuban economy. In Cuernevaca, we were housed in a motel of cottages—the Cubans on one side and our delegation on the other. As we were leaving, the housekeeper came to me and said, "Who is going to pay for the sheets, blankets, and towels taken by your friends on the other side?" I had to leave that for State Department auditors to figure out.

Our talks succeeded. Fidel Castro announced his intention to release prisoners in August. Subject to the procedures of the U.S.

Department of Justice, it was anticipated that as many as 3,000 might ultimately be freed.

The pressure to get Cuban troops out of Africa was less successful. Cuban troops did not leave Ethiopia until ten years later—in 1989—and they did not leave Angola until 1991.

One politically damaging development involved reports of a Soviet brigade in Cuba in the fall of 1979. Having constantly in mind the Cuban missile crisis of 1962, the Carter White House was sensitive to reports of possible new Soviet military moves on the island. Intelligence revealed the presence of a brigade of Soviet troops.[114] I was instructed to raise the issue with the Soviet chargé d'affaires. I encountered only the question, "What is your legal basis for raising the issue?" After I explained that such activities close to our borders were a matter of legitimate concern, the chargé promised to refer the matter to Moscow.

Because the whole matter of possible Russian bases in Cuba had been before the Congress, we felt obliged to inform congressional leaders of the intelligence. I then alerted the chairman of the Senate Foreign Relations Committee, Frank Church, who was in the midst of a tough reelection campaign in Idaho. He reacted angrily and went public with a statement urging the Carter administration to demand the withdrawal of the troops. I learned only later that Senator Church had previously been embarrassed when informed by the Kennedy administration of Russian missiles in Cuba, after previously being assured that rumors of such missiles were unfounded.

Soviet Ambassador Anatoly Dobrynin who had been in Moscow on leave returned and held a series of talks with Secretary Vance. Throughout he insisted that the brigade represented no new deployment but had been there, with the agreement of the United States, since 1962. In the emotion of the moment, and under the shadow of history, Washington was reluctant to accept this explanation. Unfortunately, however, the Soviets were right. In mid-October, McGeorge Bundy, who had been the national security adviser in the Kennedy administration, publicly revealed that as part of the agreement on the withdrawal of the Soviet missiles in 1962, the United States had agreed that the Russians could retain a brigade in the very location to guard remaining Soviet installations.[115]

The clash with domestic politics was center stage on another occasion. In April 1980, Castro, piqued at American policies toward his country, advertised that boats would be leaving the beaches at Mariel for the beaches of Florida and urged those Cubans with relatives in the United States to leave. A massive exodus of people on boats of all kinds— large and small—ensued. Grandparents, aunts, uncles, and cousins of those who had previously fled to Florida saw a new opportunity. In an effort to stop the flow, the Carter administration decided to invite leaders of the Cuban-American community in Florida to Washington. The hope was to gain the cooperation of the community in discouraging the boatlift.

The administration invited a delegation of Cuban exiles from Florida to Washington to meet with Vice President Walter Mondale. While the exiles were en route, the political operatives at the White House had second thoughts and shifted the meeting to the State Department. Instead of meeting the vice president, they met Deputy Secretary of State Warren Christopher and me in the State Department on April 26, 1980.

A not-too-happy group of about forty filed into the seventh floor conference room. Warren Christopher had uttered only a few words before one of the Florida delegation stood up and asked, "Are we here to discuss the overthrow of Castro?"

The deputy secretary sought to explain that was not the purpose of the meeting. The leader stated, firmly, "If we are not going to discuss the overthrow of Castro, then there is no use our staying."[116] The delegation stood up and headed for the door. That was the end of the diplomatic effort to shut off the Mariel boatlift, which ultimately brought 125,000 Cubans to the United States.

Every recent administration has worked in Latin America to prevent the creation of "another Cuba." The Carter government was focused on Nicaragua. A revolt was brewing against President Anastasio Somoza, fueled by charges of corruption that followed the failure to rebuild the country after a massive earthquake in 1972.[117] Taking the name of an earlier Nicaraguan rebel, the new rebels called themselves Sandinistas. Leftist in philosophy, they had support from other Latin American countries, including Cuba. In

June 1979 they were threatening action against Somoza's National Guard.

With the help of the Organization of American States (OAS), Washington sought to arrange a peaceful transition to a government of national reconciliation. Somoza believed that the United States would continue to support him and refused to cooperate in any such transition.

Two members of Congress, Charles Wilson of Texas and John Murphy of New York, were strong supporters of Somoza as a dependable anticommunist ally. I had known Murphy, who had oil interests in Indonesia, when I was living in Jakarta. When it was learned that he was encouraging Somoza to reject calls for his retirement, I was asked to call Murphy. I did not get very far. He said something like, "You are calling for democracy in Nicaragua. I know what democracy is. I am from Staten Island. And Nicaragua under Somoza is democratic."

With the mediation of an American diplomat, William Bowdler, and the help of several Latin American governments, an agreement was worked out under which Somoza resigned and flew to Miami on July 17, 1979. The Sandinistas took power. It was left to the incoming Reagan administration to pursue the elimination of Cuban influence in Nicaragua.

The Mariel boatlift was but one of several issues involving the movement of people. Because so many individuals around the world dream of the United States as a haven, the freedom of peoples to move is a constant preoccupation in the Congress and in the State Department.

By 1978, three years after the end of the war in Vietnam, the flow of refugees from Indochina was overwhelming countries in Southeast Asia. The issue had a broad bureaucratic spectrum involving the White House, the departments of State, Defense, Justice, and Health and Human Services, as well as state and city authorities and private nonprofit organizations. The situation called for establishing machinery to deal effectively with all aspects of the resettlement issue. Working with a fine officer in the Justice Department, Doris Meissner, (who later became director of the Immigration and Naturalization Service), we succeeded in creating a position in the State Department for a Special Assistant for Refugee Affairs.

In December of that year I led an American delegation to a meeting of thirty-eight nations to seek a solution to the problem. We could only begin to approach the issue and to lay the foundation for later international conferences.[118]

In 1979, when Poland was still under Soviet domination, the Polish government was blocking more than a thousand family members from leaving to join relatives in the United States. In addition, they were denying passports to Polish intellectuals who had been invited to come to the United States by the U.S. government and American academic institutions. I traveled to Warsaw and met with the vice foreign minister, Marian Dobrosielski, flanked by monitoring bureaucrats. I got nowhere. The minister replied to my raising the individual cases, saying, "If we have prevented people from leaving, we have good reason to do so. Besides, what right do your universities have to select professors to go abroad? That is our business."[119]

That night at a dinner the minister gave for me, he took me aside. "We have reviewed the cases," he said, "and I think we can agree to most of them. However, one of the professors you have invited has offended a large Eastern neighbor."[120]

Events in Poland, including the election of Karol Wojtyla to become Pope John Paul II and the shipyard strike at Gdansk in 1980, presaged major change in another Soviet satellite. I met twice in that year with George Meany, head of the AFL-CIO, to share information on the situation and to discuss possible assistance to anti-communist Solidarity elements in the country.

In my three years as under secretary I was able to witness only the beginning of dramatic developments in Eastern Europe. The adventure of experiencing those changes would fall to another team.

On November 4, 1980, President Carter lost the election to Ronald Reagan. The day after, the process of transferring power began. I had seen such transfers before from a distance. This time, as the senior State Department officer who would be "left behind," I had an intimate inside view.

The incoming administration appointed a forty-person State transition team. Several of its members were from Republican congressional staffs. In my opinion, they were more interested in fishing through the State Department files for dirt on Democrats than they were in bringing about an orderly transition. From President-elect Reagan on down, few Republicans initially showed interest in briefings on issues from the outgoing Democrats.

Late in December, General Alexander Haig was nominated to be the new secretary of state and the true transition began. He dismissed the original transition team and appointed Paul Wolfowitz, Richard Burt, and Kenneth Adelman to work with me. They were serious individuals who understood the problems.

At one point in the transition I had to intervene directly with Secretary-Designate Haig. In early January the White House transition team sent a memorandum to all executive departments saying that no Carter presidential appointee should be at his or her desk after January 20. I went to General Haig and pointed out that, in the State Department at least, many of the presidential appointees were career Foreign Service officers. To remove them from their positions would mean that after the inauguration, and for an uncertain time until others were confirmed, the department would be without most of its senior officers. The new secretary understood this and intervened with the White House. The White House agreed to leave State Department presidential appointees in office with the exception of three, two of whom had been responsible for Latin American policy. The third had been considered too politically active on behalf of the Democrats.

Misunderstandings regarding past actions, nevertheless, continued. At the time of the inauguration, I met with a group of Republican lawyers who were recommending that an agreement negotiated by Warren Christopher for the release of the hostages should be abrogated. On the basis of articles in a conservative journal, they were convinced that the United States had paid ransom for the hostages. I was, fortunately, able to convince them that, contrary to their impression, the intricate arrangements worked out to release the frozen Iranian assets actually resulted in an agreement to use those assets to pay off American claims against Iran.

Secretary of State Muskie resigned on January 18. When he descended in the secretary's elevator that day, I suddenly became a footnote to history, an interim secretary of state. The new Reaganites began carrying in their boxes on January 20, inauguration day. As they entered, we were learning from CNN that the hostages were finally boarding the Algerian airliner that would take them to freedom.

Although I was technically the secretary of state because no Reagan appointee had yet been confirmed by the Senate, the Reagan people quickly took charge. As one of my first acts under the new administration, I had to inform a disappointed Edmund Muskie that he could not use the State Department auditorium to brief the press on the agreement under which the hostages were released.

It was several days before Alexander Haig was confirmed by the Senate as the new secretary of state and before my interim status came to an end. I spent several more days briefing the new secretary and his team and, early in February, turned in my pass and walked out of the State Department for the last time as an active diplomat. Thirty-three wonderful years witnessing changes in the world scene and participating in making and implementing American foreign policy had come to an end.

18

LIFE AFTER GOVERNMENT

What does one do after nearly thirty-five years of exciting, satisfying involvement in the world of diplomacy and foreign policy? Many possibilities exist, at least in theory: academia, consulting, corporate boards, lobbying, journalism, business management, and relaxing on a golf course in Florida. After retirement I made brief excursions into the world of consulting, but my preference was academia. I had frequently dreamed of retiring as a professor on a university campus.

As I neared the end of my tour in Indonesia, I began to explore opportunities outside of government. Each potential opportunity presented problems for me. Business opportunities were obviously likely to be more lucrative, but I was not sure that I was cut out to open doors for businesses to foreign officials I had known as a diplomat. Lecture agencies were looking for far more sensational careers than mine. Full-time teaching positions in a major university required not only a Ph.D. but a record of publications as well.

I had been encouraged to continue in the diplomatic profession by none other than Henry Kissinger. I accompanied him to North Africa in 1973 on his first trip as secretary of state, and somewhere over the Atlantic we discussed my future. I was never sorry that I took his advice, and I put aside exploring other options at that moment. The future opened to the unique experience of the Philippines, the memorable years as under secretary for political affairs, and the transition in administrations that followed.

The question of my post-retirement career was solved in 1981, when Dean Peter Krogh of the Georgetown University School of Foreign Service invited me to become part of the newly organized

Institute for the Study of Diplomacy with a concurrent appointment as associate dean of the school. For the next eighteen years I would be introduced to a new culture: academe. At Georgetown that would include administration, fundraising, and teaching. At the University of Virginia to which I was invited in 1991 upon my retirement from Georgetown, the experience was confined to teaching.

I did not, however, totally escape the administrative responsibilities of the Washington institution. In June 1996, I received an unexpected telephone call from Father Leo O'Donovan, then president of Georgetown University. Peter Krogh had submitted his resignation as dean of the School of Foreign Service. Would I return to Georgetown and serve as interim dean until a successor was chosen?

How to respond to Father O'Donovan was not a simple decision. I was comfortably established in Charlottesville and had teaching obligations at the University of Virginia. I learned that Dean Krogh had made the sudden decision to retire because of a new university edict requiring "restructuring"—a further integration of the school into Georgetown College. Never one to turn down a challenge, I accepted. The next year was to represent a further education in the academic culture. I returned to Washington to face an angry staff and faculty fearful that the new requirement represented a serious threat to the independence and identity of the school.

What followed was one of the most difficult assignments of my career, requiring as much diplomatic skill as any issue involving a foreign government. Relations between individual members of the faculties of the school and the college were in some cases tense. In one instance, a professor in the college who had shared an office with one in the school placed all of his colleague's effects in the corridor when she went on sabbatical. On one of my first mornings as interim dean, I faced a tearful, unhappy professor.

During that year I negotiated twenty-five joint appointments involving tenure and merit pay, oversaw the appointment of a new dean of the school, Robert Gallucci, and generally reduced the anxieties of the faculty. A number of colleagues who served with me at that time gave me credit for saving the independence and identity of the School of Foreign Service.

The School of Foreign Service at Georgetown University was established in 1919 by Father Edmund A. Walsh, a Jesuit. Following World War I, Father Walsh saw the need for training diplomats as the United States assumed a greater role in the world. For many years thereafter Georgetown has remained one of the principal training institutions for Americans entering the diplomatic service.

The school's Institute for the Study of Diplomacy (ISD), the brainchild of R. Smith Simpson and Peter Krogh, had been founded in 1978 to enhance the understanding in Washington and beyond of the nature and importance of effective diplomacy. The eminent diplomat Ellsworth Bunker became its founding chairman. Its first director of studies and director, Martin F. Herz, a retired Foreign Service officer, died of cancer in 1983. I had succeeded him as director in 1981. In shaping the objectives of the Institute, I realized that I needed to define what I meant by "diplomacy." I discovered that there were several definitions.

Diplomacy is defined simply in Webster's collegiate dictionary as "the art and practice of conducting negotiations between nations." The Oxford dictionary defines it more broadly as "the management of international relations." In both the policy world and the academic world, however, diplomacy is interpreted in several ways. It may refer to particular problems of a diplomatic service, to interaction among nations, to the grand foreign policy strategy of a nation or group of nations, or to the particular techniques of analysis, negotiation, and persuasion that accompany one nation's efforts to influence another.

Some see "diplomacy" in pejorative terms as a weak alternative to the use of force. On one occasion I visited a West Coast corporate foundation and met with its representative, a retired general counsel of the corporation. When I explained that I was seeking support for the enhancement of our diplomatic skills, he replied rather abruptly, "We don't believe in diplomacy. If we're not going to fight the Russians we sure as hell should not talk to them."

Others view it as a game. During the 1980s' Iraq-Iran war, I spoke on the problem to the Kiwanis Club in Dallas, Texas. One of the members asked, "Which side are we on?"

I replied that we were not on either side, given the problems we had with both Iraq and Iran. He came back, "Down here we see it as like a Cowboy-Redskins game. We want to know who we are for."

In its earliest years the Institute focused on the problems of the United States Foreign Service and issued a series of monographs, such as *Contacts with the Opposition, Diplomacy: The Role of the Wife, The Consular Dimension of Diplomacy, Diplomats and Terrorists: What Works, What Doesn't,* and *The Modern Ambassador,* all edited by Martin Herz.[121]

With Dean Krogh's strong support, I expanded the mission of the Institute to add an international dimension. Ambassadors from France, Germany, Italy, and Singapore who had served in Washington became Counselors to the Institute. Diplomats from the United States and other countries were invited to become resident associates at the Institute and to teach their specialties in the university. Another program provided fellowships to student associates who would carry out projects guided by experienced practitioners. Teaching and research emphasized specific methods and talents required for effective diplomatic action. The Associates Program over the years was highly successful. Many who came to us for a year or more in Washington went on to senior positions in their governments as cabinet ministers and ambassadors. At least one became the dean of a law school in his country.

The Institute also continued a modest program of book publication, under the editorial direction of Margery Boichel Thompson, and sponsored lectures and awards, including awards for diplomatic achievement and for media coverage of diplomatic events. One of these, the Weintal Award, named for Teddy Weintal, a well-known correspondent who had covered the State Department for many years for *Newsweek,* brought to the campus prominent foreign correspondents to receive the award and speak of their experience. James "Scotty" Reston, columnist for the *New York Times,* received the award in 1992. He took issue with the request that he give "an address:"

> Mr. Chairman, let me assure you that reporters don't make addresses as advertised in this evening's program. We hate addresses. All our professional lives, we cover them by

> command and in quiet despair. The very sight of an old man mounting a platform armed with a sheaf of paper usually produces in the press box a melancholy sigh. Increasingly in this age of advertising hucksters, political manipulators, and anonymous speech writers, we listen to the mystifying clarifications of foreign policy and wonder who produce these revelations and how long will the right honorable gentleman go on.[122]

As administrator of the Institute, I also became aware of some basic facts of life. Not all space wars are fought with satellite weapons in science fiction. Many are fought over offices in academic institutions. When I joined the Institute in 1981 my office was in a conference room shared with a recently appointed research professor, Donald F. McHenry, former U.S. ambassador to the United Nations. We were both looking forward to more adequate office space in the new Intercultural Center being built with federal funds.

The financing of the center is a story in itself. Following the Vietnam War, which exposed American ignorance about Asia, the deans of the Georgetown School of Foreign Service and the Fletcher School of Law and Diplomacy at Tufts University joined together to lobby the Congress for funds to build centers for intercultural study. Georgetown, with some imagination, gained an additional $10 million under legislation for energy conservation by proposing a photovoltaic solar roof.

The expectation was that when the new center was completed in 1982, it would house the School of Foreign Service and its Institute for the Study of Diplomacy. But as the completion of the attractive new building drew near, pressures from other academic departments prevailed. Fortunately for the Institute, we had gained occupancy of a Georgetown townhouse on 36th Street and it was to that house that we were relegated, despite our dreams for the new building.

Institution-building requires money. I realized that if I was to have a meaningful new career, it would involve fundraising. Father Timothy Healy, S.J., the president of Georgetown University, was quoted as saying, "I am glad to hire anyone who can go out and raise his own salary." When I became director, the institute's total budget was $180,000. Over the years I increased that amount, and the institute's annual budget continued to grow under my successors. As of the end of 2007, it approached $1 million, with an endowment in excess of $6 million.

Peter Krogh was a superb fundraiser. With his skill at gathering resources, he gave the school an independence within the Georgetown community not always appreciated by the Jesuit establishment or by the university's development office. A core endowment for the Institute had come from Oscar Iden, an early graduate of the school, who lived modestly in Northeast Washington and contributed $1,000 annually. When Peter took over as dean, he noticed the annual gift and located Iden, a former staff member of the Senate Budget Committee. He called on Iden and his wife at their house and found they were in need of medical assistance. He also discovered that over the years the Idens had accumulated a considerable investment portfolio. He encouraged the University to attend to their medical needs and obtained a lawyer to help them write their wills—with benefit to all, including the Institute for the Study of Diplomacy. An Oscar Iden lecture remains part of the institute's program. In addition, the dean had been instrumental in raising endowments for the Weintal prize in diplomatic reporting and an award for diplomatic achievement, named for Jit Trainor, an early registrar of the school.

When I followed Peter into the realm of fundraising, I made several discoveries. In a university setting, development does not refer to improving rural agriculture but to gathering financial resources for the institution. I came to see the university's development office as both a help and an occasional impediment, when it restricted our approach to a potential donor because of a prior commitment to another part of the university.

I learned about the composition of boards of directors of nonprofit organizations. The chair and two or three others may be individuals distinguished in their fields to provide prestige and credibility, but the remaining board members in a successful organization are likely to be appointed for their generosity or their access to other potentially generous donors.

Once, when reviewing the list of ISD board members, I noticed the name Marshall Coyne, owner of the Madison Hotel in

Washington. I said to Peter, "He has no diplomatic background. What is he doing on the board?"

Peter explained that Coyne traveled widely and welcomed the prestige of association with the ISD board. Important figures (such as Mikhail Gorbachev and Anwar Sadat) had been guests at the Madison. Coyne became a generous contributor to the Institute, and his contributions were recognized when, later, I became the Marshall B. Coyne Professor of Diplomacy at Georgetown.

Finally, I discovered why people give money:

—They are personally acquainted with and respect the leader of the institution.
—They want their name publicly associated with a distinguished institution.
—They are interested in the mission of the institution.
—They are seeking a tax break.

Working on development at Georgetown led to some extraordinary experiences. One the principal donors to the School of Foreign Service was a member of the Wallenberg family of Sweden. When the scion of that family died in 1982, I was appointed to represent the university at his funeral in Stockholm. I had not anticipated when I joined the school that I would find myself at a funeral sitting behind the king and queen of Sweden in one of Stockholm's oldest churches listening to the glorious music of Sweden's finest soloists echoing in the rafters of the church.

Neither did I expect that one day I would be addressing a banquet held in the Hôtel des Invalides in Paris. A Georgetown leadership seminar created in 1985 brought thirty potential leaders from around the world each year for an intense one-week course in Washington on the politics and history of the United States. Subsequent reunions of participants were then held in various parts of the world.

In 1989 one such reunion was held in Paris, with funding from CIBA-GEIGY, a major Swiss pharmaceutical company whose executives had attended the seminar. In that year the closing event of the reunion was a dinner held in the building that housed Napoleon's tomb. Waiters in 18th century French uniforms served the meal, a delicious but cold repast—because no cooking was permitted in the ancient building. I was the principal speaker, drawing on comments about the French by early American visitors to Paris—especially those of Benjamin Franklin.

Later, when I was interim dean of the School of Foreign Service, I was witness to the conclusion of another major corporate gift. After World War II, Georgetown University had pioneered German studies through the creation of the Konrad Adenauer Chair, initially financed by the German government. It was understood, however, that after a certain number of years private money would be found to replace the government support. That private money was ultimately found in a donation from the BMW Corporation, at that time embarking upon the construction of automobile factories in the United States. Upon the conclusion of an agreement to provide $10 million to the university, a group of senior BMW executives came to Washington. As I stood with Georgetown President Leo O'Donovan awaiting their arrival, we looked out through the university gates and witnessed a procession of new BMW cars carrying the executives. Clearly, they recognized and paid respect to American colors: the first car was red, the second was white, and the third was blue.

Money came not only from corporations and individuals but also from foundations, often requiring the preparation of sometimes complex grant proposals. When successful, the results provided strong long-term support for specific projects.

The Jesuits of Georgetown had cultivated an additional source—the Congress. Two members of the order, known on campus as the "funding fathers," had developed extensive relationships in the Congress. They observed closely the passage of legislation and, when the opportunity presented itself, proposed adding an "earmark" for Georgetown University. At one point, one of the fathers noticed a congressional proposal to fund U.S. participation in an international space station. He felt that Georgetown was in a good position to train students to work in the multinational environment of such a station. Working with him, I drafted a proposal to add funds directed to Georgetown for such a purpose. We were both disappointed when one senator, noticing the proposal, suggested instead a national competition among universities. To my knowledge, the idea died in the process.

Fundraising in Washington also encounters competition not only within one's own institution but also with comparable institutions. Within Georgetown, I was frequently turned away from potential donors already under obligation to the law school or the medical school.

A special case involved the Center for Strategic and International Studies, originally founded in association with Georgetown University by a master fundraiser and respected diplomat, David Abshire. Because our objectives seemed similar, at least to the outsider, we were frequently seeking to tap the same sources. The problem came to a head over funding for a chair named for Henry Kissinger, and the two institutions were subsequently divorced.

Potential competition in funding was also a factor creating a concern among many in the international studies community over a proposal before Congress in the early 1980s to establish a United States academy of peace.[123] The movement for such an academy grew out of the rise of conflict resolution or peace studies as an academic discipline and, for some, an alternative to traditional diplomacy. A national peace academy campaign began in 1980, conducted primarily by those interested in the peace movement and academics supporting the new conflict resolution discipline.

The announced purpose was "to institutionalize the arts of peace in a national academy, just as we have institutionalized the arts of war." The letter requesting funds began:

> Imagine a world at peace. No more war, no more revolutions, no more terrorism, no more sending our sons and grandsons off to slaughter one another. Imagine a world in which the threat of nuclear annihilation no longer exists. Imagine what a world this could be!
>
> An impossible dream? Not any longer. Not now. Because for the first time in history we have within our grasp an alternative method of resolving human conflict—an alternative to force and violence.[124]

Legislation to establish such an academy was introduced in 1983. As the Senate Foreign Relations Committee, which would normally deal with such an international project, was not interested, the sponsors took it to the Senate Committee on Labor and Human Resources. The two principal sponsors were Senators Spark Matsunaga of Hawaii and Jennings Randolph of West Virginia. Senator Randolph, who had earlier sponsored legislation establishing the Air Force Academy, reportedly wanted to end his career balancing that endorsement of a war-making establishment with one making peace.

I testified as a private individual and retired diplomat before the committee considering the legislation. In a talk on the issue to a university gathering on November 3, 1983, I set forth "four questionable premises" on which the case for the legislation was based:

—that a federally funded institution can achieve insights into problems of world conflict that executive agencies with their resources and skills and the vast network of American academic institutions have not been able to achieve;
—that the techniques of domestic conflict resolution— so-called peace studies—can easily be transferred to problems of international conflict;
—that executive officials will turn to a peace academy for experts and advice in facing conflict situations;
—that other nations look to the United States and would look to a peace academy to help them in the resolution of problems.

In the course of the legislative consideration, Georgetown President Healy received a letter from the sponsoring senators requesting his support for the legislation. I drafted a letter for him that stressed his interest in peace while questioning whether this was the correct approach. I told one of my Jesuit friends that I could understand that Father Healy could not be "against peace" and asked whether there was any other factor influencing his desire to be supportive. My friend explained the other factor—Senator Randolph also chaired the Senate committee on the District of Columbia that had under consideration a grant to Georgetown University to construct a new south entrance to the university.

Ultimately the reluctance of members of Congress to be "against peace," the support of other academic institutions that saw the possibility of grants, and the Senate's courtesy to the retiring Senator Randolph overcame opposition. Legislation was passed and signed into law on October 19, 1984, as an amendment to the Department of Defense appropriations act. In the process, changes were made that reflected some of the concerns of the academic institutions. The name was changed from an academy to an institute and authorization to grant degrees and raise private funds was dropped. The United States Institute of Peace (USIP) was born.

In 1992 the restriction on USIP's raising private funds was circumvented by the creation of a foundation that raised money to construct a headquarters building, starting in 2008.

USIP's Web site in 2008 describes its peacemaking accomplishments: "Through analysis, innovation, collaboration, and expertise, USIP has successfully created an array of tools for promoting the rule of law in societies emerging from conflict, developed analytical models designed to fight extremism and terrorism, facilitated interethnic and interfaith reconciliation, and more." Although it may have served to supplement the work of private institutions in peace and conflict resolution projects, the ambitious objective of eliminating conflict set forth in the Peace Academy Campaign has yet to be realized by the U.S. Institute of Peace.

Once when speaking with someone closely associated with conflict resolution and the Institute of Peace, I commented, "I realize that the U.S. Institute of Peace and the many other efforts at conflict resolution have brought adversaries together in conferences and have contributed to clarifying the issues in a dispute; but have these efforts ever resulted in a resolution of the conflict without the involvement of governments?"

My friend replied, "The trouble with you diplomats is you want action."

In 1983 I was involved in the formation of another academy, the American Academy of Diplomacy.[125] For many years, concerns had been expressed both in the Congress and in the Foreign Service about the appointment as ambassadors of individuals from the private sector, some of whom were considered unqualified. A committee that included prominent New York banker John McCloy, Ellsworth Bunker, former under secretary of state U. Alexis Johnson, and attorney and diplomat Sol Linowitz, among others, conceived the idea of an elective organization of former officials that would provide assessments of ambassadorial candidates to the Senate, as the American Bar Association does with nominees for judgeships. Elliot Richardson, former deputy secretary of state, was the principal organizer, and I was the first president. The Institute for the Study of Diplomacy was chosen as the base for the new organization.

The Academy created a system to provide information to the Senate Foreign Relations Committee on appointees. It became clear, however, that the White House was unwilling to support the system, and very few members of the Senate or even some members of the Academy were ready publicly to oppose presidential selections. The academy continues in existence to promote excellence in diplomacy, but its efforts to judge candidates encounter the reluctance of those in the political realm to interfere with one of the last unchallenged forms of political patronage.

While starting and deflecting academies, I maintained the Institute for the Study of Diplomacy. Accepted as a member of the Georgetown faculty, I began a teaching career that continued later at Virginia, where, in 1991, I was appointed to the Hugh and Winifred Cumming Chair in International Studies. Cumming, a University of Virginia alumnus, had been the first American ambassador to Indonesia.

Both the Georgetown and Virginia institutions had a tradition of diplomats in residence, and I was welcomed in both universities. I rarely encountered the colleague whose look betrayed the question "What are you doing here?" (not unlike the attitude of some Foreign Service officers to politically appointed ambassadors). The major difference for me was that at Virginia I was no longer involved in fundraising. I could enter a reception without feeling that I had to examine the crowd for potential targets.

The two universities, Georgetown and Virginia, were different in many ways. Georgetown was a private university, Virginia a public university. Students at both were carefully selected and of high quality, although at the state university one saw a broader spectrum of backgrounds. In both I was at times shocked by the demonstrated deficiencies of secondary education in providing essential background information for the study of international affairs at the university level. For example, in one graduate class of international studies majors at Virginia I mentioned the name of Dean Acheson. I detected blank looks in the class and asked how many of the twenty-three students had ever heard of Dean Acheson—the architect of America's post–World War II policy. Three hands went up.

In 1993 I strongly supported and participated in a program to meet with groups of secondary school teachers. I found them eager to learn from those with international experience about current foreign affairs. Unfortunately the program was short-lived; but universities would do well to reach out to the high school faculties in their neighborhoods.

In both universities doubts existed within the faculty about the "academic legitimacy" of courses taught by practitioners. Georgetown, located as it is in Washington, had long accepted practitioners into the classroom. Appointing a diplomat to the faculty was rare in Virginia, and after my successor, Marshall Brement, finished his three years, the Cumming Chair funds were transferred to a more traditional academic line.

I saw my task as a teacher to convey the practitioner's view to graduate students who, because of academic requirements, were concentrating substantially on theory and models. I saw this concentration particularly when I sat on committees examining doctorate candidates. I felt often that the models and the theories oversimplified problems and were removed from the reality of the international scene.

I developed three courses:

—The Media and Foreign Policy
—Fundamentals of Diplomacy
— Foreign Policy Decision-Making

The Media and Foreign Policy course was designed to demonstrate how public officials related to the press, radio, and television and the impact of that relationship upon the making of policy. At Georgetown, which had the advantages of a Washington location, I was able to invite individual members of the press corps to participate.

The Fundamentals of Diplomacy course, modeled to some extent on the oral examination for the Foreign Service, gave students practical experience in the types of oral and written instruments essential to diplomacy. By asking them to analyze the governing structure of a city or country with which they were familiar and to designate the officials to whom a diplomat would go for decisions, I sought to introduce them to the concept of power. That brought some interesting examples. One student from Massachusetts analyzed the power structure in the city of Boston. A student from Asia suggested that if a diplomat wanted a decision on a sensitive political matter, the diplomat should go to the prime minister's brother, who controlled many political favors as director of customs.

In the Foreign Policy Decision-Making course, I sought to introduce students to the workings of institutions and networks in Washington that influence foreign policy: the executive, the cabinet, the Congress, information media, think tanks, and lobbies. I taught them to recognize important players who were not often included in textbooks on foreign policy, such as the secretary of the treasury, the attorney general, and the secretary of agriculture. I emphasized that I wanted to give them a realistic picture of how Washington works but did not want to destroy their faith in the system—especially if they were going on to employment in Washington.

I emphasized teaching students to present issues succinctly both in writing and in speaking. I wanted to convey from my own experience the importance for anyone in any career of knowing how to gain the attention of a busy executive. I discovered that developing both skills was difficult for many students. When I returned a paper of multiple pages to a student and requested that she reduce the argument to two pages, she objected, "You have to understand, Mr. Newsom, that I am a philosophy major and that in most courses I must write up to fifty pages to get a satisfactory grade." Requiring students to present a complicated issue orally in ten minutes or less proved to be equally traumatic.

In all my classes I stressed the importance to any American going into an international career of understanding the governmental structure of the United States. It is also important to understand Americans' national perspective on the world. For American diplomats, particularly those serving in countries distinctly different from the United States, communicating with Washington can be as difficult as communicating with a foreign government. The effective diplomat—or business representative—is the one who can explain to his principals the differences in the foreign environment without being seen as an advocate of a strange or unfriendly country.

In teaching, the professor encounters and helps shape a new generation. In the 1980s and 1990s—at least in the institutions in which I taught—this was a serious generation focusing on careers. There was little revolutionary zeal, and few were determined to change the world. To my great satisfaction, many kept in touch and came to see me, thanking me for what the courses had given them in preparing for their future. At least a dozen former students in my twenty years entered the diplomatic services in their respective countries. Others went into journalism, business, banking, nongovernmental relief organizations, and international organizations. I was especially touched on one occasion when two of my students who were abroad in the Foreign Service, one posted in South Africa and the other in Brussels, met up in Paris and took the time to send me a postcard.

I subsequently drew on the material from my courses to write two books, *Diplomacy and the American Democracy*, and *The Public Dimension of Foreign Policy*, both published by Indiana University Press, in 1988 and 1996 respectively.

I made further discoveries. The university teacher is a modern Abelard under a tree. What he or she teaches and how is for the individual to decide. There is no introductory training or, except for one day at the University of Virginia, no initial briefing. The mix of subjects and theories to be pursued are largely determined by the academic deans and implemented through the hiring process. At the graduate level at least, you are on your own.

I also came to understand the differences between governmental and academic professions. A government official is a member of a large institution, and his or her future lies in obligations to the institution. An article I published in the 1995–96 Winter issue of *Foreign Policy* magazine, "Foreign Policy and Academia," examined the differences: "The worlds of the professor and the policymaker meet on many occasions, yet they remain fundamentally different. Over the years, the differences between these two outlooks have been complicated by academic suspicion of government and opposition to official policies and have been made more contentious by the attitude of many in government that academia represents an irrelevant ivory tower."

In this article I also sought to address why much of current scholarship has so little impact on public policy: "[S]ome works have contributed significantly to an understanding of international events. Other works, however, disappear behind a curtain of jargon and scientific quantification that limits the readership and influence of much academic research."[126]

The academic reservations about the statements and writings of diplomats came to the fore in 1985–86, when a program recording the oral histories of diplomats was launched by retired diplomats Stuart Kennedy and Victor Wolf, with the backing of the George Washington University history department. For a time Kennedy worked out of Georgetown's Lauinger Library. Funding the program was initially difficult because of a general suspicion of the benefits of oral histories. One common criticism was that they were merely a way for diplomats to justify their mistakes. As the program continued, however, scholars gradually began to see the value of the firsthand accounts of crises and events given by the diplomats. The Association for Diplomatic Studies and Training (ADST) soon took over the program; and Stuart Kennedy, its principal interviewer, has continued to manage the program under ADST auspices. Today roughly 1,500 oral histories have been recorded and are now available on the Web site of the Library of Congress.

I also managed to find funds related to teaching. From the Pew Charitable Trusts in Philadelphia I obtained support first, for ISD's book-publishing program, and later, for a program in diplomatic case studies that currently has a worldwide clientele. The grant covered not only the preparation of cases, but also training of faculty members in the case study method of teaching common in law schools and at the Kennedy School of Government at Harvard. Under the Pew grant, the cases were to deal only with United States diplomacy.

At a meeting between Pew representatives and members of the Georgetown faculty, one professor asked, "Can we also include cases about the diplomacy of other countries? Other governments also have much to teach us about diplomacy."

The Pew representatives responded, "Not in the opinion of our board."

When I was under secretary, I used to visit then-retired Governor Averill Harriman, often joined by his wife, Pamela. Through that association, I was able to raise funds from Mrs. Harriman for a program at the Institute for students at the School of Foreign Service, designated junior fellows in diplomacy, to work on a specific project with the resident diplomatic practitioners.

At a State Department banquet in 1984 on the occasion of the 75th birthday of former Secretary of State Dean Rusk, we raised funds for a Rusk Fellowship. Taking note of the growing number of "tandem" couples, in which both husband and wife are Foreign Service officers, we dedicated the funds to enable Foreign Service couples to study and teach for a year at Georgetown.

Some efforts were less successful. When I assumed the ISD directorship, I conceived the idea of an association of former noncareer political ambassadors linked to the Institute, hoping that they would become contributors to its work. Noncareer diplomats welcomed the idea but decided they would form their own organization independent of any particular institution. Thus was the Council of American Ambassadors born, but without any meaningful association with Georgetown.

In another instance, a Foreign Service officer who had been assigned to the United States mission to the Vatican visited me, proposing that the Institute sponsor him in writing a book about the history of U.S. diplomatic relations with the Holy See. I thought immediately that this might be the basis for raising funds from the Catholic community. Then I received a summons to meet with Father Healy, a Jesuit and president of the University. He had heard of the project and expressed little enthusiasm for it. As I recall, he said, "David, right now we are not much interested in the Vatican." A few days later I discovered that at that moment the Jesuit order was in dispute with the Vatican over the appointment of the next head of the order. Our proposed Vatican project did not go forward.

When serving in Indonesia in 1974–77, I became acquainted with one of Asia's most prominent intellectuals, Soedjatmoko, and his family. "Koko," as he was known, was a prominent nationalist in the early years of the Republic, Indonesia's first ambassador to the United States, and a recognized scholar on problems of development. He was also a member of the Ford Foundation board and the Club of Rome. A chair in his name would seem an appropriate addition to an American university such as Georgetown. In 1996, I traveled to Jakarta to seek out possible donors. Koko, who died in 1989, had at various times in his career crossed Suharto, Indonesia's authoritarian president. Even some who had themselves opposed Suharto were unwilling to contribute to a project in Soedjatmoko's name. Funds that I did raise enabled Georgetown University's library to establish a special book collection in his name.

I am often asked whether, after my retirement, those who followed me in the State Department ever sought my advice. I left the department with a strong feeling, based on my experience while on active duty, that the usefulness of advice from former officials is limited. The foreign affairs process moves so rapidly that those who are not in daily contact with the communications and decisions generally lack the basis for sound advice. In the national security agencies, the additional question of security access is always present; a retired senior official retains a security clearance for only seven years. Nevertheless, opportunities existed to make use of the knowledge and insights gained in my career in diplomacy.

I was asked on three occasions to undertake lectures abroad for the United States Information Agency under their American Participants Abroad (AMPARTS) program. This gave me an opportunity to visit Foreign Service posts in areas where I had not served, particularly in the Soviet Union and Eastern Europe. My last such trip was to Hungary, Romania, and the German Democratic Republic in May 1989. The repressive regimes were still in place. In Bucharest, in contrast to my visit there as an official in 1978, I was snubbed by many Romanians. My trip report notes that of seventy Romanians invited to a reception for me by the public affairs officer, only three attended. Seven Romanians invited to a dinner with the ambassador did not attend.

The report on my lecture tour also describes a lunch with officials of the German Democratic Republic at which there was a discussion of when the Berlin Wall might come down. The earliest prediction by those present was in ten years. In the event, the Wall came down in October 1989, five months after our luncheon.

Former officials can be helpful when occasions arise requiring knowledge of past circumstances and decisions. The case of the Soviet brigade in Cuba, cited earlier, is an example. They can also provide insights into unresolved issues.

In the later years of my service, I noted how developments in science and technology were creating new international problems. I became an advocate for greater attention within the State Department to issues with a potential for international conflict, such as global warming, food security, environmental degradation, infectious diseases, and nuclear proliferation.[127] I was therefore a logical appointee to a special committee of the National Research Council on Science, Technology and Health in Foreign Policy, established by the National Academy of Sciences in 1998. For more than a year I had the stimulating experience of interacting with some of the nations leading scientists, doctors, and engineers. The committee produced a report and presented it to Secretary of State Madeleine Albright on October 4, 1999.[128]

As an individual I was active in a number of projects relating to issues of the day. Already in 1980 issues of religion were increasingly thrusting themselves into the diplomatic world. In 1984 I was asked to participate in a study on "church and state abroad," under the auspices of the Council on Religion and International affairs in New York. I disputed the premise of the group that, if we had the will, we could impose our domestic laws relating to religious freedom on other countries. This study[129] was perhaps a precursor of the enactment of the U.S. International Religious Freedom Act of 1998, which added religious freedom to the U.S. agenda. Given my many years in Muslim countries, I was called upon frequently to discuss Islam and to explain some of the bitter conflicts between Muslims and Christians that were erupting in South Asia and Africa.

Reverting to my earlier days as a journalist, for twenty years, beginning in 1982, I wrote a weekly column on international issues for the *Christian Science Monitor*.[130] I welcomed the challenge of setting forth in 600 words the complicated problems raised in the headlines and the numerous favorable comments that came to me during those years.

On a somewhat less esoteric level, I shared my experiences of other cultures as a lecturer, afloat, on four different occasions—on cruises to China, Indonesia, the Panama Canal, and the Mediterranean. On at least two of the cruises I was assigned a lecture hour just after lunch—competing with passengers' siesta time, sunbathing on the afterdeck, and blackjack in the casino. It was an impressive display of serious interest on the part of cruise passengers that I had respectable audiences on these occasions. The cruise organizers provided comfortable accommodation and passage for both my wife and myself, although, we did have to pay 50 percent of the bar bill. On one occasion our cabin was next to the anchor locker, and we were therefore quite easily awakened during early morning arrivals in port. I explained to those who looked upon our cruise lecture experiences with envy that we were actually engaged in a missionary enterprise, bringing knowledge to benighted cruise passengers. That explanation evoked little sympathy. But, all in all, I would rather be a paying passenger.

An appointment to a university position also opens the individual to a number of unexpected intellectual adventures. This was true at both Georgetown and the University of Virginia.

At Georgetown I was appointed to two committees that took my somewhat limited Protestant education into new fields: ethics and peace and conflict. President Healy named me to a group to review and coordinate the various studies of ethics that existed in the university. This led me into theology and the developing field of bioethics. The Woodstock Center at Georgetown University offered stimulating contact with scholars and specialists, who invited me to join a study group on peace and conflict, leading into the esoteric question of "just wars."

At Virginia I served on a panel appointed by President John Casteen to recommend ways to improve the university's international outreach. This involved achieving coordination among the various elements of the university with international programs. I observed again, as I had on occasions at Georgetown, the difficulty of bringing together major elements of a university into a common objective. Each major school—whether law, medicine, or engineering—has its own links abroad and its own funding sources. Deans of such schools give up their freedom of action and independence only reluctantly.

At Virginia I heard about a Rockefeller Foundation Study Center at Bellagio, on Lake Como in Italy. A number of Virginia faculty members had been residents, and I was encouraged to apply. For Jean and me it led to one of the great experiences of our lives. For four weeks in 1994 we resided in an elegant villa atop a hill overlooking the lake, interacting with scholars from every continent. Among the thirty residents there at the same time were musicians, novelists, mathematicians, and artists. Each of us had been selected on the basis of a project proposal, but I had the impression that the Rockefeller foundation was as interested in creating a stimulating mix of people as it was in any specific project.

My proposal was to study the impact of decolonization in Asia and Africa. I was able to lay the groundwork for a book that was ultimately published in 2001. I felt the book was a prescient look at the factors that would shape international life in the twenty-first century. The closing paragraph of the book, *The Imperial Mantle,* read as follows: "In the 21st century, the Third World will increasingly thrust itself into America's deliberations—through migrations, environmental degradation, disease, terrorism, and weapons. It is not too early to recognize that although the United States may not be the imperial power some claim it to be, it shares a major responsibility to respond to this thrust."[131]

Although the book was reviewed in several publications, including the *Economist,*[132] to my great disappointment, it was never seen as the explanation for so much that has happened since. Whether this was through a failure of marketing, the fact that I was not a recognized historian, or defects of which I was not aware I shall never know.

My association with the two universities also opened windows into other opportunities to spread the word about diplomacy.

Shortly after I retired from government service I was invited to spend a week with the Department of Communications at the University of Michigan in Ann Arbor. The town and the university in many respects reminded me of Berkeley, and I felt very much at home. The emphasis in this visit, as was to be expected, was on my experience as a public servant dealing with the press.

The Woodrow Wilson Foundation sponsored visits to campuses by retired diplomats. Under the foundation's auspices I traveled to colleges and universities to lecture and give short courses. These experiences brought me to parts of the United States that I had not previously seen.

At the Oklahoma Baptist University in Shawnee, Oklahoma, I encountered Native American leaders for the first time. They were particularly interested in my story of Gandhi. I was fascinated by their histories and by learning about the positions that more and more they were assuming in Oklahoma.

In another part of the West, Laramie, Wyoming, I met with high school teachers in a conference at the University of Wyoming. They faced difficulties in teaching international affairs. An ultraconservative state education official prohibited textbooks that carried the word "global." The word suggested a world regime that infringed on the sovereignty of the United States.

A similar political orientation was suggested at Lawrence University in Appleton, Wisconsin, where a statue of Senator Joseph McCarthy stood on the campus. I did not, however, find many of the students who shared his view of the world.

Kalamazoo College in Kalamazoo, Michigan, contrasted sharply with Wyoming. Through arrangements with universities around the world they sent each of the college's students to spend a semester abroad.

A similar opportunity to interact with university audiences in a different setting came in 1986, when I was appointed the John Adams Fellow at the Royal Institute of International Affairs (Chatham House) in London, under the Fulbright program. The appointment commemorated 200 years of American-British diplomatic relations. In the course of six months I visited sixteen British universities to discuss the making of foreign policy in the United States. I shortly discovered that even some American specialists had an inadequate understanding of the antiauthoritarian nature of the American political system. Such scholars believed the system to be a parliamentary pattern that had gone seriously wrong. So I began my lectures by saying, "If you have difficulty understanding our policy processes, it is partly your fault. Those who created the American Constitution were seeking arrangements that would preclude the rise of any more George IIIs."

I am proud to have spent a career serving a great nation as a diplomat, and in the years that followed, to have helped prepare a new generation to do the same.

The life of a diplomat is not an easy one. In every country, doubts exist about the loyalty of those who spend time with foreigners and seek to explain their points of view.

In every country diplomats face the stereotype of effete dilettantes living in "palaces" abroad at taxpayers expense. The frustrations of gaining access to foreign officials, the risks, the sacrifices, and the family hardships are ignored. And in an age of terrorism, diplomats are more and more walled off from the peoples of the countries in which they serve, and more and more at risk.

But the fragile world would be an even more dangerous place without those who are prepared to spend their lives, despite the risks, reaching out to other nations and cultures in the interests of establishing better understanding between governments and peoples.

And so, life after government brought new experiences and adventures—all building on those of the thirty-five years that went before.

19

REFLECTIONS

During the period covered by this memoir, significant changes have taken place in the international scene. I have been a witness to most and a participant in many:

—The United States has risen to a position of preeminence among nations.
—An increasingly united Europe has ended the cycle of wars that bloodied the twentieth century.
—India and China have emerged as major players on the world stage.
—The Cold War ended without a major clash between the Soviet Union and the West.
—The statesmanship of Nelson Mandela ended apartheid in South Africa.
—The Panama Canal is no longer a political issue at the center of relations between the United States and Latin America.

But much in the world and in the United States continues to be unaffected by fundamental change.

The region between the Mediterranean and the border of India encompassing the Arabian Peninsula, Iraq, Iran, Afghanistan, and Pakistan is, as it has been for centuries, a dangerous mix of international rivalries, ethnic quests for identity, and tribal ambitions, facilitating the rise of militant Islam. On September 11, 2001, for the first time, the United States was directly affected by struggles in this region. September 11 also revealed strong currents in American society willing to tolerate restrictions on American freedoms in the interests of security.

The ambitions of the Jewish people for a state have created a still unresolved confrontation with the peoples of Palestine and the surrounding Arab states.

The development of massive energy resources in the Persian Gulf region has made the world more dependent than ever upon the stability of a single group of countries.

Efforts of the community of nations to deal with the threat of nuclear weapons have substantially failed, although since 1945 an actual nuclear war has been avoided.

Decolonization in Asia and Africa has at least partially satisfied the demands for dignity and freedom in those continents; but unsettled boundaries and tribal tensions nurture seeds of conflict subject to constant exploitation.

The capacity of the United States to deal effectively with many of the changes in the international scene has been limited by attitudes and fundamentals of American democracy. Positive feelings toward the United States have suffered, especially in the Muslim world. Under these circumstances, conveying to policy makers the realities of politics and cultures in societies with different histories and traditions remains a problem for American diplomacy.

Exiles and ideological advocates continue their efforts to encourage forceful U.S. action in other societies. The unintended consequences for the United States and its global image of succumbing to pressure from such advocates have been demonstrated in Iraq.

Internal conflicts in Washington over policy, stirred by ideological differences, egos, ambitions, politics, and bureaucratic turf, often blunt clear messages to the rest of the world. The conflicts have frequently centered on what to do with adversarial regimes, whether state or nonstate. Each available option—conversations, sanctions, force, or isolation—has had its drawbacks.

Policy statements issued for domestic political purposes risk being contrary to the objectives of diplomacy.

Difficulties in understanding and tolerating attitudes in other societies stand in the way of effective relations, particularly with countries and cultures that seem strange or antagonistic.

Commitments to projects of war and security at the beginning of the twenty-first century limit future actions and have placed unusual strains on U.S. resources, creating increased U.S. dependence as a debtor country—especially in relation to China.

For reasons of history and patriotic emotion, substantial segments of the American public favor the use of force in confrontation with American adversaries.

The historic American desire to promote human rights and democracy has continually confronted the perceived need to cooperate with tyrannical and authoritarian regimes in the interest of security objectives.

Embargoes are still in place on Cuba. A politically active exile community in the United States closely follows the situation in the island republic.

Diplomacy and dialogue remain suspect by many in the Congress and in the public as instruments of U.S. policy. Debatable assumptions about the threats from others have led to what may have been unnecessary confrontations.

This book was completed in early 2008, when the force of an aggressive nationalistic ideology has temporarily sidetracked a more studied approach to international relations. It has always been my belief that the United States has within it a balancing wheel that saves it from the dangers of suspicion, hatred, and conflict that ravage other countries. It is my hope that the balance wheel will again be activated to save us from such a fate. I would be deeply disturbed to feel that my generation was passing on to those who follow a nation vulnerable to the tragic instability I have observed in so many other societies in the seven decades of my adult life.

NOTES

7 A New Nation

[1] *California Monthly*, Sept. 1949, 12–14.

[2] *Time*, Sept. 20, 1948, "That Man."

9 Ungovernable

[3] Agatha Christie, *They Came to Baghdad* (New York: Dell, 1977).

[4] Philip K. Hitti, *The Arabs: A Short History* (Princeton, N.J.: Princeton University Press, 1943).

[5] David D. Newsom, "Elements of Political Instability in Iraq," June 1955 (copy in author's files).

[6] From "Burned Out Post Stages Comeback," *IIA Newsletter*, July 1953, No. 26.

[7] Quoted in Waldemar Gallman, *Iraq Under Nuri* (Baltimore: Johns Hopkins University Press, 1964), 22.

[8] For a full discussion of the Baghdad Pact and its impact on Iraq, see George Lenczowski, *The Middle East in World Affairs* (Ithaca and London: Cornell University Press, 4th ed., 1980), 283–87.

[9] Author's personal recollection.

10 Tents in Blair House Garden

[10] William Taylor Fain III, *Toll Gates and Barbicans of Empire: The United States, Great Britain and the Persian Gulf Region, 1950–1968* (Charlottesville, Va.: Department of History, University of Virginia, May 2002).

[11] Fain, *Toll Gates,* 109. See also, Letter from Sir Bernard A. B. Burrows to Foreign Secretary Selwyn Lloyd, Dispatch No. 143, 22 December 1955, FO 371/120561; and "Persian Gulf," Note by the Secretary of State for Foreign Affairs, 14 May 1956, CAB 129/81, C.P. (56) 122.

[12] Fain, *Toll Gates,* 122.

[13] Letter from President Eisenhower to King Saud, August 20, 1956, U.S. Presidential Papers Concerning Saudi Arabia, 1941–1962, 241.

[14] Letter from President Eisenhower to King Saud, May 14, 1956, ibid., 238.

[15] Memorandum for the President from Secretary of State John Foster Dulles, January 15, 1957, U. S. Presidential Papers Concerning Saudi Arabia 1941–1962, 284.

[16] State Department telegram to Dhahran No. 250, January 4, 1957, U.S. Presidential Papers Concerning Saudi Arabia, 282–83.

[17] *Foreign Relations of the United States (FRUS)*, 1955–57, Vol. XIII, 757.

[18] Fain, *Toll Gates*, 201.

[19] Executive Sessions of the Senate Foreign Relations Committee, Vol. 10, July, August 1958. 600–601.

[20] Ibid., 605.

[21] Ibid., 607.

11 Unfinished Sentences

[22] For more information on Paine's bridge, see Alfred Owen Aldridge, *Man of Reason*: *The Life of Thomas Paine* (Philadelphia: J.P. Lippincott, 1959), 108–15.

12 From Piracy to Petroleum

[23] The exact citation was: "His Highness the Mushir Mohammed Es-sadek, Bey of Tunis. Portrait presented as a souvenir of his Friendship in November 1865, by his Envoy, Gen. Otman Hashem, bearer of letters of condolence for the assassination of President Lincoln and of congratulations for the termination of the Civil War."

[24] Jeffrey A. LeFebvre, "The United States, Ethiopia and the 1968 Somali-Soviet Arms Deal: Containment and the Balance of Power Dilemma in the Horn of Africa," *Journal of Modern African Studies*, 36, 4 (1998), 617.

[25] Daniel Yergin, *The Prize: The Epic Quest for Oil, Money, and Power* (New York: Simon and Schuster, 1991), 592.

13 Seeds of a Coup

[26] Dirk J Vandewalle, *A History of Modern Libya* (New York: Cambridge University Press, 2006).

[27] Recollection of Roscoe Suddarth, political officer, in e-mail to author July 20, 2007.

[28] *FRUS*, 1964–1968 Vol. XXIV, 71.

[29] Ibid., 127.

[30] Ibid., 72.

[31] Ibid., 71.

[32] Ibid., 99.

[33] Ibid, 125, fn2; see also Yergin, *The Prize*, 555.

[34] John G. Kormann, *Echoes of a Distant Clarion* (Washington, D.C.: New Academia/Vellum Books, 2007), 343–57.

[35] *FRUS*, 1964–1968 Vol. XXIV, 131.
[36] Dept. of State Airgram, June 17, 1969.
[37] Personal recollection.
[38] Letter from Donald L. Snook, dated October 30, 1999.
[39] Hearings before the Subcommittee on United States Security Agreements and Commitments Abroad, Committee on Foreign Relations, United States Senate, Ninety-First Congress, Second Session, Part 8, June 1,1970, 1888.
[40] Ibid., 1889–1900.
[41] Ibid., 1937–38.
[42] Ibid., 1940.
[43] Ibid., 1941.
[44] Ibid., Part 9, July 20, 1970, 1978.

14 Only Eight Percent of the Black Vote

[45] Memorandum from Secretary of State Kissinger to President Nixon of March 11, 1972 (declassified September 6, 2007).
[46] David D Newsom, *The Imperial Mantle: The United States, Decolonization, and the Third World* (Bloomington: Indiana University Press, 2001), chapter 13.
[47] *FRUS*, Volume E-6, Documents on Africa, 1973–1976, document 258.
[48] Roger Morris, "The Triumph of Money and Power," *New York Times*, March 3, 1974, WK1.
[49] Author's recollection.
[50] Susanna Purnell, "Kidnapping of Ambassador Cleo A. Noel and DCM George C. Moore," RAND Corporation Report No. WN(L)-9573-DOS/ARPA, November 1976 (declassified December 31, 2006); and David A. Korn, *Assassination in Khartoum* (Bloomington: Indiana University Press, 1993).
[51] Purnell, "Kidnapping," and Korn, *Assassination.*
[52] Mohamed A. El-Khawas and Barry Cohen (eds), *The Kissinger Study of Southern Africa* (Westport, Conn.: Lawrence Hill, 1976), 81-139.
[53] *New York Times*, April 2, 1972, 1 and 14.
[54] Roger Morris, *Uncertain Greatness: Henry Kissinger and American Foreign Policy* (New York: Harper & Row, 1977), 111.
[55] *FRUS*, 1969–1976, Volume E-5, Doc. No. 7.
[56] *The Star*, Johannesburg, August 28, 1969, 6.
[57] *Issue: A Journal of Opinion,* African Studies Association, Vol. 1 (Autumn, 1971), 34–44.
[58] A statement of Assistant Secretary David D. Newsom and Deputy Assistant Secretary W. Beverley Carter Jr., Bureau of African affairs,

Department of State, before the Subcommittee on Africa of the House Committee on Foreign Affairs, December 3, 1970.

[59] See, for example, Hanes Walton Jr., Robert Louis Stevenson, and James Bernard Rosser, Sr., eds., *The African Foreign Policy of Secretary of State Henry Kissinger: A Documentary Analysis* (Lanham, Md.: Lexington Books, 2007).

[60] For details of the bureaucratic infighting see *FRUS*, Vol. E-5, Nixon/Ford Administration, Documents No. 90, 92, 107, 109, 111, 121, 152, 153, 170, 173, 174.

[61] Joan Hoff, *Nixon Reconsidered* (New York: Basic Books, 1944), 246–47.

[62] For the NSC side of the story, see Roger Morris, *Uncertain Greatness*, 120–30.

[63] The Postwar Nigerian Situation, Hearing before the Subcommittee on Africa of the Committee on Foreign Affairs, House of Representatives, Ninety-first Congress, Second Session, Tuesday, January 27, 1970, 19.

[64] *FRUS*, 1969–1976, Volume E-5, Doc. No. 8.

[65] For a fuller discussion of colonialism in Africa, see Newsom, *The Imperial Mantle,* chapter seven, 96–108.

[66] For more on Idi Amin, see Thomas P. and Magaret B. Melady, *Idi Amin Dada: Hitler in Africa* (Kansas City, Mo.: Sheed, Andrews, and McMeel, 1977).

[67] Chester Crocker, *High Noon in Southern Africa: Making Peace in a Rough Neighborhood* (New York: W. W. Norton, 1993).

[68] *Issue, A Journal of Opinion,* African Studies Association, Vol. 3, no. 3.

15 Halfway between Beirut and Wellington

[69]For a full discussion of the difficult U.S.-Indonesian relations during this period see Paul F. Gardner, *Shared Hopes, Separate Fears: Fifty Years of U.S.-Indonesian Relations* (Boulder, Colo.: Westview Press, 1997), 172–99.

[70] James Warren Gould, *Americans in Sumatra* (The Hague: Martinus Nijhoff, 1961).

[71] For further information on the adventures of the early missionaries, see James Warren Gould, *American Interests in Sumatra, 1784–1873* (Medford, Mass.: Fletcher School of Law and Diplomacy, 1955).

[72] Lecture to American Embassy staff by Professor Selo Suomardjan, Head of the Department of Sociology, University of Indonesia, December 4, 1969.

[73] "Curbing Corruption in Indonesia 2004–2006," a survey of national policies and approaches by Soren Davidsen, Vishnu Juwono, and David G. Timberman (Jakarta and Washington: CSIS and USINDO, 2006), 9.

[74] Jack Anderson and Les Whitten, "The Washington Merry-Go-Round," *Washington Post*, June 16, 1976.

[75] *Congressional Record,* Vol. 121, No. 153, October 20, 1975.

[76] Quotes from Embassy Jakarta SECRET telegram No. 14946, dated December 6, 1975 (Telegram declassified by National Archives, June 6, 2001).

16 My Cousin Needs a Visa

[77] United States Senate Committee on Foreign Relations, Hearing, Tuesday, October 13, 1977, transcript by American Reporting Co., pages 47, 48.

[78] *Manila Journal*, November 11, 1977, 1.

[79] *Manila Daily Express*, December 10, 1977.

[80] David Joel Steinberg, *The Philippines: A Singular and a Plural Place* (Boulder, Colo., Westview Press, 4th ed., 2000), 115.

[81] Talking Points prepared for approach to Philippine officials, February 6, 1978, in author's files.

[82] Author's address to Manila Rotary Club, December 8, 1977 (text in author's files).

[83] Republic of the Philippines, Department of Foreign Affairs, Manila, Press Release, 14 March 1978.

[84] http://en.wikipedia.org/wiki/Benigno_Aquino,_Jr., retrieved October 11, 2007.

[85] Letter to Assistant Secretary of State Richard Holbrooke, January 13, 1978.

[86] Salvador P. Lopez, "Four American Ambassadors, 1972–1982," VIEWPOINT, *Manila Times Journal*, January 25, 1983, 4.

17 His Concerns Are Global

[87] See Cyrus Vance, *Hard Choices* (New York: Simon and Schuster, 1983), 102.

[88] Author's personal recollection.

[89] SECRET State Department telegram to Tehran, number 141224 dated June 3, 1978, declassified December 13, 2007.

[90] SECRET telegram from Tehran to Department of State No. 6551, dated July 10, 1978, declassified December 13, 2007.

[91] SECRET telegram from New Delhi to Department of State No. 10670, dated July 13, 1978, declassified December 13, 2007.

[92] SECRET telegram from London to Department of State No. 11450 dated July 19, 1978.

[93] SECRET telegram from Islamabad to Department of State No. 6903 dated July 17, 1978, declassified December 13, 2007.

[94] SECRET telegram from Jidda to Department of State No. 5314 dated July 19, 1978, declassified December 13, 2007.

[95] "Skepticism Meets Claims of Texas Businessman That He Arranged Release of 2 Employees Held in Iran," *New York Times*, February 26, 1979, A13.

[96] *New York Daily News*, October 23,1979.

[97] The most complete account of the crisis and its resolution is found in *All Fall Down* (New York: Random House, 1985), by Gary Sick, who was on the National Security Council staff at the time. Other authoritative accounts are found in *American Hostages in Iran: The Conduct of a Crisis* (New Haven and London: Yale University Press 1985), a Council on Foreign Relations book with essays by the principal participants; and Vance, *Hard Choices*, 314–97. Robert Shaplen, a *New Yorker* writer, was given special access to write a profile on the Office of the Under Secretary. The result was a three-part series dwelling extensively on the hostage crisis: Robert Shaplen, "Eye Of The Storm," *New Yorker*, June 2, 9, and 16, 1980.

[98] David D. Newsom, "The Sensitive Link: The Swiss Role in the U.S.-Iran Hostage Crisis," *Einblick in die schweizerische Aussenpolitik, Zum 65, Guburtstag von Staatsekretar Raymond Probst*, 291–303.

[99] For a full discussion of U.S. decision-making after the invasion, see Vance, *Hard Choices*, 386–90.

[100] The 1959 Agreement of Cooperation between the United States and Pakistan, signed in connection with Pakistan's adherence to the Baghdad pact, stated: "[I]n the case of aggression against Pakistan the government of the United States of America, in accordance with the Constitution of the United States of America, will take such appropriate action, including the use of armed forces, as may be mutually agreed upon and as is envisaged in the joint resolution to promote peace and stability in the Middle East [the Eisenhower doctrine] in order to assist the Government of Pakistan at its request."

[101] SECRET memorandum from NEA (Constable) to the Secretary, "Assistance for Pakistan," dated May 3, 1980, declassified Dec 6, 2007.

[102] Joseph F. Pilat (ed.), *The Non-Proliferation Predicament* (New Brunswick, N.J. and Oxford: Transitions Publications, 1985), 61.

[103] SECRET telegram from Embassy London to Department January 25, 1980, declassified November 26, 1980.

[104] Letter from President Jimmy Carter to President Nicolae Ceausescu, dated January 24, 1980, declassified December 13, 2007.

[105] SECRET telegram from American Embassy Bucharest to Department number 9070 of January 28, 1980, declassified November 21, 2007.

[106] *Washington Post*, June 26, 1980, A2.

[107] Christopher Wren, "Libya's identity blurred by ties with East, West and terrorism," *New York Times*, October 14, 1979, A1.

[108] Embassy Tripoli Secret telegram No. 0968, June 17, 1979, declassified November 13, 2007.

[109] Telegram from Department of State to American Embassy Cairo 050019 dated June 15, 1979, declassified December 13, 2007. An Israeli official, Hanan Bar-On, was similarly informed in Washington on June 16. The conversation was reported to American Embassy Tel Aviv by State Department telegram 154612 dated June 16, 1979. Declassified December 13, 2007.

[110] Memorandum for Zbigniew Brzezinski from David Aaron, dated April 13, 1978, classified top secret, declassified by National Security Council June 7, 2003.

[111] Memorandum for Zbigniew Brzezinski from David Aaron at July 20, 1978, classified as secret, declassified by NARA October 10, 2003.

[112] White House memorandum of conversation, June 15, 1978, p 9, classified secret, declassified November 26, 1996.

[113] Piero Gleijeses, *Conflicting Missions: Havana, Washington, and Africa 1959–1976* (Chapel Hill: University of North Carolina Press, 2002). See also National Security Archive Electronic Briefing Book No. 67.

[114] David Newsom *The Soviet Brigade in Cuba* (Bloomington: Indiana University Press, 1987), 20.

[115] Ibid., 49. The Soviets, although puzzled by the incident, did not attach great significance to it. For the Soviet view, see the transcript of conference number three of the Carter-Brezhnev Project, a conference of U.S. and Russian policymakers and scholars held at the Harbor Beach resort, Fort Lauderdale, Florida, March 23–26, 1995.

[116] Author's recollection.

[117] See Georgie Anne Geyer, "Nicaragua's Quake Goes On, Shakes Up Somoza's World," *Los Angeles Times*, Mar 16, 1978, D11.

[118] Henry Kamm, "Geneva Meeting Yields Few Pledges of Aid for Indochinese Refugees," *New York Times*, December 17, 1978, 16.

[119] Embassy Warsaw telegram to Department of State, No. 8044, dated October 10, 1978, declassified December 13, 2007.

[120] Author's recollection.

18 Life After Government

[121] Published by the Institute for the Study of Diplomacy between 1979 and 1983.

[122] From text of remarks by James Reston, Georgetown University, April 6, 1992.

[123] See David D. Newsom *The Public Dimension of Foreign Policy* (Bloomington: Indiana University Press, 1996), 153–56.

[124] Undated letter from National Peace Academy Campaign, signed by Milton C. Mapes, Jr,. Executive Director.

[125] R. Drummond Ayres, Jr. "In Search of Less Imperfection among Diplomats," *New York Times*, May 10, 1984, B20.

[126] David D. Newsom "Foreign Policy and Academia," *Foreign Policy*, Winter 1995–96.

[127] David D. Newsom, "The New International Agenda, Are Nations Ready?" *International Relations* (London: Royal Institute of International Affairs, 1988).

[128] *The Pervasive Role of Science, Technology and Health in Foreign Policy: Imperatives for the Department of State,* Office of International Affairs, National Research Council (Washington, D.C.: National Academy Press, 1999).

[129] J. Bruce Nichols, *The Uneasy Alliance: Religion, Refugee Work and U.S. Foreign Policy* (New York: Oxford University Press, 1988).

[130] A complete list of my columns can be found in Lexis Nexis.

[131] David D. Newsom, *The Imperial Mantle* (Bloomington: Indiana University Press, 2001), 202.

[132] *The Economist,* May 3, 2001.

INDEX

CPSIA information can be obtained at www.ICGtesting.com
Printed in the USA
BVOW08s1255270916

463439BV00001B/6/P